Command
Performance

The Harvard Business Review Book Series

Command Performance

The Art of Delivering Quality Service

With a Preface by
John E. Martin

A Harvard Business Review Book

The *Harvard Business Review* articles in this collection are available as
individual reprints. Discounts apply to quantity purchases. For information
and ordering contact Operations Department, Harvard Business School
Publishing, Boston, MA 02163. Telephone: (617) 495-6192, 9 a.m. to 5
p.m. Eastern Time, Monday through Friday. Fax: (617) 495-6985, 24 hours
a day.

The paper used in this publication meets the requirements of the American
National Standard for Permanence of Paper for Printed Library Materials
Z39.48-1984

Library of Congress Cataloging-in-Publication Data

Command peformance: the art of delivering quality service/with a preface
by John E. Martin.
       p.   cm. — (The Harvard business review book series)
    Articles originally published in the Harvard business review since 1982.
    Includes index.
    ISBN 0-87584-562-2
    1. Customer service. 2. Quality control. 3. Customer relations.
    I. Harvard business review.   II. Series.
    HF5415.5.C625 1994
     658.8'12—dc20

                                                        94-16423
                                                           CIP

Contents

compete. These changes have far-reaching implications for the way managers structure their organizations and define strategic focus. Sustainable advantage comes from developing superior capabilities in a few core service skills.

because they have designed their business around customer loyalty—a self-reinforcing system in which the company delivers superior value and reinvents cash flows to find and keep customers and employees.

became BPA's partners in making better decisions, and the agency gained authority and legitimacy.

Preface

John E. Martin

Command Performance. The very title of this book suggests action. And that is exactly what the book is all about—taking action. Action that responds to the dramatically changing needs of today's customers. Action that gives you a competitive edge. Action that sets you apart from your competition.

Unfortunately, taking action is a very frightening proposition for many companies. That is why the vast majority of organizations today continue subscribing to the notion that "if it's not broken, don't fix it." If ever there were a cliché that needed to be eradicated from our collective mind-set, this is it.

Today, companies that want to thrive must take on a "break-it" mentality. By this, I refer to a corporate culture that pursues change rather than runs from it. The break-it organization places customers at the forefront of every important strategic decision, keeping nimble, flexible, and ready to respond on a moment's notice rather than frozen by paradigms of the past.

Breaking things before they are broken in order to give our customers the very best service and products we can offer is how we at Taco Bell define "command performance." It is on the strength of this philosophy that we find ourselves moving aggressively into the future—a future in which we are committed to satisfying our customers by providing innovative ways for them to access our brand and our products the world over.

Of course, this vision of the future did not magically appear overnight. The truth is, we had to learn the hard way just how important it is to deliver quality service. A decade ago, Taco Bell was an organization in trouble. From humble beginnings the company had grown into a significant fast food competitor. Yet it had also become a classically bureaucratic, top-down, command and control organization. Then came the turning point. During the mid-1980s we began listening to our customers as never before. In doing so, we quickly learned that many of the internal processes we had considered vital to our business were expendable. They simply didn't provide the two things our customers wanted most—service and value.

Determined to respond to our customers' needs, we reexamined every aspect of our business. Nothing was sacred. If an activity or a process added value for the customer, we improved it. If it provided no value, we either changed it or eliminated it altogether. By aggressively pursuing these changes, we were soon providing our customers some of the finest value, quality, and service in the industry.

This break-it mentality also helped us realize that, when it came to service, customers wanted more than we could offer within the confines of our traditional four-wall restaurants. So we began looking for innovative ways to provide service. Today customers can find Taco Bell in an array of new places ranging from schools, airports, and stadiums to movie theaters and convenience stores—even in a subway in Moscow. They can also find us on the grocery store shelf, thanks to a rapidly growing line of retail products. Without question, it was a new-found dedication to customer service, combined with a break-it mentality, that enabled us to dramatically reshape our business.

Simply put, the lessons we learned about service changed the game for Taco Bell. Of course, the story is far from over. Indeed, it must remain a never-ending story in which we will continue to break things *before* they're broken in an ongoing effort to provide our customers with higher levels of value, quality, satisfaction, and service.

This is how Taco Bell delivers a command performance. And, as you will discover in this book, companies that are ready, willing, and able to respond to their customers with a command performance will reap the highest rewards in the years to come.

Command Performance: Practical, Logical, Specific

By focusing on four major areas—Developing a Service Strategy, The Art of Quality Service Delivery, Delivering Quality Service in the Public Sector, and Linking Service and Profit—*Command Performance* provides a range of timely, logical, specific, and practical insights into what it takes to deliver quality service profitably and competitively. An important theme running throughout this book is that those organizations that embrace continuous innovation and improvement and master change are those that will in the future enjoy a commanding position in their respective industries. Together, these companies will usher in a new era of business success.

DEVELOPING A SERVICE STRATEGY

In "Lessons in the Service Sector," Professor James Heskett writes: "Despite their diversity, leading companies in many service industries display some common themes and practices. And they yield lessons for managers in any sector of the business." The contributors to Part I of *Command Performance* look at those lessons.

The most important lesson is to put the customer first. It sounds simple, but many organizations end up providing products and services they only *think* their customers need. Successful organizations, on the other hand, begin their search for a command performance by asking customers what *they* want. These companies also stay in close contact with their customers because consumer expectations and needs can, and do, change.

In "Service Companies: Focus or Falter," William Davidow and Bro Uttal discuss the crucial step of defining your market strategy: "Without one, you don't know who your customers are, how much they value different aspects of service, how much you must spend to satisfy them, and how big the payoffs are likely to be. In short, without a strategy you can't get to first base." Davidow and Uttal also stress the importance of recognizing the "lifetime value" of your core customers—and how a clear service strategy and vision can keep you focused on fulfilling your customers' needs, not just for the present, but year after year.

At Taco Bell we discovered that over a lifetime, each of our customers represents over $11,000 in sales. We also learned that the needs and expectations of our customers change as they pass from one life stage to another. People's age and income, for example, have a powerful influence on what they eat, when they eat, and where they eat. As we defined our strategy, we also realized that we should not restrict ourselves to serving people only at traditionally defined mealtimes; we now reach out to them *anytime* they're hungry. Redefining our service strategy in this way has significantly increased the total potential lifetime value of the 50 million customers we serve each week.

In short, understanding the concept of "lifetime value" and developing a strategy to achieve it can effectively set a company on a path leading to long-term profit and competitive success. At the same time, it is essential that the company have in place both the skills and technologies to realize that potential fully.

In "Beyond Products: Services-Based Strategy," James Brian Quinn, Thomas Doorley, and Penny Paquette discuss how successful companies can build their strategies not simply around products but around highly developed service capabilities that enable them to dramatically grow their business. A service-based company "strips itself down to the essentials necessary to deliver to customers the greatest possible value from its core skills—and out-sources as much of the rest as possible."

In "Customer Intimacy and Other Value Disciplines," Michael Treacy and Fred Wiersema discuss how the companies that have taken the lead in their industries over the last decade have done so by narrowing their focus, not broadening it. Using Dell Computer, Home Depot, and Nike as examples, the authors discuss three value disciplines—operational excellence, customer intimacy, and product leadership—and show how companies that push the boundaries of one while meeting industry standards in the other two, can gain a significant lead over their competitors.

THE ART OF QUALITY SERVICE DELIVERY

There are two kinds of business strategies: espoused strategies and enacted strategies. Espoused strategies are those that get talked about, dissected, and analyzed. Enacted strategies are those that actually get taken off the drawing board and put into play. In the realm of quality service delivery, enacted strategies are the only ones that matter because customers will tell you whether or not you are actually delivering what they want in the way they want it. The articles in Part II of *Command Performance* profile companies that are "walking the talk" when it comes to quality service delivery. And I write this with great pride, knowing that Taco Bell is highlighted here as a company leading the way in quality service delivery.

In "The Service-Driven Service Company," Leonard Schlesinger and James Heskett point out that, for more than forty years, service com-

panies successfully followed an industrial model based on the principles of traditional mass production. Today that model is obsolete.
According to the authors, the reason for this obsolescence is simple.
"The old model put the people who deliver service to customers last;
the new model puts frontline workers first and designs the business
system around them."

At Taco Bell we took steps to nearly eliminate the kitchens from our
restaurants. Why? Because large, multifunctional kitchens did not
provide customers with what they wanted most—great food at a great
price delivered by people who really cared about their needs. Eliminating the kitchen—a program we call K-Minus—enabled us to reduce
an expensive operational element that was driving up our prices. It
also allowed us to achieve a more consistent level of quality. Most
important, it enabled us to bring many of our employees who once
were stuck in the back, shredding lettuce and chopping tomatoes, out
to the front where they could serve customers. Did the customers care
that we were no longer making our food from scratch? No. What they
did (and do) care about is enjoying a well-prepared meal at a reasonable price every time they patronize one of our restaurants.

In "The New Productivity Challenge," Peter Drucker takes us on a
fascinating sociological journey that compares the past to the present
and shows us to how today's sociological shifts are mandating changes
for the future. He provides compelling examples of how employee
time can be wasted, even when workers are equipped with the very
latest so-called productivity tools. He also offers a four-step plan for
"working smarter." The last of these steps, I believe, is paramount:
forming a partnership with the people who hold the jobs. As Drucker
says, "to find out how to improve productivity, quality and performance—ask the people who do the work."

In "Loyalty-Based Management," Frederick Reichheld hits a number of resonant chords when he points out the economic benefits
stemming from long-term customer loyalty. As Reichheld states, achieving and maintaining this loyalty requires a strategic plan and a unique
corporate culture. "Creating a loyalty-based system in any company
requires a radical departure from traditional business thinking. It puts
creating customer value—not maximizing profits and shareholder
value—at the center of business strategy, and it demands significant
changes in business practice—redefining target customers, revising
employment policies, and redesigning incentives."

Reichheld examines how companies such as MBNA, USAA, Entenmann's, and Honda have become "loyalty leaders," while their com-

petition struggles—and usually fails—to achieve long-term loyalty. His premise is that a company must target and retain the right customers: not necessarily those who are the easiest to attract but those who are likely to do repeat business over a long period of time. A company must also be able to extend its portfolio of products and services so that it remains the "supplier of choice" as customers move from one life stage to another.

Customer loyalty has certainly been a key driver for us at Taco Bell. For several years we have successfully focused our products and marketing on people between the age of thirteen and twenty-four. Now we are aggressively extending our portfolio to remain an attractive meal choice to our customers as they move into their late twenties and beyond. For example, through our acquisition and expansion of Chevys Mexican Restaurants (a chain of casual, sit-down restaurants) and our implementation of other new concepts, we can maintain our customers' loyalty by responding to their different needs at different stages of life.

I was inspired by Timothy Firnstahl's article, "My Employees Are My Service Guarantee," not simply because he is a restaurateur but because he is passionate about empowering people, which leads to outstanding service for his customers and success for his business. Firnstahl provides this guarantee to his patrons: "Your Enjoyment Guaranteed. Always." *Behind* this guarantee stands a re-engineered business that gives employees—at every level—absolute authority to make and keep customers happy.

Now, this setup can become very pricey for an organization whose processes are riddled with problems, and that, as far as Firnstahl is concerned, is the point. "The guarantee brings out a true, hard-dollars picture of company failures and forces us to assume full responsibility for our output. The cost of keeping a company's promises is not just the price tag on the guarantee, it is the cost of system failure."

Behind Firnstahl's success is his strongly held belief in providing employees with the proper training and environment. "People often ask us where we find such wonderful employees. While it's true that we screen carefully, I believe our employees are better than most because they have the power and the obligation to solve customer problems on their own and on the spot."

At Taco Bell we also believe in the power of people and we are aggressively working to promote empowerment across all levels. The most telling example is our creation of Team Managed Units (TMUs) in which crew members take ownership of a wide range of management responsibilities, effectively enabling the crew to run a restaurant without the full-time supervision of a manager. Do TMUs work? The answer is a resounding yes. We now enjoy lower costs, lower turnover, higher morale, and, most important of all, higher customer satisfaction than at any other time in our history. Today, 90 percent of our company restaurants operate at top efficiency without dedicated management supervision.

Intense clarity. That's what came to mind when I read "Service Comes First," Thomas Teal's interview with Robert F. McDermott, former CEO of United Services Automobile Association (USAA), the nation's fifth-largest insurer of privately owned automobiles and homes. McDermott, a retired U.S. Air Force Brigadier General, is a no-nonsense leader who approaches business head on. There is nothing mysterious or vague about his thinking—his commitment to quality service delivery stands above all else as the reason for his company's tremendous success. "The mission and corporate culture of this company are, in one word, service. As a company objective, service comes ahead of either profits or growth."

McDermott is a leader who cares deeply about corporate culture: during his twenty-two years at USAA's helm, he worked hard to create an environment that challenged and enriched his people. From establishing a four-day workweek to developing training and education programs that far exceed the industry's standard, McDermott's strategy was clear: provide great service to your people and they will, in turn, provide great service to your customers.

McDermott is clear about the powerful service benefits that are realized through technology. "Information technology has to be a strategic competitive weapon, not just a cost center . . . we're not interested in technology for its own sake, only if we can turn it into better service and more satisfying jobs."

At Taco Bell we take this warning to heart. As we continue to incorporate more and more technology—whether for information collection and analysis or for production—we always ask ourselves whether a proposed technological enhancement will help us serve our customers. Only when the answer is an unequivocal "yes" do we proceed.

DELIVERING QUALITY SERVICE IN THE PUBLIC SECTOR

Regardless of the industry or market, and regardless of whether the enterprise functions in the private sector or the public, quality service delivery is a critical part of any strategic plan and its implementation. In "How I Turned a Critical Public into Useful Consultants," Peter Johnson shares both the turmoil that greeted him and the triumph that followed during his years as head of the Bonneville Power Administration (BPA) in Portland, Oregon. In the early 1980s, BPA—much like Taco Bell during the same period—was an organization in trouble. "By first making decisions and then explaining them, we were essentially telling people that we knew what was good for them. Meanwhile, the people affected by our decisions were telling us in any way they could . . . by aiming rifles at us . . . that the father-knows-best approach to decision making was completely unacceptable."

After spending far too much time in litigation and disputes, Johnson set out to create a solution at the point where all sound business decisions must begin—by communicating with the customer. In the years that followed, many of BPA's most important decisions emerged as the outcomes of open and candid two-way discussions with the public—its customers. The result was a consistent history of "win-win" situations. The public won by making its voice heard and becoming part of the solution; BPA won by making decisions based on customer needs and thereby developing a highly supportive customer base.

I found "Crime and Management," Alan Webber's interview with then-New York City Police Commissioner Lee P. Brown, uplifting yet sobering. The challenges Brown faced in delivering quality service are the very challenges faced by a society fighting crime, drug addiction, illiteracy, poverty, and lack of opportunity. Brown chose a fresh, businesslike approach to New York City's law enforcement challenges. His vision of community policing called for training and empowering officers to provide unique solutions, while enlisting the involvement and support of the city's citizens. As an executive, I appreciated Brown's creative, intelligent, and far-reaching approach.

At Taco Bell we are striving to bring new business opportunities into America's inner cities. I was therefore inspired by Ron Grzywinski's article, "The New Old-Fashioned Banking," chronicling the tremendous challenges he and his management team faced at Chicago's South Shore Bank in the early 1970s. It is a classic story with, fortunately, an un-classic ending.

In the late 1960s, Chicago's South Shore had become a community in decline. Banks that had once prospered in the region were now faltering and looking to get out. "Old-fashioned banking"—local establishments serving local needs—was disappearing at an alarming rate. Rather than becoming part of the problem, however, Grzywinski and his partners—though vastly undercapitalized—became part of the solution by taking over as managers of South Shore Bank in August 1973. Driven by their great entrepreneurial spirit and their philosophy that banks have a responsibility to serve communities at the local level, the South Shore Bank managers began to learn, try, discover, fail, triumph, struggle, learn, and ultimately succeed. That the South Shore Bank flourished under Grzywinski's leadership reminds us that certain values, such as focusing on the needs of the community, can lead to prosperity. And while acting on those values can be challenging, it can also be tremendously rewarding—both financially and personally.

It is refreshingly clear that many of this country's top administrators in the public sector share not only a solution-oriented approach to business but quality of life values as well. This observation is reinforced in "Profits with a Purpose," Nancy Nichols' interview with Tom Chapman, the CEO of Greater Southeast Community Hospital in an impoverished suburb of Washington, D.C. Nearly one-quarter of the area's residents live near the poverty line, yet Greater Southeast is thriving, thanks to highly innovative programs that, at first glance, would appear to have little in common with traditional health care. "We don't just treat our patients' illnesses. We treat the diseases racking our community—poverty, illiteracy, drugs, and violence. . . .we try to create services that are relevant to the needs of the people. In business, this might be called being close to the customer. In health care, we call it responding to the needs of the community."

What Tom Chapman and the other leaders profiled here have in common is a refusal to believe that quality service delivery in the public sector is an oxymoron—and they are inspiring examples of leaders who have changed, and continue to change, the rules of the service game.

LINKING SERVICE AND PROFIT

Profits are the heartbeat of any business, a point that is clearly underscored in this final segment by five leading authorities, Harvard Business School's James Heskett, Thomas Jones, Gary Loveman, W. Earl Sasser, Jr., and Leonard Schlesinger, who have joined forces in "Putting the Service-Profit Chain to Work." The authors remind us that customer satisfaction stems from a series of interconnected causes and disciplines: customer loyalty drives profitability and growth; value drives customer satisfaction; employee productivity drives value; employee loyalty drives productivity; employee satisfaction drives loyalty, and internal quality drives employee satisfaction.

In the second part of the article, "Service-Profit Chain Audit," the authors provide a framework for understanding an organization's assets and liabilities with regard to service delivery. The audit is the beginning of a process that can give managers at all levels a thorough understanding of what customers and employees think about current procedures—and how those procedures must change in order to deliver world-class service and outstanding profits.

A Final Thought

As I review the many insights to be found in *Command Performance*, one thing stands out from all the rest: while quality service is easy to talk about, it is a difficult thing to deliver. The truth is, delivering quality service is hard work requiring tremendous energy, skill, wisdom, and determination. If it could be achieved through anything less, the world would be full of satisfied customers and—believe me—it isn't. But in this book are ideas to apply to your business, ideas that will enable you to turn the art of delivering quality service into a competitive advantage. The only question, then, is—will you?

Command
Performance

PART

I

Developing a Service Strategy

1
Lessons in the Service Sector

James L. Heskett

A large food and lodging company creates and staffs more general management jobs than any ten manufacturers of comparable size. This company, like many others dispensing high customer-contact services, has eliminated functional lines of responsibility between operations and marketing. In its planning the company routinely combines operations and marketing with what I call a strategic service vision.

The most profitable large American company assumes daily the task of managing a work force of window washers, cooks, and maintenance personnel. An almost single-minded concentration on people—their jobs, their equipment, their personal development—accounts for much of its success.

The quality control process in a decentralized oil-field services business involves careful selection, development, assignment, and compensation of employees working under varying conditions and in widespread locations where close supervision is impossible. In this prosperous company, the process builds shared values and bonds people together.

An international airline, by paying more attention to market economies than to production scale economies, reduces the average size of its aircraft and increases its net income.

Products introduced since 1982 by a well-known financial service generated 10% of its revenues in 1985. The raw material for these products is data already existing in other forms in the company's vast data base.

These examples give a glimpse of forward-looking management practice. When examined closely, they offer insights into the ideas on which successful competitive strategies have been fashioned in the much-maligned and little-understood service sector.

It's no coincidence that dominant industries have cutting-edge management practices. Some U.S. railroads in the nineteenth century pioneered in divisionalized management of their far-flung systems and in good procurement procedures to support their sizable construction and operational needs. At the turn of the century, basic industries led the way in experimenting with scientific management. Then the rise of the large consumer goods manufacturer, epitomized by the auto industry, spawned concepts of decentralization and a full product line aimed at carefully segmented markets.

Today service industries have assumed the mantle of economic leadership. These industries, encompassing trade, communications, transportation, food and lodging, financial and medical services, education, government, and technical services to industry, account for about 70% of the national income and three-fourths of the nonfarm jobs in the United States. In generating 44 million new jobs in the past 30 years, they have absorbed most of the influx of women and minorities into the work force, softened the effects of every post–World War II recession, and fueled every recent economic recovery.

In view of this leadership role, now is a good time to look at the exemplars in the service sector for insights into ways of boosting productivity and altering competitive strategies. Despite their diversity, leading companies in many service industries display some common themes and practices. And they yield lessons for managers in any sector of business. Let's look first at the way the best service companies are structured.

Integrated Functions

Most goods-producing businesses follow the traditional organizational pattern of separate and equally important marketing and manufacturing functions, with coordinating authority at high levels. Some service businesses do the same thing, but the pattern is much less common in service companies where contact with customers is close, as in retailing, passenger transport, and food and lodging. In these businesses, service is marketed and produced at the same place and time, and often by the same person. Naturally, close coordination between marketing and operations management in these cases, regardless of reporting relationships, is essential.

Integration of marketing and operations is often found at very low levels in these organizations. In fact, more than 90% of all field managers in four multisite service companies surveyed in one study claimed responsibility for operations, personnel, and marketing, could not say which was most important, and paid great attention to each.[1]

Even where operations are buffered from marketing activities in organizations offering little customer-contact service, there are ways to break down the traditional functional barriers. Several years ago, the Chase Manhattan Bank launched an effort to upgrade its nonloan products, improve its external communications and customer service, and make its back-office (production) operations more market based. A weak spot was Chase's international business. In the highly visible "product" of international money transfer, differences of viewpoint between marketing—embodied in the account relations manager in the field—and the back office in New York had frustrated communication. Errors were frequent, a large backlog of inquiries about balances and transactions had piled up, and morale in the operations group was poor.

A study ordered by the executive put in charge showed that headquarters accounted for operational errors in only about one-third of all the inquiries and that the marketing people had little idea what operations could offer the bank's customers. The executive traced the backlogged errors to their sources, often a correspondent bank, and resolved them. He launched a campaign to improve operations staff morale around the theme "We make it happen" and formed a new group, the customer mobile unit, consisting of the bank's most experienced international operations people. The unit visited Chase customers at their businesses to help resolve problems and smooth operations. The executive brought the marketing and back-office people together to talk about ways to improve the flow of information. Perhaps most important, the bank revised reporting relationships so that operations units serving specific market segments reported to both the customer relationship manager and the head of operations—a move that improved functional coordination.[2]

The product manager's job was created in many manufacturing organizations to address the problem of coordinating manufacturing and marketing. But in most cases, product managers have had profit responsibility without the authority to coordinate. Assignment to these positions has been regarded as temporary, which encourages decisions with a short-term orientation.

Because of their importance, the high-contact service company

Exhibit I.   Externally Oriented Strategic Service Vision

Target market segments ◀▶	Positioning ◀▶	Service concept ◀
What are common characteristics of important market segments?	How does the service concept propose to meet customer needs?	What are important elements of the service to be provided, stated in terms of results produced for customers?
What dimensions can be used to segment the market?	How do competitors meet these needs?	How are these elements supposed to be perceived by the target market segment? By the market in general? By employees as a whole?
Demographic?	How is the proposed service differentiated from competition?	
Psychographic?		
How important are various segments?	How important are these differences?	
What needs does each have?	What is good service?	How do customers perceive the service concept?
How well are these needs being served?	Does the proposed service concept provide it?	What efforts does this suggest in terms of the manner in which the service is:
In what manner?	What efforts are required to bring customer expectations and service capabilities into alignment?	Designed?
By whom?		Delivered?
		Marketed?

Basic element ▬▬▬

Integrative element ▭▭▭

Lessons in the Service Sector *Lessons in the Service Sector*   7

Value–cost leveraging	Operating strategy	Strategy-systems integration	Service delivery system
To what extent are differences between perceived value and cost of service maximized by:	What are important elements of the strategy?	To what extent are the strategy and delivery system internally consistent?	What are important features of the service delivery system, including:
Standardization of certain elements?	Operations?	Can needs of the strategy be met by the delivery system?	The role of people?
Customization of certain elements?	Financing? Marketing? Organization? Human resources? Control?	If not, what changes must be made in:	Technology? Equipment? Layout? Procedures?
Emphasizing easily leveraged services?	On which will the most effort be concentrated?	The operating strategy?	What capacity does it provide?
Management of supply and demand?	Where will investments be made?	The service delivery system?	Normally? At peak levels?
Control of quality through–	How will quality and cost be controlled?	To what extent does the coordination of operating strategy and service delivery system ensure:	To what extent does it:
Rewards? Appeal to pride? Visibility and supervision? Peer group control?	Measured? Incentives? Rewards?	High quality?	Help ensure quality standards?
Involving the customer?	What results will be expected versus competition in terms of:	High productivity? Low cost?	Differentiate the service from competition?
Effective use of data?	Quality of service?	High morale and loyalty of servers?	Provide barriers to entry by competitors?
To what extent does this effort create barriers to entry by potential competition?	Cost profile? Productivity? Morale and loyalty of servers?	To what extent does this integration provide barriers to entry to competition?	

makes a point of developing numbers of marketing-operations managers, often carrying the title of store or branch manager. At hand, therefore, is a large cadre of talent from which the company can draw senior managers already trained for administrative responsibilities.

Strategic Service Vision

The need of most service organizations to plan as well as direct marketing and operations as one function has led to the formation in leading companies of what I call a strategic service vision. Its elements consist of identification of a target market segment, development of a service concept to address targeted customers' needs, codification of an operating strategy to support the service concept, and design of a service delivery system to support the operating strategy. These basic elements are shaded darker in Exhibit I.

A company naturally tries to position itself in relation to both the target market and the competition. The links between the service concept and the operating strategies are those policies and procedures by which the company seeks to maximize the difference between the value of the service to customers (the service concept) and the cost of providing it. This difference, of course, is a primary determinant of profit. And the link between the operating strategy and the service delivery system is the integration achieved in the design of both. These integrative links are shaded lighter in Exhibit I.

To see how the strategic service vision works, examine the Hartford Steam Boiler Inspection & Insurance Company. For many years, HSB has been in the business of insuring industrial and institutional equipment. Its market targets are organizations using boilers and related pieces of equipment with high operating risk. It offers the same risk reduction as many other insurance companies but positions itself against the competition by emphasizing cost reduction as well.

HSB concentrates on a few types of equipment and has built a large data base on their operating and performance characteristics. (Manufacturers of the equipment often turn to HSB to get wear and maintenance data.) The information furnishes the actuarial base on which HSB prices its insurance. The company's engineers, who inspect customers' equipment before and after it is insured, are also qualified to give advice on preventing problems and improving utilization rates, and through many years of association they often get very close to their customers. As a service manager of one HSB client told me, "If I tried to replace that insurance contract, my operating people in the plant would let me know about it."

This practice enhances the perceived value of the service to the customer at little extra cost to HSB. Of course, by reducing the risk to the customer HSB can improve its own loss ratio.

HSB has a larger cadre of engineers than any of its competitors. These engineers, in tandem with the big data base, make up a service delivery system that capitalizes on the knowledge of marketing and operating managers at all levels of the organization.

The net result is a strategic service vision (though HSB doesn't use the term) that is highly valued by its customers and very profitable for its provider. It addresses implementation issues as part of the strategic plan, and it requires agreement and coordination among marketing and operating managers throughout the organization.

Inner-Directed Vision

High-performance service companies have gained their status in large measure by turning the strategic service vision inward: by targeting important groups of employees as well as customers. In the head offices of these organizations, questions such as those listed in Exhibit II are heard often. The questions parallel those in Exhibit I; but in asking them about employees, management shows it's aware that the health of the enterprise depends on the degree to which core groups of employees subscribe to and share a common set of values and are served by the company's activities.

The basic elements, shaded darker as in Exhibit I, start with the service concept designed with employee's needs in mind. The operating strategy is set to meet these needs in a superior fashion at the lowest cost, a result often achieved through the design of the service delivery system. The integrative elements, shaded lighter, include positioning of a service concept, which it is hoped will lead to low turnover, low training costs, and the opportunity to develop shared goals and values. High-performance service organizations invariably have operating strategies designed to maximize differences between operating costs and value perceived by employees in their relations with the company. And delivery systems designed with the operating strategy in mind can form the foundation for remarkable gains in productivity.

A case in point is the ServiceMaster Company, based in Downers

Exhibit II. *Internally Oriented Strategic Service Vision*

Target employee group	Positioning	Service concept
What are common characteristics of important employee groups?	How does the service concept propose to meet employee needs?	What are important elements of the service to be provided, stated in terms of results produced for employees and the company?
What dimensions can be used to describe these employee groups?	How do competitors meet such needs?	How are these elements supposed to be perceived by the targeted employee group?
Demographic?	How are relationships with employees differentiated from those between competitors and their employees?	
Psychographic?		
How important are each of these groups to the delivery of the service?	How important are these differences?	How are these elements perceived?
What needs does each group have?	What is "good service" to employees?	What further efforts does this suggest in terms of the manner in which the service is:
How well are these needs being served?	Does the proposed service concept provide it?	Designed?
In what manner?		Delivered?
By whom?	What efforts are required to bring employee expectations and service capabilities into alignment?	

Basic element

Integrative element

▶ Value-cost leveraging	◀▶ Operating strategy	◀▶ Strategy-systems integration	◀▶ Service delivery system
To what extent are differences between returns to employees and the level of effort they put forth maximized by:	How important is direct human contact in the provision of the service?	To what extent are the strategy and the delivery system for serving important employee groups internally consistent?	What are important features of the service delivery system, including:
The design of the service concept?	To what extent have employees been involved in the design of the service concept and operating strategy?	To what extent does the integration of operating strategy and service delivery system ensure:	The role of people? Technology? Equipment? Layout? Procedures?
The design of the elements of the operating strategy?			
Job design?	How desirable is it to:	High quality?	What does it require of target employee groups?
The leveraging of scarce skills with a support system?	Increase employee satisfaction?	High productivity? Low cost?	Normally?
The management of supply and demand?	Increase employee productivity?	High morale and "bonding" of the target employee group?	At peak periods of activity?
Control of quality through —	What incentives are provided for:		To what extent does it help employees:
Rewards? Appeal to pride? Visibility? Supervision? Peer group control?	Quality? Productivity? Cost?		Meet quality standards? Differentiate their service from competitors?
Involving the customer in the delivery of the service?	How does the strategy address employee needs for:		Achieve expectations about the quality of their work life?
Effective use of data?	Selection? Assignment? Development? Evaluation? Compensation? Association?		

Grove, Illinois, which manages support services for hospitals, schools, and industrial companies. It supervises the employees of customers' organizations engaged in housekeeping, food service, and equipment maintenance. These are services that are peripheral to the customers' businesses and therefore get little management attention.

Many of the people whom ServiceMaster oversees are functionally illiterate. To them, as well as its own managers, ServiceMaster directs a service concept centered around the philosophy stated by its CEO, "Before asking someone to do something you have to help them be something." ServiceMaster provides educational and motivational programs to help these employees "be something."

To its own supervisors the company offers training leading to an ambitious "master's" program taught in part by the chief executive. New responsibilities and opportunities present themselves via the rapid growth of the company, approximating 20% per year, nearly all of it from expansion of existing operations rather than acquisition. Elaborate training aids and a laboratory for developing new equipment and materials enhance the employee-managers' "be something" feeling.

For customer's employees ServiceMaster tries to build the "be something" attitude and improve their productivity by redesigning their jobs and by developing equipment and pictorial, color-coded instructional material. In most cases it is the first time that anyone has paid attention to the service of which these employees are a part. ServiceMaster also holds weekly sessions to exchange ideas and offers educational programs to, among other things, develop literacy. ServiceMaster also recruits up to 20% of its own managers from the ranks in jobs it handles. The service concept clearly is improved self-respect, self-development, personal satisfaction, and upward mobility.

Another company slogan, repeated often, is "to help people grow." When a hospital served by the company decided to hire a deaf person, ServiceMaster's local head didn't object. Instead he authorized three of his supervisors to take a course in sign language.

It should be no surprise that the turnover rate among ServiceMaster's 7,000 employees is low. Further, the turnover rate in organizations it services is much lower than the averages for their industries. And when ServiceMaster takes a job, the productivity achieved by supervised support workers invariably rises dramatically.

Now a billion-dollar company, ServiceMaster had a return on equity from 1973 through 1985 that was the highest of all the largest service or industrial companies in the United States, averaging more than 30% after taxes. It oversees the support service employees for 15 hospitals in Japan, which probably makes it the largest exporter of managerial talent to Japan. According to one ServiceMaster executive, "The Japanese immediately recognize and identify with what we do and how we do it." This company turns its strategic service vision inward with dramatic results.

The Vision Applied

In addition to building a strategic service vision, the best service companies apply it to customers and to those who deliver the service and oversee its delivery—in new or different ways. From my study of organizations like Hartford Steam Boiler and ServiceMaster, I've gathered a series of lessons useful for service providers to consider. These lessons can furnish goods producers food for thought too.

RETHINK QUALITY CONTROL

Executives whose careers have spanned service as well as manufacturing agree that reaching a consistently high quality level is tougher in services. In high-contact (so-called high-encounter) services, the interaction between two people or more varies with each transaction. In low-contact services, people many miles from the customer have to rely on their own judgment in handling orders and other transactions and in fielding complaints.

Those who have tried to solve the quality control problem by adding more supervision have found that it limits effectiveness. A service transaction cannot be halted, examined, and recycled like a product.

The most effective approaches to the problem have included restructuring of incentives to emphasize quality, designing jobs to give service providers higher visibility in dealing with customers, and building a peer group to foster teamwork and instill a sense of pride.

One incentive that is often effective in organizations ranging from rapid transit companies to hotels is the employee-of-the-month award—especially if based on customer feedback. Both monetary and nonmonetary incentives have been used successfully. What's more, the cost is low.

Making the person who delivers the service more visible is another technique. In England, at the Lex Service Group's luxury auto dealerships, the customer is encouraged to go directly to the mechanic working on the car. The Shouldice Hospital near Toronto, Canada specializes in the repair of hernias using only local anesthetic—a practice that allows the doctor to talk with the patient during the operation. Defective work is referred to the doctor responsible. The remission rate for hernias performed at Shouldice is less than one-tenth that of the average North American hospital. At Benihana, the U.S. chain of Japanese-style steak houses, the chef cooks at a grill in front of the restaurant guests. The chef's visibility and proximity to customers promote a consistently high quality of service and a consistently high level of tips.

Incentives and visibility may be insufficient for those tasks performed without supervision and out of view of the customer. In these cases, some companies rely on careful selection and thorough training of employees and the development of programs to build both a sense of pride in the service and a sense of identification with the company. This bonding process can be hard for rivals to emulate and can thereby contribute to competitive advantage.

Schlumberger's wire-line service has roughly 2,000 geological engineers, each responsible for a mobile rig equipped with more than $1 million worth of computers and electronic gear that helps predict the outcome of petroleum producers' drilling efforts. Each year the company recruits those it considers the brightest of the crop of college engineering graduates, spends months teaching them how to use the equipment, and goes to great lengths to make them feel a part of a special tradition. As one engineer put it recently, "Indoctrination is just as important as technical training." This is all in preparation for an assignment to represent Schlumberger in the field, without direct supervision, often in a remote part of the world. Two measures of the success of this program are Schlumberger's dominant share of the world's wire-line business and the profit-to-sales ratios for this company, which consistently exceed others in its industry in good times and bad.

Often effective in achieving and maintaining quality is peer group control, supported by incentives, training, job design, and service delivery system design. In cases where professional standards have been established for a task, they reinforce peer group control.

In an architectural firm, the mere existence of a policy requiring partners' review of every piece of work can keep partners and associates on their toes. Surgeons are sometimes assigned in teams to foster

Exhibit III. How Success Builds High-Contact Services

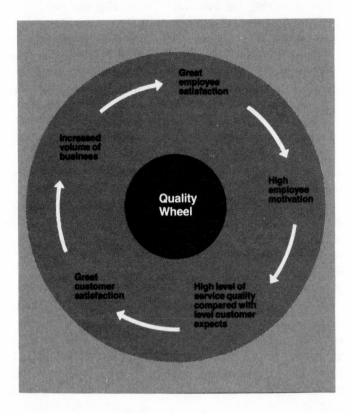

the learning process and encourage peer group control. A partner of a leading real estate development company told me, "There are three things I'm most concerned about in my work. In this order, they are not to embarrass my colleagues, not to cast a bad light on the company by inadequately serving my clients, and making money." It's not surprising that this company has a strong sense of shared values, reinforced by a policy of encouraging partners to invest in the projects that they propose and carry out.

Recent research suggests that the internal strategic service vision, quality control, and success are connected, especially in those providers of high-encounter service requiring judgment in delivery. I show it as the "quality wheel" in Exhibit III. Studies directly link customer satisfaction and the resulting sales volume to the satisfaction derived by the person serving the customer.[3] Naturally, the more motivated the employee, the better the service.

The selection and development of employees, care in assignment, and the layout and equipment of the facility (in a high-contact environment) are all integral elements of the design of the service encounter, which in turn is based on the company's assessment of customer needs. Preconditioning of the customer may also be part of the design of the service encounter. Review and redesign of the encounter go on continually as the organization assesses how well it is meeting those needs.

A part of the internal service vision is the design of policies and performance measures that further the fulfillment of customers' needs. For example, the server's well-being in the job apparently depends, at least in part, on the extent to which his or her superiors emphasize the solution of problems for customers rather than strict adherence to a set of policies and procedures.[4]

Driving the self-reinforcing elements of the wheel of quality takes a great deal of executive time and requires an honest interest in people across the organization. The senior vice president for finance of Delta Airlines, an organization well regarded for its service and its employee programs, remarked recently, "I would guess that 25% of the time of the finance department officers is spent listening to people problems."

For most service companies, people obviously are more important than machines in the control of quality. But even where the machines employed carry an unusually high value, as in Schlumberger and Delta, developing and building the dedication of people takes precedence.

REASSESS THE EFFECTS OF SCALE

In service organizations, scale economies are often much more important at the company level than at the operating unit level. This is particularly true for companies that have many units over wide areas connected by a common identity. Such scale gives McDonald's and Hertz great purchasing clout and General Cinema the advantage of selling soft drinks of its own manufacture.

Large scale at the company level is important for exploiting network effects, a phenomenon much more important in the service than in the manufacturing sector. To a point, the addition of new network links augments volume for those parts already in place, thus building average network capacity utilization. The addition of service to Las Vegas from its Memphis hub gave Federal Express more volume on the Memphis–New York link. When Visa adds a large retailer to its network of card-accepting establishments, it increases the attractiveness of its credit card to present and potential cardholders and the potential volume to be realized by retailers already accepting the card.

Bigger is not better in those service industries in which the factory must be taken into the marketplace to sell a more accessible, visible, and convenient product that meets customers' needs. Factories operated by the Hyatt and Marriott organizations (called hotels) have not, on average, grown in size for years. These companies have settled on a range of hotel dimensions that can be designed, located, and operated effectively to achieve the capacity utilization, quality of service, and financial performance they want. The range describes sizes at which diseconomies resulting from poor supervision and inflexibility tend to outweigh advantages of larger scale. In the design and siting of hotels, Hyatt and Marriott give the less quantifiable advantages of market flexibility weight equal to operating economies of scale.

At the unit operating level, many service companies have found that the loss of flexibility and greater difficulty in supervising those delivering the service far outweigh any savings realized in operating costs as unit size grows. In the rush to cut costs per seat-mile, for example, many of the world's airlines bought large, wide-bodied aircraft like the Airbus 300 and McDonnell DC-10. While these planes performed admirably, their effective utilization required funneling large numbers of passengers into the airline's hub. Moreover, because business travelers, who represent the most attractive market segment, are prone to choose an airline on the basis of times and frequency of flights, the load and schedule consolidation necessary for effective employment of wide-bodied aircraft worked against the goal of building traffic.

When Jon Carlzon became CEO of Scandinavian Airlines System in 1980, wide-bodied aircraft were used extensively between the airline's hub at Copenhagen and major cities like London and Paris. With smaller DC-9s, SAS funneled travelers between the hub and other Scandinavian cities. To reclaim the business travelers SAS had lost, Carlzon relegated most of the wide-bodies to charter work and offered nonstop flights using DC-9s between Scandinavian and principal European cities.

A size question confronts nearly every power utility in the United States today. For years it was industry gospel that the more power-generating capacity concentrated in one place, the greater the economies of scale. This was the case until the 1970s, when ever-larger units began encountering reliability problems. Furthermore, construction schedule stretch-outs, at times fomented by environmental groups' agitation against big plants, caused the expected power-generating economies to vanish. Finally, an improved capability for transmitting excess energy from one market to another made it possible to buy energy for less than the big units could afford to charge. So many utilities today are meeting the needs of smaller markets' fluctuating demands more economically through new means.

REPLACE AND CREATE ASSETS WITH INFORMATION

For decades, manufacturers have sought ways of substituting information for assets. Foremost among these are forecasting and inventory control techniques. For many service operations, information offers creative new ways to substitute for assets.

Heating oil dealers, by maintaining data on the capacity of their customers' tanks, on habitual consumption rates, and on weather, program fuel oil deliveries to provide 100% availability while reducing delivery times and the number of trucks and drivers. These companies substitute information for assets.

The Rural/Metro Fire Department extends effective fire protection at a fraction of the cost of most municipally run fire departments. This Scottsdale, Arizona-based company analyzes data on past fires and uses much smaller, less expensive trucks staffed with smaller crews and equipped with a large-diameter hose that can shoot a lot of water on a fire very fast. On the way to a fire, a truck crew can learn the floor plan of the building to which it is going. While speeding through the streets, the crew examines a microfiche of the layout on a screen. Rural/Metro substitutes information for assets.

Many service industries are information driven, beginning with familiarity between the server and the served. In many (not all), assets have never been allowed to become dominant, perhaps because of limited capital. But with the development of new technologies for processing and communicating information, companies in these industries have advanced far beyond the use of information as a substitute for assets. They are instead using the information they have collected in one business as the basis for new services.

Companies servicing manufactured goods, for example, have built data bases on the types, wear rates, and failure rates of various parts of a furnace, appliance, or automobile. A company can use this information for sending timely service reminders to customers and also to manage parts inventories to reflect the age and condition of the particular machine serviced. In the process, the data have taken on great value for the producers of the goods—and they're willing to pay for the information.

A credit card service builds expenditure profiles for its customers; broken patterns may signal a problem like stolen cards. Theft is sometimes suspected when a large expenditure is made far from the cardholder's address. Instead of outright disallowance of a retailer's request for a big charge, one major travel card issuer tries to determine whether the cardholder indeed is traveling in the retailer's area. Information collected for this service yields person-specific data about travel patterns that often is valuable to airlines and hotel chains (to name two businesses). But the company limits the use of such information to ways that benefit its cardholders.

Dun & Bradstreet's $2.7 billion enterprise is centered on its data base, a file of credit information describing businesses in 30 countries. Through development and acquisition, the file steadily grows. D&B has consistently realized about 10% of its revenues from business that did not exist three years before. Nearly all of these services use the same data base but package the information in different ways. A potential competitor would have to spend an estimated $1 billion— nearly half D&B's net asset value—to duplicate the data base.

Though a data base may constitute a service provider's most important asset, it doesn't appear on the balance sheet and can't be depreciated. But the degree to which many such companies rely on an accumulation of knowledge as their chief competitive weapon and source of new business development suggests opportunities for their counterparts in the manufacturing sector.

Harlan Cleveland has pointed out that information, unlike most manufactured products, is often infinitely expandable (as it is used), compressible, substitutable (for capital, labor, or physical materials), transportable, diffusive (hard to keep secret), and sharable (as opposed to exchangeable).[5] If it is infinitely expandable, those who possess it are limited only by their imagination in creating new ideas, revenue sources, and job opportunities. As the demand for creative exploitation of information grows, so will job creation in the service sector.

The Service Economy

Many successful service providers have strategies in common that offer lessons to other companies. Among these are:

Close coordination of the marketing-operations relationship.

A strategy built around elements of a strategic service vision.

An ability to redirect the strategic service inward to focus on vital employee groups.

A stress on the control of quality based on a set of shared values, peer group status, generous incentives, and, where possible, a close relationship with the customer.

A cool appraisal of the effects of scale on both efficiency and effectiveness.

The substitution of information for other assets.

The exploitation of information to generate new business.

Why these particular lessons among all I might cite? For one reason, they feature characteristics that distinguish many service industries from goods-producing industries. Notice the emphasis on people, ideas, and information instead of things. For another, they promise twin benefits as part of a business strategy. Each can further differentiation of the service product as well as lower costs.

These lessons have significance for the economy too. While the service economy has wrought a gigantic social restructuring of the United States, it has come in for unwarranted criticism for its low rate of productivity gains. Companies like those I have described, however, have created new jobs while raising productivity. If other companies learn these lessons, job opportunities in the service sector will continue to expand and productivity continue to rise. These developments will ease the pressures for the inflation of service prices, sharpen the already respected competitiveness abroad of U.S.-based services, and contribute to the partnership between services and manufacturing that is crucial to a healthy, balanced national business base.

Notes

1. Christopher H. Lovelock, Eric Langeard, John E.G. Bateson, and Pierre Eiglier, "Some Organizational Problems Facing Marketing in the Service Sector," in *Marketing of Services*, ed. James H. Donnelly and

William R. George (Chicago, Ill.: American Marketing Association, 1981), p. 168.

2. See James F. Loud, "Organizing for Customer Service," *The Bankers Magazine*, November–December 1980, p. 41.

3. Benjamin Schneider and David E. Bowen, "New Services Design, Development, and Implementation and the Employee," in *New Services*, ed. William R. George and Claudia Marshall (Chicago, Ill.: American Marketing Association, 1985), p. 82; and Eugene M. Johnson and Daniel T. Seymour, "The Impact of Cross Selling on the Service Encounter in Retail Banking," in *The Service Encounter*, ed. John A. Czepiel, Michael R. Soloman, and Carol F. Surprenant (Lexington, Mass.: D.C. Heath, 1985), p. 243.

4. This is the implication of John J. Parkington and Benjamin Schneider in "Some Correlates of Experienced Job Stress: A Boundary Role Study," *Academy of Management Journal*, June 1979, p. 270.

5. Harlan Cleveland, "Information as a Resource," *The Futurist*, December 1982, p. 37.

2
Service Companies: Focus or Falter

William H. Davidow and Bro Uttal

In an industry bedeviled by rising costs, Shouldice Hospital near Toronto, Canada is a model of cost-bashing productivity. Surgery patients stay at Shouldice for 31/2 days compared with 5 to 8 days at most hospitals. Its doctors perform many more operations a year than elsewhere, yet they are paid less than they would make in private practice; nurses attend to several times as many patients as they would in most other hospitals. Patients care for themselves; they get to the operating room on their own steam, walk to the recovery room, and take their meals in a common dining room.

Does this sound like a low-quality, uncaring production line? It's just the opposite. Measured by how often patients need repeated treatment for the same problem, Shouldice is ten times more effective than other hospitals. Ex-patients are so delighted with the Shouldice experience that they hold an annual reunion to commemorate it. The January 1988 jamboree at the Royal York Hotel in Toronto attracted some 1,500 "alumni."

There's something else unusual about this picture of great service: most sick people couldn't get admitted to Shouldice. If you have a broken bone, gallstones, or clogged arteries, apply elsewhere. Shouldice accepts only one type of patient—people whose single complaint is a hernia. Even then, the hospital will reject hernia victims who have histories of heart trouble or who have undergone surgery in the last 12 months or who weigh more than Shouldice recommends.

A tightly focused service strategy is the key to Shouldice's performance. By segmenting the market of sick people according to their complaints, then concentrating on one segment that is inexpensive to serve, Shouldice has optimized its operations, fulfilled its mission—and enjoyed a handsome return.

After doing hundreds of hernia repairs a year using a special technique, Shouldice's doctors have become highly proficient and productive. The hospital usually can avoid using general anesthesia because local anesthesia, which is safer and cheaper, works well for hernia repair. Patients recover from surgery faster if they're up and about, so Shouldice avoids paying for a fleet of wheelchairs and gurneys, armies of aides to push them, and banks of wide elevators. Instead, it gives patients hallways with comfortable carpeting, staircases with low risers, and acres of well-groomed grounds on which to stroll. The central location of television sets and toilets encourages patients to walk around even as it saves the hospital money.

Concentration on hernias enables Shouldice to produce a highly competitive core service. But that's not the main reason for Shouldice's success. Other organizations, notably the Lichtenstein Hernia Institute of Los Angeles, do low-cost repairs that work at least as well. Consumers, most of whom have medical insurance, are somewhat insensitive to health care costs. And those who have personal physicians tend to follow their advice, which normally is to get a hernia fixed at a hometown hospital.

No, people flock to Shouldice mainly because they hear from former patients that being there is a great experience. The hospital earns this enthusiastic word of mouth because it adds significant (though intangible) value to its core service. Most people can't accurately judge the quality of a hospital's core service. What they can and do appraise, at least when they're not very sick, are experiences like the welcome received at check-in, the behavior of fellow patients, and the attentiveness and perceived competence of doctors and nurses.

Could Shouldice produce outstanding customer service absent its clear strategy? Probably not without completely redesigning its physical and social systems and sending its rates sky high. Shouldice is ill-suited for treating people with broken legs or weak hearts, those who can't walk much or who have had major surgery and need intravenous feeding, or patients recovering from plastic surgery (they seldom want to socialize). Shouldice managers have thought about undertaking minor eye surgery and repairing varicose veins and hemorrhoids—procedures fairly similar to hernia repair in their demands on facilities. But "fairly similar" isn't close enough. Shouldice has decided to stick with the segment it knows best and serves most effectively.[1]

In contrast, fuzzy or conflicting strategies make good customer service impossible. Look at People Express. In 1981, it focused tightly on budget travelers—students, back-packers, vacationers, and others willing to sacrifice convenient schedules and airport gates for low fares. Customers actually enjoyed the airline's widely advertised "no frills" service, which gave them the options of bringing their own food or paying extra for a snack in flight, of carrying their luggage or paying $3 a bag to check it, and of buying a ticket on board instead of in advance. In five years, People Express's fleet grew from 3 airplanes to 117, and its revenues soared from $38 million to nearly $1 billion.

But People had overexpanded. Every day, the airline had thousands of seats available, but its steady customers wanted to fly mainly on weekends and during the summer and other vacation times. The glut of empty seats produced a $3.7 million loss in 1984. So People scrambled to get more revenue from its fleet. It scheduled each plane for as many flights as possible and it grossly overbooked to compensate for customers who made reservations but didn't show up. The airline also went after business travelers, whose demand is heaviest Monday through Friday and nicely complements the weekend demand pattern of budget fliers. To attract executives, the airline pitched its luxurious first-class service, complete with leather seats.

Nearly everything People Express had done to serve the budget-minded conflicted with this new strategy. Businesspeople intensely dislike inconvenient schedules and gates, paying extra for checked baggage and for meals, and waiting until the last minute to buy tickets. People's tight scheduling meant that many flights were late, and over-booking meant that it often turned away customers who had reserved seats. The carrier earned a new name, "People Distress."

Business travelers stayed away, and the airline racked up a $300 million net loss in 1986, when Texas Air took it over. If it had continued to focus tightly on budget fliers and had sold off or leased planes to cut capacity, People Express might still be around. But it broadened, and irrecoverably blurred, its original winning strategy.

Markets and Market Segments

To some managers, developing a strategy for customer service may sound like a waste of time. How much strategy do you need to send out a repairperson or to adjust an erroneous bill? Yet even those seemingly simple activities won't do much for customer satisfaction or corporate profits unless they are part of a considered strategy. Without one, you don't know who your customers are, how much they value different aspects of service, how much you must spend to satisfy them, and how big the payoffs are likely to be. Without a strategy, you can't develop a concept of service to rally employees or catch conflicts between corporate strategy and customer service or come up with ways to measure service performance and perceived quality. In short, without a strategy you can't get to first base.

Developing a service strategy is an essential step toward choosing an optimal mix and level of service for different customer sets. Provide too little service, or the wrong kind, and customers will leave; provide too much, even the right kind, and your company will go broke or price itself out of the market.

Proof of that truism comes from a General Electric experiment that varied the levels of repair service for out-of-warranty appliances over a two-year period. GE discovered that repair service is very sensitive to the law of diminishing returns. At a certain point, each incremental investment in service starts to yield lower returns than the previous investment. The only way to find that point is to segment customers, find out how much they value different levels of service, and estimate the costs and benefits of serving them well.

Simply charging ahead with extraordinary service doesn't guarantee a high return, as Service Supply Corporation of Indianapolis, the "house of a million screws," should know. If Service Supply had a cogent customer service strategy, it would stratify its 15,000 customers according to their sensitivity to stockouts of different classes of fasteners, then adjust its inventory levels and prices to address those tiers with the highest potential returns. As it is, Service Supply gives outstanding service to *all* its customers, regardless of what service they need or their willingness to pay, and it can't charge enough on average to bring profits up to industry norms.

The essence of any customer service strategy is to segment the customers to be served. As with classic market segmentation, the goal is to isolate a reasonably homogeneous set of customers that can be served at a profit. But customer service segments differ from the usual market segments in significant ways. For one thing, they tend to be narrower. While many different kinds of customers may be happy to buy the same product, they're less likely to feel that their expectations have been met or exceeded if the service they receive is standardized and routinized. Service expectations, after all, are highly personal.

Moreover, marketing segmentation focuses on what people and

organizations *need*, while customer service segmentation focuses on what they *expect*. Marketers tend to use immediate sales to judge whether a segment is valid. Since purchasing decisions look binary—the sale is made or it isn't—the validity of marketing segments seems easy to assess.

Occasionally, marketing segments and customer service segments are the same, especially for service companies that have well-focused, comprehensive marketing strategies. Those strategies can meet a broad range of service expectations. Federal Express's strategy, for example, is to meet expectations for all the actions and reactions that customers perceive they have purchased, including not only pickup and delivery but also documentation and information about shipments.

More often, though, defining customer service segments means rethinking overly broad market segments and the ways in which they impede superior service. Intelligent segmentation can transform the productivity and profitability of customer service operations, as Shouldice's strategy shows.

It's hard to get big productivity gains by substituting capital and technology for labor, since high-touch customer service by definition means lots of flexible, warm, human contact. So managers often seek to substitute low-touch service for the high-touch kind—offering, for instance, automatic checkout from the hotel instead of the usual front-desk checkout.

The problem is that some customers welcome low-touch substitutes while others view them as cost-cutting measures that seriously reduce the quality of service. Compared with business travelers, tourists staying at a grand hotel have a far less favorable view of automatic checkout. They may see it as a jarring, impersonal note in their hotel experience. Veteran users of large home appliances may prefer getting repair instructions over the telephone, while novices expect a human repair expert to show up. Only after a company has segmented its customers and chosen which ones to serve can it figure out where to substitute low touch for high, thus improving productivity without imperiling customer satisfaction.

Segmentation also is key to solving one of the thorniest problems in customer service—matching supply and demand. Manufacturers with overcapacity will produce for inventory or shut down machines and lay off workers. When demand exceeds supply, they draw down inventory, run their factories continuously, hire extra shifts, and call on the capacity of other suppliers.

Service providers have fewer options. Service can't be stored in inventory. Seldom can you substitute another company's service for your own and keep meeting customer expectations, since those expectations refer to a unique experience, not an interchangeable product. A sudden addition to or reduction in capacity (people, mainly) ensures shoddy quality, or even a breakdown of the service "factory," as anyone can attest who has stayed at a large hotel when it's hosting a convention. Since demand for customer service isn't homogeneous— every customer demands somewhat different versions of excellent service—service organizations need idle capacity for adapting their product to mixed demand. By some estimates, service quality drops off sharply when demand exceeds as little as 75% of theoretical capacity.[2]

Until it segments, a hotel or a field force of computer engineers may see huge and apparently random fluctuations in demand. But segmenting usually shows that the overall pattern is made up of several smaller, more predictable, and therefore more manageable patterns. For instance, convention visitors, ordinary business travelers, foreign tourists, and vacationing families all contribute to variations in demand for hotel service. The distinctive patterns of their demands can be forecast.

Segmenting may even reveal that some kinds of demand are undesirable and should be finessed, like the demand on a bank to make change for noncustomers and the demand on a fire department to rescue cats from trees.[3] But simply ignoring demand is nearly always dangerous. Disgruntled noncustomers, like the grandmother whose cat is up a tree, can spread as much bad word about a company as genuine customers can. Better than ignoring inappropriate demand is lowering the expectations of noncustomers, say by broadcasting to cat owners how busy the fire department is fighting fires or by creating disincentives like a $20 charge for restoring arboreal cats to earth.

Among the most powerful ways to vary service capacity with demand is to expand the role of customers in producing service, in effect making them coproducers. To some degree, the customer always helps produce service, by reading a manual, returning an appliance for repair, filling out an air bill, or participating in the service ritual at a fancy restaurant. Finding opportunities to expand the customer's role and move toward self-service often depends on savvy segmentation.

Automated teller machines, for example, increase the role of customers in producing some banking services and thus represent highly flexible capacity. The greater the demand on the machines, the greater the capacity customers provide (at least until the waiting line gets too long). But targeting the right kinds of customers for ATMs is crucial.

Retirees and other older people, expecially in smaller towns, tend to resist the machines. So do many of the very wealthy, who expect the attention of human beings in return for their lucrative business.

Carving out segments is a matter of life and death for some companies. A good example is banking, whose core services are close to being pure commodities. Pundits have forecast the death of the small-town bank ever since the early 1980s, when deregulation started opening local markets to more efficient regional and money-center banks. Many local banks have in fact closed their doors or disappeared into the maws of acquisition-hungry superregionals.

Some local banks, though, have prospered despite the competition by focusing on certain customer segments whose service expectations the big boys don't satisfy. University National Bank & Trust of Palo Alto, California has just one office. The bank discourages small depositors by setting a high monthly fee for checking accounts, $20, and waiving it only for average monthly balances of at least $3,000. Deadbeats need not apply: the bank accepts new customers only with a referral or after a credit check. Bounce two checks and UNBT will close your account.

Yet UNBT keeps gaining market share and consistently earns a return on assets more than twice the average for California banks. Like its mammoth competitors Wells Fargo, First Interstate, and Bank of America, UNBT has targeted individuals with high net worth, generally more than $500,000. Unlike its competitors, UNBT serves *only* those customers, and it serves them with an array of services that includes free traveler's checks, cashier's checks, and stop-payment orders, streamlined approval of large loans, free shoe shines on visits to the bank, and a sack of sweet onions gratis every July. UNBT successfully targeted the people in the community who wanted lots of hands-on service.

More important than any of these features, however, says CEO Carl J. Schmitt, "was the concept of keeping the 1/2 of 1% of customers who are bad guys out of the bank's customer base. It is that 1/2 of 1% that causes the large banks to create the arbitrary rules that in turn create the hassle experienced in the large bank."

The "two bad checks and you're out" policy improves the bank's service in an interesting way. For one thing, local merchants know all UNBT checks are good, so they honor them as if they were cash. For another, tellers don't have to spend time checking the customer's credit. In almost all cases, the bank cashes customer checks without inquiring whether they have money in their accounts. This reduces lines at the teller windows. So the bad-checks policy leads to better credit outside and faster service inside the bank.

If you can carve out a niche by offering platinum service, can you also carve out a niche by offering virtually no service? Sure, if you spot the niche and handle it right. One market segment that is too "cheap" to pay for service is the college population. The East Lansing State Bank has prospered mightily by taking on Michigan State students with no-minimum-balance, all-ATM checking accounts. The students get five checks a month for a monthly service charge of $1, and they pay 50 cents for each window transaction. The bank knows where it wants the students—and it isn't at the teller windows clogging up service to its regular customers.

Classifying Customers

In reality, most companies can't segment their customers as sharply as Shouldice Hospital and University National Bank & Trust do; the set of existing customers is usually too diverse to be stuffed into a single pigeonhole. The problem is most difficult, of course, for manufacturers because they usually sell to a wide range of buyers and use distribution channels that insulate them from direct knowledge about their customers.

Nonetheless, any company can carve out useful segments, rank their attractiveness, and develop a focused service strategy by examining a few key characteristics of its customers and its business. The traits to look at first are obvious financial ones. How do the typical size of a sale and the likelihood of repeat sales vary among customers? What are the costs of giving superior service to different types of customers? Approximating the answers produces a rough segmentation and a working notion of the benefits and costs of different service strategies.

In any well-run business, service levels normally correlate closely with size of sale. For a $150 suit off the rack at a discount store, you won't get free alterations, let alone any advice from a salesperson about fashion trends, the fit of the suit, or appropriate accessories. But in keeping your appointment with Bijan, which sells $1,500 suits behind barred storefronts on Rodeo Drive in Beverly Hills and on Fifth Avenue in New York, you can expect head-to-toe fashion advice, any alteration you care to name, and a phone call after the sale to make sure that everything fits as well as you thought it would.

Note that people who buy discount suits don't necessarily get worse service. They do get less of it, but whether they perceive that consequence as low-quality service depends on their expectations.

When automotive analyst Martin Stein examined 26 auto service programs and their impact on customer satisfaction, he was not surprised to find that the more expensive the car, the more elaborate the service. The manufacturers of Mercedes and Acura take the "open pocketbook" approach: whatever customers want, they get, including 24-hour roadside assistance.

The companies with the worst service quality and the lowest customer satisfaction weren't those making the lowest priced cars or offering the lowest absolute levels of service, but those lacking a service strategy and failing to match service levels with the size of sale. Except in the case of Cadillac, General Motors took a cosmetic approach: it sent service managers through a training program where they learned to refuse requests for service politely, and it used "800" numbers to field complaints. "This approach backfires," according to Stein. "Customers say that General Motors is 'supercilious' and that 'they are overly courteous but don't want to fix your car.' Polite evasion antagonizes people more than if you just say you can't do it. Tactically, there's nothing wrong with '800' numbers, but given GM's lack of a service strategy, its managers don't see any positive change in customer satisfaction."

When their product permits it, sophisticated companies look for customer segments that are less costly to serve. Part of Shouldice's secret is that basically well people cost less to serve than the seriously ill. Older, more conservative car owners who live in the suburbs are less costly to serve than people in their twenties who live in urban and rural areas, a fact that canny auto dealers and insurance companies appreciate. Companies with strong central-purchasing offices tend to be less expensive to serve than those that let each branch or division make its own buying decisions.

Besides traits like health, age, and geographical location, some segments have other characteristics that cut the costs of serving them. Many customers are happy to share the burdens of service, like shoppers at self-service stores and industrial buyers who order parts and supplies through computers linked directly to their suppliers. Other customers are willing to adjust their demand for service to accommodate the supplier, like the budget-minded who accepted People Express's no-frills tack, like Shouldice patients who shave their own groins and abdomens before surgery, and like utility customers who limit their electrical usage during peak demand hours.

The cost of service also is affected by customers' knowledgeability and by their ability and willingness to cooperate in getting service. Buyers of semiconductor chips expect the products to meet their specifications, and living up to specs is a crucial aspect of the service that chip makers offer. But unless the buyer adjusts its automated test equipment to perform the same way the chip maker's does, the buyer will reject batch after batch of chips for being out of spec, even though, according to the chip maker's test equipment, the parts were fine when they left the factory.

Competent customers are what Network Equipment Technologies seeks for its communications multiplexers. The California manufacturer focuses on large companies, with sophisticated communication needs and able communication management teams. Its equipment is designed with diagnostic features that make it easy for NET to diagnose failures remotely. With telephone support, most customers can fix the equipment themselves. As a result, service engineers stay at home; the company needs to dispatch them on a customer call in only about 240 of every 1,000 incidents. NET can extend service to competent customers cheaply, and on top of that, customers get their equipment up and working again faster. That makes for happier customers.

Classification of customers by the value they place on service and by their service expectations often generates a rough idea of the cost of satisfying them. But which customers are the best targets? Those who are the most valuable compared with the likely costs of serving them. While, as we suggested, size and frequency of purchase are good indicators of value, there are many others, such as: customers whose demand is likely to grow faster than average; influential customers, who will generate powerful word of mouth; and loyal customers. Buyers who are especially demanding, sophisticated, or technologically advanced often go to the top of the list because serving them gives a supplier insight into the needs of more ordinary customers.

Ranking customers by their value is essential for any service operation that must live with big swings in aggregate demand and can't adjust capacity quickly to meet those swings. Ranks or tiers are the key to allocation. When capacity is short, smart suppliers give top-tier customers first claim on service and cut back on service to lower value customers. That's what popular restaurants do at peak dining times by finding tables for regulars and keeping newcomers waiting, and it's what American and Japanese semiconductor makers do when capacity is short and they fill the orders of long-term customers first.

Without assigning its customers to tiers, a company that serves numbers of segments has difficulty getting the most out of its service capacity. Stretching and straining to satisfy every segment, it may end up giving low-quality service to all customers, not just to the less desirable ones in lower tiers.

Service companies have discovered through painful experience that using the same organization to serve different market segments, or to provide very different services to the same segment, seldom works. Frito-Lay, the PepsiCo subsidiary that leads the potato chip business, is famous for its customer service. A corps of 10,000 route drivers visits most stores, many of them small grocers, two or three times weekly to ensure that the stock is fresh—and prominently displayed. At one point, the company decided to add packaged cookies that they would deliver in the same way and at the same time.

The attempt failed. Frito-Lay's service infrastructure, very efficient for potato chips, was too specialized to handle cookies well. As Leo Kiely, senior vice president for sales and marketing, explains it: "On the surface it looked easy, but there were underlying problems. Our other products turn over in about seven days, which is very rapid. Cookies have a much slower turn, with a 60- to 90-day shelf life. That's a different inventory problem for our drivers, so our regular visit two to three times a week proved inefficient for cookies."

While handling many customer segments piles on complexities, few companies can afford the luxury of addressing just one segment. The challenge of exploiting service capacity forces them to diversify at least a little, as airlines do in targeting both business and vacation travelers. Moreover, the same customer is often a different type of customer at different times. Business executives go on vacation. New bank customers, who value location and convenience most, quickly become established bank customers and start giving the highest rankings to different criteria, like operational accuracy, dependability, and friendliness.

The best practice is to pick segments that are as similar as possible and to keep your priorities straight. People Express failed to do that.

What Do Customers Expect?

After segmenting your market so that you can target your customers, the next step is to find out what they want and expect. This takes research and analysis.

The payoffs for good analysis are tangible sales and profits. In Norway, where customers are particularly sensitive to service, Toyota used to think of cars as simply products. Then the company began looking into the total car experience and asking what kinds of service customers expected. Discovering that they were concerned not just about reliability and performance but also about the difficulties of buying cars and car insurance and about the anxieties of repair, Toyota used its large customer base to bargain for very competitive financing and insurance services, and it started offering free diagnostic service. In 1985 and 1986, Toyota's sales in Norway rose more than 30% and its earnings went from the equivalent of $12 million to $22 million.

It's tempting to forgo analysis because you assume you know what customers expect. But assumptions don't make effective customer service strategies. Inward-looking companies that are guided by industry norms and their own past practices end up with inappropriate strategies, lower market shares, and anemic profits. Time after time, studies have shown large differences between the ways that customers define service and rank the importance of different service activities and the ways that suppliers do.[4]

Numbers of companies have triumphed by filling the gap between what customers see as good service and what competitors think it is. Tom Ford, founder and head of the Ford Land Company, perceived that most developers of office buildings see their businesses as financial plays where return on assets is paramount. Most commercial tenants, he noted, are convinced that their landlords are trying to squeeze the last penny of return from their properties.

So Ford decided to stress tenant service in the 34 office and industrial buildings he put up and operates on the peninsula south of San Francisco. He doesn't charge for extras like installing electrical outlets, laying computer cable, or changing names on doors and building directories. When remodeling creates a racket that disturbs neighboring tenants, Ford brings the neighbors wine and flowers to show he's at least aware of the problem.

The result? Since 1977, Ford's properties have been 100% leased, a remarkable record in an area where vacancy rates have been running between 10% and 30%. A competitor who opened an office building next to Ford's flagship property in Menlo Park tried to draw away Ford's tenants by offering months of free or reduced rent. None of the tenants would bite, and the new building was only 50% occupied 15 months after opening.

Good service has nothing to do with what the provider believes it is; it has to do only with what the customer believes is true. Good service results when the provider meets or exceeds the customer's expectations. Do less than the customer expects and the service is bad. Do what is expected and the service is good. Exceed by a great amount what is anticipated, as Tom Ford does, and the service will be superior. This is why the providers of good service have to be extremely careful to set the customer's expectations at the proper level.

Levels of expectation are why two organizations in the same business can offer far different levels of service and still keep customers happy. It is why McDonald's can extend excellent industrialized service with few employees per customer and why an expensive restaurant with many tuxedoed waiters may be unable to do as well from the customer's point of view. It is why diners like the folksy service at New York City's upscale steak house, Christ Cella, and would perhaps be disappointed with the same type of service at a fancy French restaurant.

Setting customer expectations at the right level can be a very tough job even for service experts. Consider Nordstrom, the most service-oriented large fashion retailer in the United States. Nordstrom's reputation for good service has gotten out of control. Stories about heroic service deeds of Nordstrom employees, fueled by the word of mouth spread by enthusiastic customers, are threatening to ruin Nordstrom's service. Why? Because customers enter the store with unrealistically high expectations.

In an effort to rein in expectations, Nordstrom has stopped talking about service to the press. Too much publicity about a company's good service can be bad. Likewise, fire departments should stress their expertise in fighting fires, and keep mum about rescuing animals, if they want to lower the expectations of owners of tree-climbing cats.

There are severe limits to any company's ability to set expectations. The strictest one is reality. Few patrons of a high-priced hotel can be led to expect anything other than luxury service, and few people who have experienced bad service can be persuaded to expect anything else. As Martin Stein, the auto-industry analyst observes, "General Motors's advertising campaign for Mr. Goodwrench, the GM dealer's mythical service expert, doesn't work because people doubt that the quality of service being advertised will be available. They may be looking for Mr. Goodwrench, but they aren't finding him." Trying to set expectations that vary widely from the realities customers perceive is futile.

Expectations are formed by many uncontrollable factors, from the experience of customers with other companies and their advertising to a customer's psychological state at the time of service delivery.

Strictly speaking, what customers expect is as diverse as their education, values, and experience. The same advertisement that shouts "personal service" to one person tells another that the advertiser has promised more than it possibly can deliver.

Yet some straightforward tactics can help bring expectations into line with the service strategy. The job is basically the same as positioning a company or product in the marketplace. Service positioning starts with four givens: the segments targeted, the expectations of those segments, the strategy for exceeding those expectations, and the positions of competitors, that is, the images they have created for their companies in customers' minds.

A winning service position meets two criteria. It uniquely distinguishes a company from the competition, and it leads customers to expect slightly less service than a company can deliver. That's what Avis did years ago by positioning itself as the second-place car rental company that has to try harder, and it's what Avis is doing today by portraying itself as the rent-a-car outfit that tries harder because the employees own the company. Maytag has done the same, positioning its washing machines as so reliable that the Maytag repairman is bored to death.

The tools used to position customer service operations are the same communication tools any marketer uses—advertising, promotion, public relations, and everything else that affects the all-important word of mouth. But sending messages about service is different from most forms of marketing communication. Since service is intangible, advertising has a special mission to dramatize service in ways that make the benefits clear and real.

All forms of communication should be tightly focused on the target segment because customers' expectations about service are affected strongly by the other kinds of customers they see. Reaching the wrong segments can be a disaster. A business traveler checking into a budget motel revises her expectations radically if she sees a drunk asleep in the lobby.

Positioning customer service differs from normal positioning in other ways as well. Customers are hypersensitive to tangible service clues like uniforms, repair trucks, brochures, and hotel lobbies. Often they can't tell that a service has been performed without some additional evidence like the elaborate receipts car mechanics make out or the strip of paper hotels wrap around toilet seats to let guests know the toilet has been cleaned. Customers' expectations of service rise and fall markedly because of seemingly minor clues or tip-offs like these.

The key to successful positioning of customer service is not to create expectations greater than the service your company can deliver. The whole organization must be together on this. Network Equipment Technology, for one, disciplines salespeople who overpromise. NET realizes that keeping expectations at just the right level—slightly below perceived performance—is a constant challenge.

Three Steps to Take

Great service providers inform customers about what to expect and then exceed the promise. Not all customers want or deserve high levels of service, but they are entitled to what they have been promised, explicitly or implicitly.

The strategy of great service providers has a rather familiar ring. Almost all of these companies have taken the same three steps:

First, they segmented the market carefully and designed core products and core services to meet the needs of the customer base. They realized that not all customers who bought the same product or service had the same service needs.

Second, they realized that only the customer knew what he or she wanted. Therefore, they researched the needs of the customer base thoroughly, both with formal programs and by paying close attention to what the customer was saying.

Third, they were careful to set the customer's expectations at the right level. They underpromised and overdelivered.

Providing good service is a towering challenge. There are many reasons businesses and professions fail in the endeavor, even when they have a perfect strategy. Without a focused service strategy, however, meeting the challenge becomes impossible.

Notes

1. See James L. Heskett, *Managing in the Service Economy* (Boston: Harvard Business School Press, 1986).

2. Ibid., p. 38.

3. The cats come courtesy of Christopher H. Lovelock, *Services Marketing* (Englewood Cliffs, N.J.: Prentice-Hall, 1984).

4. See, for example, Norman E. Marr, "Do Managers Really Know What Service Their Customers Require?" *International Journal of Physical Distribution and Materials Management*, vol. 10, no. 7, 1980, p. 433.

3

Beyond Products: Services-Based Strategy

James Brian Quinn, Thomas L. Doorley, and
Penny C. Paquette

When communication was limited to telephones and letters, and transportation took weeks or months instead of hours or days, concentrating on a few products—and the vertical integration that let managers control every step of their production processes—made real sense. Now such traditional strategic formulas no longer hold.

Thanks to new technologies, executives can divide up their companies' value chains, handle the key strategic elements internally, outsource others advantageously anywhere in the world with minimal transaction costs, and yet coordinate all essential activities more effectively to meet customers' needs. Under these circumstances, moving to a less integrated but more focused organization is not just feasible but imperative for competitive success.

Companies that understand this new approach—Honda, Apple, and Merck among them—build their strategies not around products but around deep knowledge of a few highly developed core service skills. In such companies, the organization is kept as lean as possible. The company strips itself down to the essentials necessary to deliver to customers the greatest possible value from its core skills—and outsources as much of the rest as possible. As a result, management focuses on what it does best, avoids distractions, and leverages its organizational and financial resources far beyond what traditional strategies allow.

The Power of Services

To rethink their strategies objectively, managements need to break out of the mind-set that considers manufacturing (or goods production) as separate from (and somehow superior to) the service activities that make such production possible and effective. In fact, most companies—product manufacturers and service providers alike—are largely service operations. U.S. employment and output statistics reflect this clearly, as do internal company cost figures. Upon analysis, so do most manufacturers' value chains.

First consider some numbers. Approximately 76% of all U.S. workers are employed in industries commonly thought of as services: communications, transportation, health care, wholesale and retail distribution, financial services, and professional firms. Of those working in manufacturing industries, 65% to 75% perform service tasks ranging from critical production-related activities like research, logistics, maintenance, and product and process design to indirect staff services like accounting, law, financing, and personnel. Overall, services account for over three-fourths of all costs in most U.S. industries.

The role of services in providing value is ever more important. Not long ago, most of a product's value added came from the production processes that converted raw material into useful forms (steel into auto bodies, for example, or grain into edible cereals). Now, however, value added is increasingly likely to come from technological improvements, styling features, product image, and other attributes that only services can create.

This occurs in part because systemization and automation have driven production costs steadily downward, thus diminishing their relative importance in most companies' value chains. More and more companies are beginning to look like those in the personal computer industry, where producing the actual "box" is a low-margin activity, and software and service-support activities create most of a product's value to customers. In fact, nonmanufacturing services are so preeminent in many pharmaceutical, clothing, food, and sports equipment companies (to name just a few) that even classifying them as manufacturers seems open to question.

In pharmaceuticals, for example, value is added primarily by service activities like drug development in R&D, carefully constructed patent and legal defenses, thorough clinical and regulatory clearances, and effective drug detailing and distribution systems. With production costs a trivial portion of a drug's value, leading companies' strategies concentrate on specialized activities within the value chain. Merck, for example, focuses on a powerful research-based patent position, while Glaxo targets rapid regulatory clearance of drugs.

SCI Systems, the world's largest electronics subcontractor, is a less obvious case in point. SCI produces a wide variety of communications, computer, and advanced instrumentation equipment that it sells both to value-added resellers and on an OEM basis. The company has been growing at a rate of 35% per year in its cutthroat business by outsourcing as much of its production processes and nonessential services as possible. Management concentrates its resources on design and development, logistics management, quality control, and the company's special expertise—low-cost assembly technologies for surface mounting components on both sides of the circuit board. The thin overhead structure such outsourcing allows (130 managers for 7,000 employees) lets SCI respond flexibly, rapidly, and precisely, with lower bureaucratic costs than its competitors or its customers themselves would incur.

In addition to enhancing the leverage of services inside companies, new technologies have significantly increased the relative power of service enterprises. For both manufacturers and service companies, this presents important opportunities and challenges.

On the one hand, services technologies offer astute managers new options for lowering costs, restructuring their organizations, and redefining their strategic focus. On the other hand, those who ignore the opportunities that services technologies create will surely sacrifice competitive advantages to their more farsighted rivals. Our three-year study of technology's impacts provided us with examples of both phenomena time and time again. (The insert, "The Impact of Services Technologies," describes this research.)

At the most basic level, technology has made it possible for independent companies to specialize in particular service activities, automate them, and create higher value added at lower costs than all but a few integrated companies can attain. Automatic Data Processing provides a good example.

ADP developed a flexible payroll-handling system that is so low cost it now processes payrolls for more than 10% of its potential client base. From this initial service, ADP expanded into routine bank accounting and tax filings for its customers and their employees, then into ERISA reporting, personnel records, and financial analyses, and finally into personalized communications like printing slogans, messages, or logos on checks and including notes with employees' paychecks. ADP's customers get expertise they could not afford in-house, lower overhead costs thanks to ADP's substantial economies of scale, and an objective check on their own costs for these services.

Similarly, the $1.5 billion ServiceMaster uses its system economies and specialized management skills to raise the quality of its customers' maintenance services while at the same time lowering their costs. ServiceMaster's database, which covers 14 years of maintenance history on 17 million pieces of equipment at thousands of locations, enables the company to determine objectively how its customers' facilities should be maintained, when equipment purchases and preventive maintenance will pay off, and when parts should be replaced. So effective are its systems that ServiceMaster and its customers often invest jointly in new equipment and share the resulting productivity gains.

As these examples suggest, many service companies have become large, capital-intensive, technology-dominated organizations on which companies from almost every industry depend for specialized knowledge and assistance. Service companies are now among the most important suppliers, customers, market innovators, coalition partners, and repositories of market knowledge available to manufacturers.[1] A prime illustration is Toys "R" Us, which sells at year-round discount prices the largest selection of toys available nationwide.

To maintain inventories of 18,000 items in each store at lowest cost, Toys "R" Us must make huge off-season purchases, respond rapidly to developing fads, yet minimize systemwide storage and handling costs. It does this through what is perhaps the most detailed materials management and movement system in retailing, combining daily updates from its electronic point-of-sale system with an expert system linked to its sophisticated supplier information models.

The power of this system does not stop with Toys "R" Us. The 350-store system is so effective that the company knows more about toy sales than any of its manufacturer-suppliers, who often use their spring and summer Toys "R" Us sales to gauge production levels and to redesign products for their Christmas lines. With its market share approaching 20%, Toys "R" Us is so powerful that it can strongly influence product offerings and require manufacturers to meet its needs (for example, providing special packaging and four-sided product markings for its open, high-stack displays).

Shifting Strategic Focus

True strategic focus means that a company can concentrate more power in its chosen markets than anyone else can. Once, this meant owning the largest resource base, manufacturing plants, research labs, or distribution channels to support product lines. Now physical facilities—including a seemingly superior product—seldom provide a sustainable competitive edge. They are too easily bypassed, reverse engineered, cloned, or slightly surpassed. Instead, a maintainable advantage usually derives from outstanding depth in selected human skills, logistics capabilities, knowledge bases, or other service strengths that competitors cannot reproduce and that lead to greater demonstrable value for the customer.

Recognizing this, smart strategists no longer analyze market shares and their associated cost positions ad infinitum, nor do they build integrated companies to exploit them. Instead, they concentrate on identifying those few core service activities where their company has—or can develop—unique capabilities. Then they aggressively seek ways to eliminate, limit, or outsource activities where the company cannot attain superiority, unless those activities are essential to its chosen areas of strategic focus.

Apple Computer illustrates the value of this kind of activity-based focus. Like many other now-large companies, Apple initially succeeded by organizing itself as an intellectual holding company that purposely manufactured as little internally as possible. Because its business strength lay in creating the friendly look and feel of its software and hardware, Apple's management concentrated on designing and controlling its products' concepts, appearance, and key software, especially Apple DOS, which was not even made available for license. Other components and activities were outsourced wherever possible.

Apple bought microprocessors from Synertek, other chips from Hitachi, Texas Instruments, and Motorola, video monitors from Hitachi, power supplies from Astec, and printers from Tokyo Electric and Qume. (The Apple II was estimated to cost less than $500 to build, of which $350 was for purchased components.[2]) Similarly, Apple kept its internal service activities and investments to a minimum by outsourcing application software development to Microsoft, promotion to Regis McKenna, product styling to Frogdesign, and distribution to ITT and ComputerLand.

While this strategy may have been essential in Apple's early days, when it lacked both the time and the capital to build factories or hire a sales force, even today it is structured less like a traditional manufacturing company and more like a $4 billion service company that happens to have limited manufacturing facilities. Yet it has produced spectacular employee productivity and profitability: in 1988, Apple had $377,000 in sales per employee and $57,400 in profits per employee, outperforming the more vertically integrated IBM ($154,200 and $22,600) and DEC ($101,900 and $10,600).

To develop an activity-focused strategy, management needs to concentrate its competitive analyses not on market share but on the relative potency of the services undergirding its own and its competitors' product positions. Too much attention has been paid to high market share, especially since it often is bought by inappropriate pricing and short-term marketing strategies. High market share and high profitability together come from having a high activity share, or the most effective presence in selected services that the market truly desires.

Defining each activity in the value chain as a service that can be either produced internally or sourced externally is the first step in this new competitive analysis. Next management must ask a series of questions about each activity: Do we have or can we achieve best-in-the-world capabilities for this service? If so, should we make it a part of our core strategy? If not, what possibilities exist for outsourcing the activity or forming a strategic alliance with someone who does have superior capabilities? Finally, management needs to focus the organization's energies on two sets of activities: those where it can create unique value and those it must control to maintain its supremacy in the critical elements of its value chain.

In recent years, outsourcing has been disparaged for "hollowing out" companies and making them uncompetitive. Approached strategically, as we suggest, the effects of outsourcing are just the opposite. Whenever a company produces something internally that others can buy or produce more efficiently and effectively, it sacrifices competitive advantage. Conversely, the key to strategic success for many companies has been a carefully developed coalition with one or more of the world's best suppliers, product designers, advertising agencies, distributors, financial houses, or other service providers. Apple is one company that profits from such an approach. Honda Motor Company is another.

Soichiro Honda's personal commitment and engineering skills led him to create the world's finest team for designing small, efficient engines, first for bicycles, then for motorcycles. In the company's early years, limited capital resources and the cost-competitiveness of the motorcycle market forced Honda to develop very small, efficient assembly operations and to outsource as much of its nonengine fabrication work as possible. At the same time, Honda's president, Takeo Fujisawa, used innovative financing to build the strongest motorcycle distribution network in Japan.

Once Honda's motorcycles had succeeded at home, the company parlayed these same core service capabilities into building a steadily broader line of motorcycles, automobiles, and household machines sold worldwide. Its successes in the United States and elsewhere are still based on its unique depth in small engine design, moderate-scale assembly management, superb outsourcing logistics, and creative marketing and distribution coalitions. It has avoided many of the investments and inflexibilities that its major competitors have been saddled with, while building itself a number one share of the U.S. foreign car market and a number three share of all cars sold in Japan.

While both Apple and Honda began by outsourcing critical activities, other companies have adopted this strategy later in life. Intel Corporation, for example, at first relied heavily on its internal production prowess to lower costs, increase reliability, and open new markets. Now it focuses primarily on its extraordinary competencies in chip design and development. When its chips move toward commodity status, Intel often withdraws from the manufacturing process, subcontracting that to silicon foundries and other producers that concentrate on volume manufacturing and may have inherent cost advantages.

Similarly, in a lower tech industry, E&J Gallo Winery shifted to outsourcing an activity many vintners consider the core of their business—growing the specialized grapes for its wines. Gallo devotes its resources and management attention to maintaining the legendary marketing and sales strengths that give the company its volume advantages and to using the deep knowledge base its 31% market share can provide to purchase grapes with the precise qualities its wines require. An important side benefit is that Gallo has avoided the investments and risks inherent in growing grapes.

What Stays, What Goes?

The great part of most companies' costs (other than those for purchased materials) typically occur in overhead categories. Even in manufacturing, more than two-thirds of all nonmaterial costs tend to be indirect or overhead expenses. Yet most overhead is merely services that the company began to buy internally. Reconceptualizing internal staffs and overhead costs as services that could be bought externally exposes a powerful, unexploited source of competitive advantage for most companies. Management can ask activity by activity: Are we really competitive with the world's best here? If not, can intelligent outsourcing or coalitions improve our productivity and long-term competitive position?

Competitive analyses should consider not just competitors in the company's own industry or the exclusive providers of a service (like insurance companies or communications companies) but *all* the potential providers and industries that might cross-compete in the activity, using "best in the activity" as the relevant benchmark. This approach broadens the analytical process and gives it a much more external, market-driven orientation. It also introduces new objectivity into the evaluation process and, at a minimum, generates strong pressures for productivity gains if management decides to continue sourcing internally. In many cases, managers discover that specialized sources are so much more cost-effective than their internal groups that they outsource activities long considered integral to their business.

Clearly, however, not all overhead is worthless—and therefore to be eliminated. Many of the most essential activities that modern companies perform are in what could be considered overhead categories. The objective is not to slash costs simplistically but rather to produce or buy needed services most effectively.

By limiting or shedding activities that provide no strategic advantage, a company can increase the value it delivers to both customers and shareholders and, in the process, lower its costs and investments. Conversely, if a company performs activities that it could buy more effectively, costs tend to balloon, and it loses competitive advantage. The company may also become more vulnerable to takeovers by outsiders who see in these activities the potential for margin gains.

Determining which core activities to emphasize is not always easy or obvious. Often a company's true strengths are obscured by management's tendency to think in divisional or product terms and by each functional group's need to see itself as the main source of the enterprise's success. But careful analysis will identify the few critical activities that drive (or could drive) the company's strategy and that it therefore must dominate.

Consider recent developments in the credit card industry. Processing customer charges and transactions is obviously an important activity in this business. Yet both MasterCard and Visa have clearly decided that their distinctive advantage lies not in this costly and complicated activity—which they often outsource to arch-competitor American Express—but in their large customer bases, retail networks, and ability to market effectively to both.

Managers must, of course, plan and control outsourcing so that the company does not become overly dependent on—and hence dominated by—its partners. In most cases, this means consciously developing and maintaining alternative competitive sources. It also means the company may have to perform activities at certain critical stages of its value creation process that it would otherwise outsource if efficiency were the sole criterion.

As Apple demonstrates, a company need not fabricate many components itself to control manufacturing. But it must dominate the strategic steps in the manufacturing process and develop technological knowledge, logistics systems, and commercial intelligence networks about the other steps that are second to none. That is why Honda still manufactures key engine parts in Japan and does all of its critical engine-related R&D there, although it outsources body parts overseas and shares responsibility for body design with its affiliates worldwide.

One way to avoid becoming too dependent on critical suppliers is to seek alliances with outstanding but noncompeting enterprises. Seagate Technology, the world's leading manufacturer of hard disk drives for personal computers, provides a good example. To gain competitive advantage against Japanese rivals, Seagate decided to absorb the cost of delivering its products to customers and to guarantee delivery within four days. To handle this crucial service, the company developed a special relationship with Skyway Freight Systems to make deliveries from its California distribution center to customers all over the United States. On a per unit basis, Seagate's payments to Skyway amounted to less than 1% of each disk drive's total cost. Yet in six months and thousands of shipments, only three deliveries arguably were late.

On rare occasions, companies can even outsource some strategic components to potential competitors—as Apple did with its microprocessor chips—provided that they develop and protect other key elements in the value creation process and control the critical information linkages between their various suppliers and customers—as Apple did by controlling Apple DOS and its marketing interfaces.

This kind of refocusing and strategic hollowing out goes well beyond mere tactical redeployment for efficiency's sake. By avoiding investments in vertical integration and by managing "intellectual systems" instead of workers and machines, companies decrease total investment and leverage resources substantially. They also minimize certain unavoidable risks.

For example, if one unit in an outsourced system underperforms, management can substitute another competitor's components or services more quickly than it could shut down an internal operation or develop an alternative itself. Similarly, if new technologies suddenly appear, it is easier to switch among outside sources than to forsake internal investments. Lastly, if there is a cyclical or temporary drop in demand, the coordinating company is not saddled with all the idle capacity and inventory losses.

With strategic outsourcing, companies have at their disposal the world's best talent, offering both higher quality and greater flexibility than internal groups could provide. For this reason, many large manufacturers now rely on smaller, state-of-the-art product and service suppliers to shorten product-development cycle times. While the larger company must typically maintain strong R&D efforts in its core technologies—and be willing to share its longer term plans with suppliers to ensure that its new products make the best use of suppliers' designs—it can substantially leverage its R&D funds through inputs from specialized technical vendors. Dramatic savings, totaling some 70% to 80% of the cost of key components or designs, are common when joint development is managed properly.

In the early 1980s, General Motors, like many other large companies, realized that the rigidities and costs of its internal suppliers were not only raising its cost per unit against its competitors' but also cutting off the company from the R&D support and innovations that outside suppliers could provide. In a policy reversal, GM began to encourage more extensive outsourcing and, among other initiatives, turned to PPG Industries to handle the painting of auto bodies. Today PPG manages and operates the paint shops in GM assembly plants, lowering GM's cost per unit and offering the latest advances in robotics and materials research related to painting.

Perhaps most important, strategic outsourcing allows a company to focus all its attention on the areas in which it adds the most value per unit of input. This creates entry barriers for would-be competitors in a variety of ways. Because they are leaner, these companies can respond faster to customers and move more easily to form the cross-functional teams that best provide innovative products for new market needs. Because they have fewer management levels, less bureaucracy, and more opportunities for employees' personal and entrepreneurial development, they can often attract better people. Finally, they can leverage managerial talent—their most limited and most crucial resource—because their executives no longer need to waste time and attention on peripheral activities.

Service-Driven Competition

Global sourcing, volatile currency fluctuations, fast-changing communications and information technologies, and the increased leverage of services are combining to restructure entire industries as well as individual companies. As an example, consider biotechnology.

The industry is becoming a loosely structured network of service enterprises built around specialized core competencies and joined together (often temporarily) for one undertaking, while remaining suppliers, competitors, and customers in others. Many research groups and companies focus only on identifying and patenting biological organisms (often proteins) at the laboratory level. Others develop and license cell lines that can reproduce these organisms. Still others have developed processes for using these cell lines to make particular proteins in sufficient quantities for clinical tests and commercialization. Some enterprises specialize in running clinical trials, others concentrate on having the marketing expertise and distribution channels to bring new products to market, and so on.

Because of the high risks involved, the scarcity of expensive expertise, and the relatively small scale required at each of these stages, it is hard for a single company to support the full chain of activities in-house. As a result, the industry is developing a series of multilevel consortia in which each enterprise—and each new product introduced—has its own network of contract relationships with research, clinical, production, and marketing groups around the world.

The semiconductor and electronics industries are becoming similarly structured, with independent design, foundry, packaging, assembly, industrial distribution, kitting, configuration, system analysis, networking, and value-added distributor groups essentially acting as service units that perform specialized tasks for one another. Because of services' high value added and extremely low shipping costs, the most powerful consortia now seek and coordinate the world's best suppliers on a truly global basis.

In another set of major restructurings, large service companies are exploiting their technological power and size in ways that have erased many traditional industry boundaries and distribution patterns. This process is most apparent in banking and financial services, where specialists of all sorts have captured important segments of familiar value chains and cross-competition is rampant. But this process is very much alive in other service and manufacturing sectors.

For example, retailing, wholesaling, and manufacturing companies now partner and cross-compete on many levels. Many large retailers like Sears, K mart, and Wal-Mart design or produce their own products worldwide, run their own distribution operations, and compete directly with wholesalers, drugstores, and supermarkets. Wholesalers like McKesson are also large manufacturers of private brands, and they support extensive independent retail networks with electronic accounting, billing, merchandising, planning, and control systems. Broad-line manufacturers like Matsushita control thousands of wholesale and retail outlets, which they use both to gather better market information and to assure rapid market access for new products.

Similarly, boundaries between transportation, communications, and travel-service industries are disappearing as airlines begin to provide direct reservations, tours, conferences, auto and hotel arrangements, in-flight telephone service, electronic retailing, and package delivery services in competition—and coalition—with thousands of other service units. Accounting, software, and professional service firms are also breaking all traditional industry boundaries as they openly compete and cooperate to develop and supply new and better products and services to each other and to a wide variety of common customers.

The bottom line is simple but powerful: whenever a company outsources, sets up a joint venture, or enters into a strategic partnership with a major service company—as most will—it is likely to encounter a totally new set of potential competitors and competitive interests. Under these circumstances, an activity-focused competitive analysis, which includes all possible cross-competitors, provides a much clearer basis for assessing the opportunities, relationships, and threats these complex new situations offer. Conversely, defining the company's industry and competitors in product rather than in service-activity terms can lead to strategic disasters.

The capacity to command and coordinate services activities, supplier networks, and contract relations across the globe has become perhaps the most important strategic weapon and scale economy for many of today's most successful enterprises. Indeed, our study suggests that one reason large Japanese export manufacturers have been so successful is that they have avoided the controlled vertical integration of U.S. companies. Instead, they have moved directly to a kind of quasi-integration similar to what we are describing here: coordinating many independent suppliers through strong contractual and strategic relationships. U.S. industry, with its more efficient service sector, now has an opportunity to jump to a higher level of coordinated disaggregation and thus to regain its strategic advantage.

Appendix

THE IMPACT OF SERVICES TECHNOLOGIES

In a three-year study begun under the auspices of the National Academy of Engineering, we explored the important impacts of technology in the service sector. Following the dictionary, we defined technology broadly as the systematic application of knowledge—particularly knowledge of physical, chemical, and systems phenomena—to useful purposes. We studied not just information technologies but all the other systems, operations, software, and hardware technologies developed specifically for service functions or applied in them. Among those included were: the diagnostic techniques, treatment devices, and specialized procedures developed for health care; advanced cargo handling and passenger movement equipment; specialized food distribution and preparation systems for restaurant chains; and automatic teller machines and satellite communication systems used in banking.

We examined the way such technologies are affecting industry structures, corporate strategies, and organizations. Our findings are based on an analysis of all relevant databases (including the Strategic Planning Institute's PIMS unit, Standard & Poor's COMPU-STAT tapes, as well as databases from the U.S. Departments of Commerce and Labor), a series of case studies, and numerous interviews with key technical and senior managers in companies identified as outstanding developers or users of services technologies. We gratefully acknowledge the support of the following companies in financing this project: Bell & Howell, Bell Atlanticom, Bankers Trust, Royal Bank of Canada, Braxton Associates, and American Express.

Notes

1. James Brian Quinn, Jordan J. Baruch, and Penny C. Paquette, "Exploiting the Manufacturing-Services Interface," *Sloan Management Review*, Summer 1988, p. 45.

2. William H. Davidson and Edward F. Colby, Jr., "Apple Computer, Inc.," University of Virginia Darden Graduate Business School Foundation Case Study, 1983 (UVA-BP219).

4

Customer Intimacy and Other Value Disciplines

Michael Treacy and Fred Wiersema

How was Dell Computer able to charge out of nowhere and outmaneuver Compaq and other leaders of the personal computer industry? Why are Home Depot's competitors losing market share to this fast-growing retailer of do-it-yourself supplies when they are all selling similar goods? How did Nike, a start-up company with no reputation behind it, manage to run past Adidas, a longtime solid performer in the sport-shoe market?

All three questions have the same three answers. First, Dell Computer, Home Depot, and Nike redefined value for customers in their respective markets. Second, they built powerful, cohesive business systems that could deliver more of that value than competitors. Third, by doing so they raised customers' expectations beyond the competition's reach. Put another way, these industry leaders changed what customers valued and how it was delivered, then boosted the level of value that customers expected.

The idea that companies succeed by selling value is not new. What is new is how customers define value in many markets. In the past, customers judged the value of a product or service on the basis of some combination of quality and price. Today's customers, by contrast, have an expanded concept of value that includes convenience of purchase, after-sale service, dependability, and so on. One might assume, then, that to compete today, companies would have to meet all these different customer expectations. This, however, is not the case.

Companies that have taken leadership positions in their industries in the last decade typically have done so by narrowing their business focus, not broadening it. They have focused on delivering superior customer value in line with one of three value disciplines—operational excellence, customer intimacy, or product leadership. They have become champions in one of these disciplines while meeting industry standards in the other two. (For a discussion of companies that excel at more than one discipline, see "Masters of Two.")

By operational excellence, we mean providing customers with reliable products or services at competitive prices and delivered with minimal difficulty or inconvenience. Dell, for instance, is a master of operational excellence. Customer intimacy, the second value discipline, means segmenting and targeting markets precisely and then tailoring offerings to match exactly the demands of those niches. Companies that excel in customer intimacy combine detailed customer knowledge with operational flexibility so they can respond quickly to almost any need, from customizing a product to fulfilling special requests. As a consequence, these companies engender tremendous customer loyalty. Home Depot, for example, is better than any other company in its market at getting the customer precisely the product or information he or she wants. And product leadership, the third discipline, means offering customers leading-edge products and services that consistently enhance the customer's use or application of the product, thereby making rivals' goods obsolete. Nike excels in product leadership in the sport-shoe category.

Masters of Two

While market leaders typically excel at one value discipline, a few maverick companies have gone further by mastering two. In doing so, they have resolved the inherent tensions between the operating model that each value discipline demands. A decade ago, Toyota successfully pursued an operational excellence strategy; today, it retains its mastery in operational excellence, and, through its breakthroughs in automobile technology, it is moving ahead in product leadership as well.

USAA, a Texas-based insurer that caters mainly to people in the military, has mastered both customer intimacy and operational excellence. USAA is everything an operationally excellent company would want to be: centralized, highly automated, and incredibly disciplined. Its immense, state-of-the-art information system is an information technologist's wish come true. By virtually eliminating paperwork, it allows the company to be quick and responsive. The information system at USAA *is* the process.

Other insurance companies—Northwestern Mutual and Allstate come to mind—have been building equally excellent operations. But USAA continues to set the pace by doing a better job of tailoring its services to customers' particular needs. USAA segments its customer base by, among other characteristics, life stage—at what point a customer is in life—and develops products, services, and servicing approaches for each of those segments. In addition to execution, USAA has mastered customer intimacy.

Staples, the office supply giant, also has become adept at both operational excellence and customer intimacy. Staples achieves the lowest net-landed cost in the entire office stationery business, but it also has become intimate with a particular market: companies employing fewer than 50 people. To further the intimacy with that market segment, it has created a club. Customers join it at no cost and get at least a 5% discount on the fastest moving items. But to get the discount, customers have to show their club card, which means Staples can track sales by customer, and that gives the company all kinds of data it can use in satisfying its market. Store managers now have incentives based on customer retention.

Toyota, USAA, and Staples are today's rare exceptions. But mastery of one discipline will eventually become the minimum that a company will need to get itself into the game. Chances are that the big winners of the future will have mastered two.

Companies that push the boundaries of one value discipline while meeting industry standards in the other two gain such a lead that competitors find it hard to catch up. This is largely because the leaders have aligned their entire operating model—that is, the company's culture, business processes, management systems, and computer platforms—to serve one value discipline. Knowing what they want to provide to customers, they have figured out what they must do to follow through. And with the hard work of transforming their organizations behind them, they can concentrate on smaller adjustments that produce incremental value. Less focused companies must do far more than simply tweak existing processes to gain this advantage.

Companies that pursue the same value discipline have remarkable similarities, regardless of their industry. The business systems at Federal Express, American Airlines, and Wal-Mart, for example, are strikingly similar because they all pursue operational excellence. An employee could transfer from FedEx to Wal-Mart and, after getting oriented, feel right at home. Likewise, the systems, structures, and cultures of product leaders such as Johnson & Johnson in health care and pharmaceuticals and Nike in sport shoes look much like one another. But across two disciplines, the similarities end. Send people from Wal-Mart to Nike, and they would think they were on a different planet. Moreover, homogeneity exists only among *leaders* in the same value discipline; mediocre performers are not distinctive enough to look like anything except other mediocre performers in their own industries.

The conclusions we've drawn about the value disciplines are based on a three-year study of 40 companies that have redefined performance expectations in their markets. Through this research, we have come to understand what each value discipline demands of an organization and why.

Operational Excellence

The term "operational excellence" describes a specific strategic approach to the production and delivery of products and services. The objective of a company following this strategy is to lead its industry in price and convenience. Companies pursuing operational excellence are indefatigable in seeking ways to minimize overhead costs, to eliminate intermediate production steps, to reduce transaction and other "friction" costs, and to optimize business processes across functional and organizational boundaries. They focus on delivering their products or services to customers at competitive prices and with minimal inconvenience. Because they build their entire businesses around these goals, these organizations do not look or operate like other companies pursuing other value disciplines.

Dell Computer is one company that has focused on such operational excellence and, in doing so, has shown PC buyers that they do not have to sacrifice quality or state-of-the-art technology in order to buy personal computers easily and inexpensively. In the mid-1980s, while Compaq concentrated on making its PCs less expensive and faster than IBM's, college student Michael Dell saw the chance to outdo both IBM and Compaq by focusing not on the product but on the delivery system. Out of a dorm room in Austin, Texas, Dell burst onto the scene with a radically different and far more efficient operating model for operational excellence.

Dell realized that Compaq's marketing strategy—selling PCs through dealers to novices—could be outperformed by a model that cut dealers out of the distribution process altogether.

By selling to customers directly, building to order rather than to inventory, and creating a disciplined, extremely low-cost culture, Dell has been able to undercut Compaq and other PC makers in price yet provide high-quality products and service. While Dell has risen to $1.7 billion in revenue in less than ten years, Compaq has been forced to cut prices and overhead.

Other leaders in operational excellence include Wal-Mart, American Airlines, and Federal Express. Yet another, less well-known example, is General Electric's "white goods" business, which manufactures large household appliances. It has focused on operational excellence in serving the vast market of small, independent appliance retailers.

In the late 1980s, GE set out to transform itself into a low-cost, no-hassle supplier to dealers, and it designed its so-called Direct Connect program in pursuit of that objective. The Direct Connect program was ambitious. It required that GE reengineer several of its old business processes, redesign its information systems, reconfigure its management systems, and create a new mind-set among employees. In effect, General Electric reinvented its white goods business to embody its operational excellence discipline. As a result, the company has lowered dealers' net-landed cost of appliances and simplified its business transactions.

Historically the appliance industry had endorsed the theory that a loaded dealer is a loyal dealer. If a dealer's warehouse were full of a manufacturer's product, went the argument, the dealer would be committed to that company's product line because there was no room for goods from anyone else. Manufacturers' programs and pricing had been built around the idea that dealers got the best price when they bought a full truckload of appliances and were offered the best payment arrangements if they adhered to the manufacturer's floor plan.

But changes in the retail end of the industry caused GE to question that assumption. For one, the loaded-dealer concept was costly for independent appliance dealers, whose very existence was being threatened by the growing clout of low-price, multibrand chains like Circuit City. Independent stores could hardly afford to carry a large stock of appliances, especially when faced with competition from multibrand chains. Moreover, the chains could put price pressure on manufacturers, causing makers' margins to shrink.

Realizing that it had to supply high-quality products at competitive prices with little hassle, General Electric abandoned the loaded-dealer concept and reinvented its operating model—the way it made, sold, and distributed appliances. Under the company's new Direct Connect system, retailers no longer maintain their own inventories of major appliances. They rely instead on General Electric's "virtual inventory," a computer-based logistics system that allows stores to operate as though they had hundreds of ranges and refrigerators in the back room when in fact they have none at all.

To make Direct Connect work, retailers acquire a computer package that gives them instantaneous access to GE's on-line order-processing system 24 hours a day. They can use the system to check on model availability and to place orders for next-day delivery. The dealers get GE's best price, regardless of order size or content. Direct Connect dealers also get, among other benefits, priority over other dealers in delivery scheduling plus consumer financing through GE Credit, with the first 90 days free of interest. In exchange, Direct Connect dealers make several commitments: to sell nine major GE product categories while stocking only carryout products, such as microwave ovens and air conditioners; to ensure that GE products generate 50% of sales and to open their books for review; and to pay GE through electronic fund transfer on the 25th of the month after purchase.

Under the Direct Connect system, dealers have had to give up some float time in payables, the comfort of having their own back-room inventory, and some independence from the supplier. In return, they get GE's best price while eliminating the hassle and cost of maintaining inventory and assembling full truckload orders—and their profit margins on GE products have soared.

Virtual inventory, it turns out, works better than real inventory for both dealers and customers. "Instead of telling a customer I have two units on order," says one dealer, "I can now say that we have 2,500 in our warehouse. I can also tell a customer when a model is scheduled for production and when it will be shipped. If the schedule doesn't suit the customer, the GE terminal will identify other available models and compare their features with competitive units."

Meanwhile, GE gets half the dealers' business and saves about 12% of distribution and marketing costs. And since dealers serve themselves through the network, GE saves time and labor in order entry and in responding to inquiries. At GE, the new Direct Connect system *is* the order-entry process. Most important, GE has captured a valuable commodity from its dealers: data on the actual movement of its products. Most appliance manufacturers have been unable to track consumer sales accurately because they can't tell whether dealers' orders represent requests for additional inventory or actual customer purchases. With Direct Connect, GE knows that vendors' orders are, in fact, actual sales to customers.

GE links its order-processing system to other systems involved in forecasting demand and planning production and distribution. The company now, in effect, manufactures in response to customer demand instead of to inventory. It has reduced and simplified a complex and expensive warehousing and distribution system down to ten strategically located warehouses that can deliver appliances to 90% of the country within 24 hours.

Other businesses that vigorously pursue a strategy of operational excellence have reinvented their companies in similar fashion. They have reengineered the process that begins with order entry and ends with product or service delivery in a way that emphasizes efficiency and reliability. Specifically, they have adopted automated inventory replenishment and invoiceless payments and have integrated formerly disparate logistics systems. Companies that have adopted a strategy of operational excellence also have built their operations around information systems that emphasize integration and low-cost transaction processing.

Customer Intimacy

While companies pursuing operational excellence concentrate on making their operations lean and efficient, those pursuing a strategy of customer intimacy continually tailor and shape products and services to fit an increasingly fine definition of the customer. This can be expensive, but customer-intimate companies are willing to spend now to build customer loyalty for the long term. They typically look at the customer's lifetime value to the company, not the value of any single transaction. This is why employees in these companies will do almost anything—with little regard for initial cost—to make sure that each customer gets exactly what he or she really wants. Nordstrom is one example of such a company; IBM in its heyday was another; Home Depot is a third.

Home Depot clerks spend whatever time is required with a customer to figure out which product will solve his or her home-repair problem. The company's store personnel are not in a hurry. Their first priority is to make sure the customer gets the right product, whether its retail price comes to $59 or 59 cents.

Individual service is Home Depot's forte. Clerks do not spend time with customers just to be nice. They do so because the company's business strategy is built not just around selling home-repair and improvement items inexpensively but also around the customer's needs for information and service. Consumers whose only concern is price fall outside Home Depot's core market.

Other companies that have embraced a strategy of customer intimacy include Staples in office-supply retailing, Ciba-Geigy in pharmaceuticals, and Kraft and Frito-Lay in consumer packaged goods. These companies have designed operating models that allow them to address each customer or small subsegment of their market individually, as much for the sake of the company's profitability as for the customer's satisfaction. Their infrastructures facilitate multiple modes of producing and delivering products or services. They gladly split hairs when segmenting a market.

One principle that such companies understand well is the difference between profit or loss on a single transaction and profit over the lifetime of their relationship with a single customer. A leading financial brokerage firm, for instance, knows that not all customers require the same level of service or will generate the same revenues. The company's profitability, then, depends in part on its maintaining a system that can differentiate quickly and accurately among customers based on both the degree of service they require and the revenues their patronage is likely to generate. The company recently installed a telephone-computer system capable of recognizing individual clients by their telephone numbers when they call. The system routes investors with large accounts and frequent transactions to their own senior account representative. Other customers—those who typically place only an occasional buy or sell order, for instance—may be routed to a trainee, junior rep, or whoever is available. In either case, the customer's file appears on the rep's screen before the phone is answered.

The new system, which embodies this company's pursuit of customer intimacy, lets the firm segment its services with great efficiency. If the company has, say, just 400 clients around the country who are interested in trading in a particularly arcane financial instrument, it can group them under the one account rep who specializes in that instrument. It does not have to train every rep in every facet of financial services. Moreover, the company can direct certain value-added services or products to a specific group of clients whose interest it knows to be strong. It could, for instance, search its customer database for affluent retirees interested in minimizing inheritance taxes, customize a service or a product just for them, and train a rep in the new offering's sale and use.

In its move toward customer intimacy, Kraft USA has created the capacity to tailor its advertising, merchandising, and operations in a single store or in several stores within a supermarket chain to the needs of those stores' particular customers. Kraft has the information systems, analytical capability, and educated sales force to allow it to develop as many different so-called micro-merchandising programs for a chain that carries its products as the chain has stores. The program can be different for every neighborhood outlet. But to accomplish this, Kraft had to change itself first. It had to create the organization, build the information systems, and educate and motivate the people required to pursue a strategy of customer intimacy.

Like most companies that choose this strategy, Kraft decentralized its marketing operation in order to empower the people actually dealing with the customer. In Kraft's case, this was the sales force. Instead of pushing one-size-fits-all sales promotion programs, Kraft salespeople now work with individual store managers and regional managers to create customized promotional programs from an extensive computerized menu of program models.

Kraft does not just give its salespeople permission to work with customers, it also is giving them the data they need to make intelligent recommendations that will actually work. To do so, Kraft has assembled a centralized information system that collects and integrates data from three sources. The data it collects from individual stores break out consumer purchases by store, category, and product and indicate how buying behavior is affected by displays, price reductions, and so forth. They also provide profiles of customers who have bought particular products over the past several years and their rates of purchase. A second database contains demographic and buying-habit information on the customers of 30,000 food stores nationwide. A third set of data, purchased from an outside vendor, contains geo-demographic data by nine-digit zip code.

At Kraft headquarters, its trade marketing team sorts and integrates the information from these three databases and uses the results to supply sales teams with a repertoire of usable programs, products, value-added ideas, and selling tools. For instance, the trade marketing team sorted all shoppers into six distinct groups, with names such as full-margin shoppers, planners and dine-outs, and commodity shoppers. Kraft then determined for its major accounts which shopper groups frequented each of their stores. A Kraft sales team even persuaded one chain to create a drive-through window in stores where planners and dine-outs—people who plan their shopping trips and dine out often—were a large segment, making it more convenient for them to pick up staples between big shopping trips.

Kraft is also able to develop promotion packages for store clusters for special events like the Superbowl. It can design a product mix more likely to succeed in one cluster than another. Pinpointing which store gets which product reduces inventory and delivers the right product to the right place at the right time.

In reinventing itself, Kraft emulates other companies in different industries that also choose to pursue the strategy of customer intimacy. Its business processes stress flexibility and responsiveness. Its information systems collect, integrate, and analyze data from many sources. Its organizational structure emphasizes empowerment of people working close to customers, and its hiring and training programs stress the creative decision-making skills required to respond to individual customer needs. Its management systems recognize and utilize such concepts as customer lifetime value, and the rules and norms that management fosters among employees are consistent with the "have it your way" mind-set that must prevail in a company built on customer intimacy.

Product Leadership

Companies that pursue the third discipline, product leadership, strive to produce a continuous stream of state-of-the-art products and services. Reaching that goal requires them to challenge themselves in three ways. First, they must be creative. More than anything else, being creative means recognizing and embracing ideas that usually originate outside the company. Second, such innovative companies must commercialize their ideas quickly. To do so, all their business and management processes have to be engineered for speed. Third and most important, product leaders must relentlessly pursue new solutions to the problems that their own latest product or service has just solved. If anyone is going to render their technology obsolete, they prefer to do it themselves. Product leaders do not stop for self-congratulation; they are too busy raising the bar.

Johnson & Johnson, for example, meets all three of these challenges. J&J seems to attract new ideas, but it is not happenstance that brings good ideas in, develops them quickly, and then looks for ways to improve them. In 1983, the president of J&J's Vistakon, Inc., a maker of specialty contact lenses, heard about a Copenhagen ophthalmologist who had conceived of a way of manufacturing disposable contact lenses inexpensively. At the time, the company's Vistakon unit generated only $20 million each year in sales primarily from a single product, a contact lens for people who have astigmatism.

What was unusual was the way Vistakon's president got his tip. It came from a J&J employee whom he had never met who worked in an entirely different subsidiary in Denmark. The employee, an executive for Janssen Pharmaceutica, a J&J European drug subsidiary, telephoned Vistakon's president to pass along the news of the Danish innovation. Instead of dismissing the ophthalmologist as a mere tinkerer, these two executives speedily bought the rights to the technology, assembled a management team to oversee the product's development, and built a state-of-the-art facility in Florida to manufacture disposable contact lenses called Acuvue.

By the summer of 1987, Acuvue was ready for test marketing. In less than a year, Vistakon rolled out the product across the United States with a high-visibility ad campaign. Vistakon—and its parent, J&J—were willing to incur high manufacturing and inventory costs even before a single lens was sold. Its high-speed production facility helped give Vistakon a six-month head start over would-be rivals, such as Bausch & Lomb, Inc. and Ciba-Geigy. Taken off guard, the competition never caught up. Vistakon also took advantage of the benefits of decentralization—among them, autonomous management, speed, and flexibility—without having to give up the resources, financial and otherwise, that only a giant corporation could provide. Part of the success resulted from directing much of the marketing effort to eye-care professionals to explain how they would profit if they prescribed the new lenses. In other words, Vistakon did not market just to consumers. It said, in effect, that it's not enough to come up with a new product; you have to come up with a new way to go to market as well.

In 1991 Vistakon's sales topped $225 million worldwide, and it had captured a 25% share of the U.S. contact-lens market. But Vistakon is not resting on its laurels. It continues to investigate new materials that would extend the wearability of the contact lenses and even some technologies that would make the lenses obsolete.

J&J, like other product leaders, works hard at developing an open-mindedness to new ideas. Product leaders create and maintain an environment that encourages employees to bring ideas into the company and, just as important, they listen to and consider these ideas, however unconventional and regardless of the source. "Not invented here" is not a part of their vocabularies. In addition, product leaders continually scan the landscape for new product or service possibilities;

where others see glitches in their marketing plans or threats to their product lines, companies that focus on product leadership see opportunity and rush to capitalize on it.

Product leaders avoid bureaucracy at all costs because it slows commercialization of their ideas. Managers make decisions quickly, since in a product leadership company, it is often better to make a wrong decision than to make one late or not at all. That is why these companies are prepared to decide today, then implement tomorrow. Moreover, they continually look for new ways—such as concurrent engineering—to shorten their cycle times. Japanese companies, for example, succeed in automobile innovation because they use concurrent development processes to reduce time to market. They do not have to aim better than competitors to score more hits on the target because they can take more shots from a closer distance.

Companies excelling in product leadership do not plan for events that may never happen, nor do they spend much time on detailed analysis. Their strength lies in reacting to situations as they occur. Fast reaction times are an advantage when dealing with the unknown. Johnson & Johnson's Vistakon managers, for example, were quick to order changes to the Acuvue marketing program when early market tests were not as successful as they had expected. They also responded quickly when competitors challenged the safety of Acuvue lenses. They distributed data combating the charges, via Federal Express, to some 17,000 eye-care professionals. Vistakon's speedy response to the concerns raised by its competitors engendered goodwill in the marketplace.

Vistakon can move fast and take risks because it is organized like a small, entrepreneurial company. At the same time, it can call on the resources and capabilities of a multibillion-dollar corporation. This combination makes Vistakon—and J&J—a powerhouse competitor and strong product leader.

Product leaders have a vested interest in protecting the entrepreneurial environment that they have created. To that end, they hire, recruit, and train employees in their own mold. When it is time for Vistakon to hire new salespeople, for example, its managers do not look for people experienced in selling contact lenses; they look for people who will fit in with J&J's culture. That means they do not first ask about a candidate's related experience. Instead, they ask such questions as, "Could you work cooperatively in teams?" and "How open are you to criticism?"

Product leaders are their own fiercest competitors. They continually cross a frontier, then break more new ground. They have to be adept at rendering obsolete the products and services that they have created because they realize that if they do not develop a successor, another company will. J&J and other innovators are willing to take the long view of profitability, recognizing that whether they extract the full profit potential from an existing product or service is less important to the company's future than maintaining its product leadership edge and momentum. These companies are never blinded by their own successes.

One final point about product leaders: they also possess the infrastructure and management systems needed to manage risk well. For example, each time J&J ventures into an untapped area, it risks millions of dollars as well as its reputation. It takes that chance, though, in part because its hybrid structure allows it to combine the economies of scale and resource advantages of a $12 billion corporation with the cultural characteristics of a start-up company. In the case of Acuvue, J&J could manage the tremendous risk associated with developing and launching the lens because it represented only a small portion of the company's outlays.

Sustaining the Lead

Becoming an industry leader requires a company to choose a value discipline that takes into account its capabilities and culture as well as competitors' strengths. (For more on choosing a value discipline, see "Choosing Disciplines or Choosing Customers?") But the greater challenge is to sustain that focus, to drive that strategy relentlessly through the organization, to develop the internal consistency, and to confront radical change.

Choosing Disciplines or Choosing Customers?

When a company chooses to focus on a value discipline, it is at the same time selecting the category of customer that it will serve. In fact, the choice of business discipline and customer category is actually a single choice.

One set of potential customers defines value within a matrix of price, convenience, and quality, with price the dominant factor. These customers are less particular about what they buy than they are about getting it at the lowest possible price and with the least possible hassle. They are unwilling to sacrifice low price or high convenience to acquire a product with a particular label or to obtain a premium service. Whether they are consumers or industrial buyers, they want high-quality goods and services, but even more, they want to get them cheaply or easily or both.

These are the customers who shop for retail goods at discount and membership warehouse stores. They buy PC clones directly from manufacturers. They seek basic transportation when they buy a car and discount commissions when they buy or sell stocks and other investments. The business that succeeds by serving these customers focuses on operational excellence.

The second set of customers is more concerned with obtaining precisely what they want or need. They are willing to make some sacrifice—in price or delivery time, for instance—if the sacrifice helps them acquire something that meets their unique requirements. The specific characteristics of the product or the way the service is delivered is far more important to them than any reasonable price premium or purchase inconvenience they might incur.

Customers in this group ascribe value to a product or service according to how closely it appears to be designed just for them. Chain stores—whether in the food, book, or music business—that customize their inventories to match regional or even neighborhood tastes serve this category of customer. Other retailers and catalogers attract this customer type by offering the largest imaginable range of products. They won't carry just standard Scrabble, for instance, but every version of the game. An industrial distributor we know carries 12 pages of water heaters in its catalog. Its breadth of inventory is a strategic asset in appealing to this second customer category. These customers require a company to focus on customer intimacy.

To the third category of customers, new, different, and unusual products count most. These are customers who, as clothing buyers, are primarily interested in fashion and trends. In an industrial context, they are buyers who value state-of-the-art products or components because their own customers demand the latest technology from them. If they are service companies, they want suppliers that help them seize breakthrough opportunities in their own markets. For a company to succeed in serving these customers, it has to focus on product leadership.

One point to bear in mind: the same people can be found in all three customer categories, depending on what they are buying. An individual might buy office supplies primarily on price, groceries strictly on the basis of personal taste, and clothes as fashion dictates. The same people will define value differently as it applies to different goods and services.

Many companies falter simply because they lose sight of their value discipline. Reacting to marketplace and competitive pressures, they pursue initiatives that have merit on their own but are inconsistent with the company's value discipline. These companies often appear to be aggressively responding to change. In reality, however, they are diverting energy and resources away from advancing their operating model.

Sears is a good example. Under enormous pressure from Wal-Mart and other competitors, Sears's retailing division in the late 1980s launched a number of initiatives aimed at winning back customers and boosting its sagging bottom line. First came "everyday low prices," a component of an operational excellence discipline. For that gambit to pay off, Sears needed to cut costs—which it did to some extent by eliminating many in-store employees and slashing front-office expenses. But the cost cutting did not go nearly far enough, in part because Sears had not consciously focused on the discipline of operational excellence. Had it done so, it would have scrutinized each part of its organization, including the order-fulfillment process, to see where it could realize savings. The consequence of not focusing meant, among other things, that Sears failed to restructure its end-to-end distribution costs, as Wal-Mart, for instance, has done.

In another attempt to regain market share, Sears inaugurated "Brand Central," whereby the retailer would carry branded products in addition to its house brands, Kenmore and Craftsman. Creating more product variety in an attempt to meet the needs of different market segments is a component of a customer intimacy discipline. But again, Sears did not go far enough. By just plucking Brand Central from a quiver of random ideas, Sears shot wide of the target. Brand Central only confused existing customers, who did not know which brand to buy. Sears's strategy also cut into sales of its own brands. And since the move did not give Sears any more product variety than competitors had, it did little to boost sales.

Sears's third initiative, meant to give the retailer a trendy image, was to have models and actresses endorse its fashion line. This tack, which corresponds to a product leadership discipline, also had little impact on profits. One problem was that Sears struck just one deal, with model Cheryl Tiegs. The second problem: J.C. Penney was following the same strategy but was outdoing Sears with more endorsements, slicker advertising, better catalogs, more sophisticated marketing, and better product design. In trying to be all things to all people, Sears pursued strategies that steered it away from its chosen value discipline and into unproductive dead ends. It tried to fuse together incompatible philosophies and practices and got predictable results. In its time, Sears was a value leader, but to regain that distinction in today's competitive market, the company will have to pick one value discipline and vigorously pursue it while meeting industry standards in the other two.

The key to gaining and sustaining value leadership is focus, but the management of a company that's a value leader must stay alert. The operating model that elevated a company to value leadership—Compaq's model, for instance—is superior and worth exploiting only until a better one—Dell's distribution model, say—comes along.

Companies that sustain value leadership within their industries will be run by executives who not only understand the importance of focusing the business on its value discipline but also push relentlessly to advance the organization's operating model. They will personally lead the company's drive to develop new capabilities and to change the imbedded work habits, processes, and attitudes that prevent them from achieving excellence in the discipline they have chosen. By leading the effort to transform their organizations, these individuals will be preparing their companies to set new industry standards, to redefine what is possible, and to forever change the terms of competition.

This article is based on our consulting work and the research that we have conducted in Index Alliance, a research and advisory service of CSC Index. Jay Michaud, principal of CSC Index and director of Index Alliance, contributed significantly to this article.

PART

II

The Art of Quality
Service Delivery

1
The Service-Driven Service Company

Leonard A. Schlesinger and James L. Heskett

For more than 40 years, service companies successfully followed an industrial model based largely on the principles of traditional mass-production manufacturing. Today that model is obsolete, as dangerous a threat to the long-term health of the service sector and the U.S. economy as it has already proved to be in manufacturing. It leads inevitably to degradation in the quality of service a company can provide. And it sets in motion a cycle of failure that is uniformly bad for customers, employees, shareholders, and the country. Among its symptoms are customer disaffection, high employee turnover, flat or falling sales, and little or no growth in productivity for individual companies and for services overall.

As an example, consider the situation McDonald's now faces. From the day that Ray Kroc opened his first hamburger stand in 1955, the company's operating system has been a model of efficient service, not only for fast-food operators but also for hotels, retail stores, banks, and scores of other businesses in which personal contact is an essential part of delivering value to customers. Every aspect of the operation is designed to assure quick service, clean surroundings, and uniform products. Nothing is left to chance or individual discretion: a McDonald's franchisee can no more decide to sell tuna sandwiches (the kitchen has no place to prepare them) than a counterperson can scoop too many (or too few) french fries.

The rewards of this mass-production approach have been enormous. For years, no one in the industry could match McDonald's growth and profitability. Then, at the end of the 1980s, things changed. McDonald's had a harder time finding satisfactory employees, especially in the suburbs. Construction costs shot up, as did prices. For the first time ever, sales and operating income in many of the U.S. stores began to stagnate or even fall. Attracted by competitors that offered more varied menus, lower prices, or both, customers defected and continue to defect. And while McDonald's is working hard to win them back, its own systems are constraining its ability to respond.

Production-line thinking cannot help traditional service companies like McDonald's that are now facing unprecedented pressure from new competitors. Attracting and retaining today's customers demands a fundamentally different approach, one that reverses what we call the cycle of failure. The basic premise is simple: the old model puts the people who deliver service to customers last; the new model puts frontline workers first and designs the business system around them. The consequences of this reversal are profound, as senior managers are discovering at companies like Dayton Hudson and Fairfield Inn, which have made service delivery the centerpiece of their competitive strategy.

A new model of service is emerging, replacing the old model of industrialization in every element of the business. In this new model, companies:

- value investments in people as much as investments in machines, and sometimes more;
- use technology to support the efforts of men and women on the front line, not just to monitor or replace them;
- make recruitment and training as crucial for salesclerks and housekeepers as for managers and senior executives;
- link compensation to performance for employees at every level, not just for those at the top.

Finally, to justify these investments, the new logic uses innovative data that traditional accounting and measurement systems do not track: the aggregate costs of customer or employee turnover, for example, or the greater profit margins that repeat customers can provide.

As yet, no single company has put all the pieces of this new service model together. But its internal logic is already becoming clear: capable workers who are well trained and fairly compensated provide better service, need less supervision, and are much more likely to stay on the job. As a result, their customers are likely to be more satisfied, return more often, and perhaps even purchase more than they otherwise would. For individual companies, this means enhanced competitiveness. For the United States overall, it means the creation of front-line service jobs that can bring more working people into the mainstream of economic life.

More than 45 million people (or roughly 42% of the U.S. work force) are employed in serving food, selling merchandise in retail stores, performing clerical work in service industries, cleaning hospitals, schools, and offices, or providing some other form of personal service. These are the occupations that accounted for most of the U.S. job growth in the 1980s, a pattern that will continue at least until the turn of the century. Yet for the most part, these jobs are poorly paid, lead nowhere, and provide little if anything in the way of health, pension, or other benefits. Many are truly dead-end jobs. (See Exhibit I, "Dead-End Jobs.")

For a long time, demographics masked this reality. As baby boomers and married women streamed into the work force, it was plausible to believe that these were mostly first jobs for teenagers or a source of supplementary income for two-earner families. Now, however, that is no longer the case. The number of young people coming into the job market has fallen sharply, while many if not most of the women are breadwinners and often single parents as well. The reality is that the people behind the cash registers, sales counters, and vacuum cleaners are adults. The work they are doing is increasingly likely to be their permanent form of employment.

Moreover, for many service workers, it is the work itself that is permanent, not a particular job. The old industrial logic has created a new class of migrant workers in the United States—some 16 million service workers, according to figures derived from Department of Labor data. Like field hands moving from farm to farm, these people travel from one short-term job to another, becoming more demotivated with every move. Sometimes they are fired because their performance is inadequate. But often they are purposely let go just before they qualify for the five or ten cents more an hour that three or six month's seniority would command.

CEOs and their senior managers are responsible primarily for the well-being of their companies, not the well-being of society. But in the cycle of failure, the two coincide. Today a handful of pioneers have chosen to break the cycle by recognizing and rewarding the value their frontline service workers provide. The results so far are encouraging. Employees typically earn more and enjoy their jobs more than their peers in comparable companies. Employers report higher rates of customer satisfaction and retention, lower employee turnover, and higher

Exhibit I.

Dead-End Jobs Dominated Many of the Service-Sector Industries That Grew the Most in the 1980s...

	Jobs Added 1979-1989	Dead-End Jobs*	Average Hourly Real Wage Growth 1979-1989	Productivity Growth 1979-1989
Restaurants	1,857,000	93.7%	– 2.1%	– 0.5%
Grocery Stores	887,000	91.7	– 3.1	N/A
Personnel Supply	824,000	81.2	– 0.3	– 4.4
Hotels	529,000	91.5	– 0.2	– 1.1
Building Services	321,000	95.9	– 1.3	– 2.1
Department Stores	178,000	91.7	– 1.3	N/A

Source: United States Department of Labor, Bureau of Labor Statistics.
* In jobs we classify as dead-end, the average employee has at most a high school diploma.

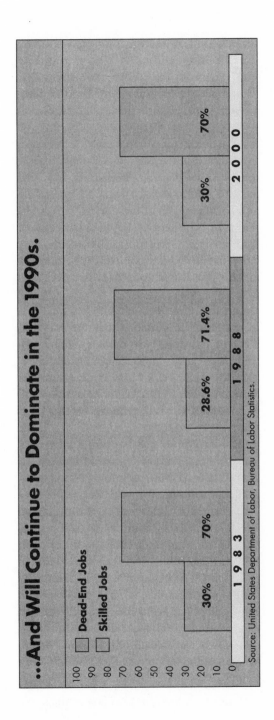

...And Will Continue to Dominate in the 1990s.

Source: United States Department of Labor, Bureau of Labor Statistics.

sales. Employers of choice in their industries, these companies are staking out strong competitive positions based on a system that produces uniformly good service—and that competitors bound to the old industrial model will be unable to match.

Poor Service by Design

The industrial approach to services is on display virtually every hour of every day in supermarkets, airports, banks, hotels, government offices, and more. But its effects may be easiest to see in the department store, that warehouse of goods where all too frequently the typical customer experience is aggravation.

Imagine that you have just walked into the men's department of almost any big store in the United States to buy a pair of slacks. You might spot a seemingly unoccupied salesperson standing at a distance. More likely, you see racks of clothes, counters filled with accessories, and other shoppers equally in need of help. Undeterred when no one offers to wait on you, you begin the search on your own. You find the pants section, choose a few pairs to try on, and search out a dressing room. You may first have to find someone to unlock it or give you a numbered tag to monitor the merchandise—and you. Should you want a different size, color, or style, you'll have to get it for yourself. And when, at last, you are ready to pay, you still have to track down a cashier in the right department. Special requests—"Could you see if another store has these slacks in my size?"—take time, if they can be accommodated at all. Returns, exchanges, and other problematic transactions (like register errors) take more time and the intervention of a manager who is authorized to respond.

What is astonishing about this scenario is not the poor service it depicts. What is astonishing is that these service failures are not failures, they have been designed into the system by the choices senior management has made. Like their peers in many other service industries, the department store's managers have created, and continue to run, a self-reinforcing system that establishes an inevitable cycle of failure. Ironically, the system's assumptions and operating practices virtually guarantee the degradation of the services the business exists to provide.

The cycle of failure begins with a set of interlocking assumptions about people, technology, and money derived from old industrial models. Today these assumptions are rarely made explicit, even in manufacturing where they had their birth. But their internal logic still drives a great many companies and managers. Simplifying somewhat, that logic goes like this: all things being equal, it is better to rely on technology, on machines and systems, than on human beings. Machines are more efficient and productive. They cost less in the long run. And they are infinitely less trouble to manage since, unlike people, they do not need to be recruited, supervised, trained, and motivated.

The human resource policies and practices that follow from this industrial logic effectively treat people as though they were machines. Frontline, customer-contact jobs are designed to be as simple and narrow as possible so that they can be filled by almost anyone—idiot-proof jobs. Employers ask little of potential employees. They use minimal selection criteria (often nothing more than the ability to show up on time) and set abysmally low performance expectations. At the same time, these employers offer little in return. They keep wages as low as possible, typically just above the legal minimum. The training they offer new hires is rudimentary at best, a reasonable policy in a system that gives workers no room to exercise discretion or judgment. Opportunities to advance are rare.

Unfortunately, however, this industrial model flies in the face of what service-sector customers many times value most: the things that technology cannot do at all or as well as thinking human beings. Automated-teller machines are one exception. But on the whole, consumers have shown little liking for restaurants without servers, hospitals without nurse's aides and orderlies, hotels without front-desk clerks, or department stores without salespeople. In fact, the more that technology becomes a standard part of delivering services, the more important personal interactions are in satisfying customers and in differentiating competitors.

Recent research on customer loyalty in the service industry conducted by the Forum Corporation shows that only 14% of customers who stop patronizing service businesses do so because they are dissatisfied with the quality of what they bought. More than two-thirds defect because they find service people indifferent or unhelpful. Yet helpful, attentive service is out of reach for companies that follow the traditional industrial model.

Sears is a good example. Like other big merchandisers, Sears has faced strong competitive pressure from a variety of sources for years. Specialty shops and catalogs have used superior service and product knowledge to attract customers willing to pay full price. Breakthrough fashion retailers have reaped enormous cost advantages by using technology and just-in-time inventory methods to slash design-to-market cycle times. Off-price and warehouse stores sell identical branded goods at deeply discounted prices. Even the department stores' own efforts to compete have contributed to the problems they face: markdowns and almost continuous sales have lowered revenues, eroded margins, and accustomed shoppers to year-round bargain hunting.

In this environment, improving (or even maintaining) profitability is a daunting task. Despite its extensive and growing base of retail outlets, revenue gains at Sears have averaged only 4.3% per year since 1986, while operating margins in the same period have deteriorated significantly, dropping from 4.9% in 1986 to 1.2% in 1990. (In contrast, arch-rival Wal-Mart Stores maintains a 4% net margin on its operations, and its average sales growth over the past five years has exceeded 28%.) Perhaps worst of all, Sears is widely perceived to have lost the loyalty of its target market, middle-income consumers.

Sears has tried to reverse these declines by upgrading its buying organization, introducing new merchandising strategies such as "Everyday Low Pricing," and cutting costs throughout the organization. Since 1989, the giant retailer has eliminated over 33,000 nonselling positions for a projected savings of $600 million to $700 million. But despite these efforts, management still seems not to have realized how critically important its salespeople are to turning things around, and how long-standing human resource policies have seriously eroded the sales force's ability and will to compete.

For example, in the labor market, Sears has consistently followed the basic tenet of the old industrial mind-set to keep labor costs as low as possible. During the 1970s and early 1980s, Sears shifted the composition of the sales force from 70% full-time employees to 70% part-timers. In the short run, this change undoubtedly reduced the aggregate wage bill and cut benefit costs dramatically. Over time, however, it led to rising rates of turnover and a sharp drop in customer satisfaction.

The chain of consequences that is the cycle of failure explains these unintended outcomes: with fewer, less knowledgeable salespeople on the floor, customers will get less and lower quality help. Impatient, dissatisfied customers have no reason to hide their feelings from employees. And since discontent breeds discontent, sooner or later even the most conscientious salespeople become demotivated. Then the best leave, the mediocre hang on until they are fired, and the cycle starts over with a new crop of recruits who are likely to be even less capable than the people they have replaced.

"Cycle-of-failure" companies cannot attract job hunters with good skills or experience to fill vacancies because quality employees will naturally be attracted to positions offering better prospects and pay. So they must use new technology mostly to monitor employees' work (electronic time clocks, for example, and sophisticated countertheft systems) rather than to give customers better service. Total expenses rise because more supervisors and managers are needed to deal with situations marginal employees cannot be trusted to resolve. Overall, service quality ratchets down another notch or more.

Obvious as these connections may be once they have been stated, many service company managers do not make them. The assumptions reflected in the cycle of failure contribute largely to this myopia. In fact, the harder managers push to resolve performance shortfalls using tools derived from the industrial model, the less likely they are to make real long-term progress. Moreover, the day-to-day performance measures commonly used in most companies only reinforce this vicious circle.

The Economics of Service

Managers in labor-intensive service companies cannot track the real performance of their operations with traditional measurement systems. Determining the costs of customer turnover or the economics of service recovery requires metrics that generally accepted accounting principles do not provide. It also requires senior managers who are willing to abandon conventional wisdom about how and where profits are created.

In service companies that have stores, restaurants, or other facilities in many locations, two assumptions are common. One is that location strategies, sales promotions, and advertising drive the top line.

The other is that cost control is the unit-level manager's primary responsibility. Both assumptions are right in part. Prominent locations, catchy sales promotions, and memorable ads are fine ways to bring in trade. And no business can operate profitably for long without careful cost controls at every level. But what these assumptions omit is the role that workers who are in direct contact with customers play in enhancing or diminishing customer satisfaction and therefore profits.

Research into the economics of problem resolution and service recovery highlights the critical role of customer-contact employees. Data collected by Technical Assistance Research Programs for the U.S. Department of Consumer Affairs show a close link between resolving a customer's problem on the spot and the customer's intent to repurchase. When customers experience minor problems, 95% say they will repurchase if the complaint is resolved speedily. If the resolution process takes even a little time, however, the number drops to 70%. A spread of 25 percentage points can easily mean the difference between spectacular and mediocre operating performance. (Indeed, studies on the effects of customer loyalty have shown that even a 5% increase in customer retention can raise profitability by 25% to 85%.[1]) Yet the old industrial model virtually guarantees poor on-the-spot problem solving because it assumes that only managers can solve problems. As a result, it has created a generation of service workers who are either uninterested in customers' difficulties or unable to assist them if they do care. Even if they want to, managers cannot confidently rely on workers hired under the cycle-of-failure model to do the right thing.

The economics of turnover are another area in which new metrics are needed—and where traditional accounting practices reinforce the cycle of failure and invisibly undermine a business's profits. To illustrate the scope of the problem, consider some data from Sears.[2] In 1989, 119,000 sales jobs turned over in the retail network of the Sears Merchandise Group. The cost of hiring and training each new sales associate was $900, or more than $110 million in the aggregate (a figure that represents 17% of the Merchandise Group's 1989 income).

Costs of this magnitude often lead managers to make cuts in training. The explanation is the absence of relevant information: while wages and training costs are universally measured and known, the return on these investments in employee development is not because the incremental value of better service has long been considered unknowable. Now, however, that assumption is breaking down. Managers are looking for measures that will help them evaluate the relationship between training and employee retention, for example, or the value of the consistency of service that comes from lower turnover. In sum, they are beginning to factor in the new economics of service.

In 1989, Sears surveyed customers in 771 stores as part of its routine service-monitoring activities. Its findings throw new light on the critical importance of employee turnover as well as on the value of employee morale overall. First, the data make it clear that employee turnover and customer satisfaction are directly correlated. In stores that were given relatively high customer-service ratings, 54% of the sales force turned over in a year compared with 83% at the poorer scoring stores. Second, customer satisfaction correlates directly with the composition of a store's sales force. The more a store relied on a continually changing group of part-timers (a staple in many service businesses), the lower the customer ratings it received. The higher its percentage of full-time and regular part-time workers, the more satisfied customers said they felt.

Evidence from companies that are mounting innovative efforts to measure the full costs of employee turnover adds to the impact of these findings. For example, two divisions at Marriott Corporation undertook a study to quantify the links among turnover, customer retention, and profitability. As a working hypothesis, management estimated that a 10% reduction in turnover would reduce customer nonrepeats by 1% to 3% and raise revenues by $50 million to $150 million. The study's conclusions are striking: even with high-end estimates for recruitment and training costs and low-end estimates for the cost of lost customers, reducing turnover by 10% yielded savings that were greater than the operating profits of the two divisions combined.

The inefficiencies in day-to-day operations created when employees leave are another hidden cost of turnover. Merck & Co. found that disruptions in work relationships and the transactional costs of getting employees on and off the payroll raised the total costs of employee turnover to 1.5 times an employee's annual salary. Further, the analysis concluded that, from an investment of 50% of an employee's salary in activities to eliminate turnover, Merck could reap a one-year payback.[3]

Finally, in a study done in 1988 and 1989, Ryder Truck Rental discovered that another hidden cost of turnover is its impact on workers' compensation claim rates (a significant component of benefit costs). In the 16 districts with annual voluntary turnover of less than 10%, the workers' compensation claim rate was just over 16%. In the 20 districts where voluntary turnover ranged between 15% and 20%, the rate rose to 23%. In addition, Ryder found that increased training led to decreased turnover. Among employees who participated in the company's new training program, the turnover rate was 19%. Among employees who did not participate, the rate soared to 41%.

Documenting the critical relationships among customers, profits, and employees presents a measurement challenge to be sure. The economics of customer loyalty are only now beginning to be worked out, despite overwhelming evidence of their importance. The economics of employee loyalty are still largely unexplored. But thoughtful managers at companies such as Marriott, Merck, and Ryder are making measurable strides in factoring the new economics of service into their strategies and their general accounts.

Design for Service

Companies cannot design new standards of service by following old routines. In many service industries, one or two leading companies have realized this and begun to do business in a radically different way that represents a 180-degree turnabout from the old industrial paradigm. Its consequences are apparent to everyone—customers, employees, managers, and competitors.

At the heart of this new approach to service are the needs and expectations of customers as the customers themselves, not the operating system and its constraints, define them. Fast-food patrons who expect instant service as well as variety will not be satisfied if new menu options leave them watching the clock. Shoppers who want to consider purchases from several departments at the same time need salespeople who can help them do so, not clerks who are tied to one department and one register.

As these examples indicate, putting customers first means focusing on how and where they interact with the company. That, in turn, means focusing on the workers who actually create or deliver the things that customers value—a spotless hotel room, a quick and easy refund, a fresh, inexpensive sandwich. In companies that are truly customer oriented, management has designed (or redesigned) the business to support frontline workers' efforts and to maximize the impact of the value they create. New job definitions and compensation policies are critical parts of these redesigned systems. So are new organization structures and systems. The product is economic performance that is startling compared with the performance of traditional industry competitors.

Consider Taco Bell. Over the past three years, in an overall market that has been flat to declining, sales growth at company-owned Taco Bells has exceeded 60%. Profits have grown by well over 25% per year (compared with under 6% annually at McDonald's U.S. restaurants). All of Taco Bell's financial success has come while it has dramatically cut prices for its core menu by over 25%.

The media and industry analysts attribute this success to Taco Bell's "value strategy." The chain offers the most popular menu items such as tacos and burritos at prices as low as 99 cents, 79 cents, 59 cents, and recently even 39 cents. But this analysis begs the question of how the restaurant can perform so well financially while carrying on such aggressive price cutting. The answer lies in the way Taco Bell's management has chosen to operate its business. If McDonald's is the epitome of the old industrialized service model, Taco Bell represents the new, redesigned model in many important respects.

Taco Bell's new model is based on a very simple premise: customers value the food, the service, and the physical appearance of a restaurant, and that is all. Everything that helps the company deliver value to customers along these dimensions deserves reinforcement and management support. Everything else is nonvalue-adding overhead. The brilliance of this strategy lies in its execution: Taco Bell's management examined every aspect of the restaurant operation, then fundamentally altered roles and responsibilities at every level of the corporate hierarchy.

At the outset, management realized that the company could not execute the new strategy as long as its old, seven-layer organization remained in place. To compete on service and maintain low prices, the stores had to be staffed with talented, motivated people supplied with timely, accurate information about how their units were performing. Such people would need far fewer supervisors: in fact, the span of control has gone from one supervisor for every 5-plus stores in 1988 to one for every 20-plus stores today. Management would require different things from those supervisors: coaching and support, for example, rather than direction and control. And it would need new information systems to help raise quality and sales as well as to monitor mistakes.

To meet these needs, management initiated changes in almost every part of the business. By expanding the company's sophisticated information technology to the store level, for example, it freed restaurant managers from more than 15 hours of nonproductive paper work each week while providing real-time performance data on costs, employees, and customer satisfaction. Management also restructured the store's operating processes to reflect the fact that fast-food customers value fresh, tasty food served in clean surroundings and don't particularly care where the work of preparing that food is done.

The back room of any fast-food operation is a complex, high-volume manufacturing system. By outsourcing much of the preparation work that had been done in the restaurants (like shredding lettuce and chopping tomatoes), Taco Bell shifted its factory operation from manufacturing to assembly. Now while more automated facilities perform the tasks that lend themselves to economies of scale, Taco Bell's employees concentrate on customers and their needs. In contrast, the back room of the average McDonald's is becoming increasingly complex. The more that management adds items such as pizza and fresh muffins to appeal to a broader set of customers, the more complicated the store's manufacturing operation becomes, and the more managerial attention and control it demands.

By making these changes, Taco Bell's management drove down costs and removed more than 15 hours of back-room labor per day from the average operation. Even more important, it shifted the focus of both frontline workers and their managers from manufacturing meals to serving customers. The ratio of front-of-the-house personnel to back-room factory workers has been turned upside down, and employee job descriptions increasingly focus on the limited but crucial service dimensions that drive the bottom line. Patronage from high-frequency fast-food consumers has skyrocketed, and consumer perceptions of Taco Bell's value outstrip all competitors.

These front-of-the-house jobs cannot be done by incompetent, uncommitted workers. They require men and women who can take responsibility, manage themselves, respond well to pressure from customers—in short, the kind of people who rarely come to mind when most service managers think about candidates for frontline service jobs. Taco Bell's management does not make that mistake. It assumes that service workers—like everyone else—come to the workplace with a wide variety of attitudes, assumptions, and expectations. Some will have the potential to be high performers; others will not. To differentiate among them, Taco Bell uses a selection process that is designed to elicit prospective employees' values and attitudes toward responsibility, teamwork, and other "life themes" that have been shown to correlate with successful service work. Far from being discriminatory, the selection process has demonstrated its value in identifying high-potential candidates without regard to race, sex, ethnicity, or age. Oftentimes, detailed preliminary interviews between managers and candidates are conducted over the phone.

These selective hiring policies are a critical component of the new human resource model that Taco Bell is developing. Training efforts are another. Revised job descriptions for the company's restaurant managers require them to spend more than half their day (or twice the time they used to) on human resource matters, such as developing their unit's employees. To help them with this task, they are now receiving training and support in communication, performance management, team building, coaching, and empowerment that they, in turn, pass on to the front line.

Changes in job design and supervisory style have stimulated marked improvements in employee morale. In a recent companywide survey,

62% of the respondents said they felt more empowered and accountable; 55% felt they had more freedom to act independently; 66% felt they had the authority they needed to act; and 60% felt a strong sense of accountability.

More capable people with the responsibility and freedom to act inevitably require better pay. Dramatic changes in compensation have yet to hit Taco Bell's front line. But already, workers behind the counter take home paychecks that are above the industry average. Moreover, even as the company's pay system evolves, the perception is growing among employees and competitors alike that it is disrupting the industry's traditional practices. For example, store managers are eligible for bonuses that allow them to earn up to 225% of the industry average based on the restaurant's economic and service performance. And those numbers are slated to rise as more funds are generated from incremental profitability and from further increases in the company's spans of control. (Exhibit II, "Pay for Supervision or Pay for Service?" shows how dramatic such a redistribution of funds can be.)

Precisely how these new policies and attitudes will translate into greater employee loyalty remains to be seen, although it is reasonable to expect marked reductions in turnover and continuing improvement in the quality of new hires. But it is clear that Taco Bell's success comes from more than lowering its prices. The company has explicitly rejected the prevailing model of service organization in favor of a redesigned system with service at its core. Human resource management is a central component of this new model as well as a critical part of Taco Bell's competitive strategy overall.

While all these changes have been taking place at Taco Bell, McDonald's has focused on more of the same: more advertising and promotion efforts, more new products, more new locations. But more of the same no longer works. Competing against Taco Bell and other redesigned service businesses demands a shift in management's mind-set as well as a new appreciation for the real value of service and the value that service employees create.

Reversing the Cycle of Failure

Senior managers at companies like Dayton Hudson, Marriott, and ServiceMaster (which provides health-care, educational, and industrial facilities with services ranging from materials management to food service) know there is no single strategy for competing on serv-

Exhibit II.

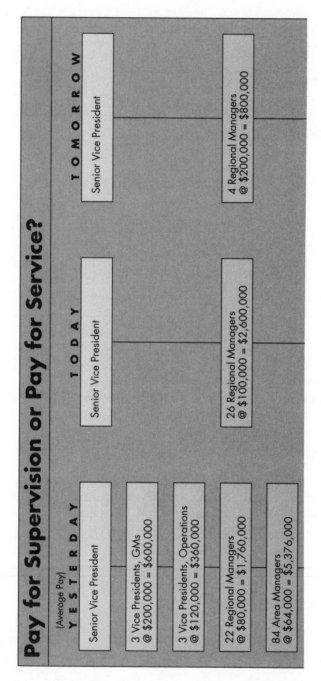

Pay for Supervision or Pay for Service?

(Average Pay)

YESTERDAY	TODAY	TOMORROW
Senior Vice President	Senior Vice President	Senior Vice President
3 Vice Presidents, GMs @ $200,000 = $600,000		
3 Vice Presidents, Operations @ $120,000 = $360,000		
22 Regional Managers @ $80,000 = $1,760,000	26 Regional Managers @ $100,000 = $2,600,000	4 Regional Managers @ $200,000 = $800,000
84 Area Managers @ $64,000 = $5,376,000		

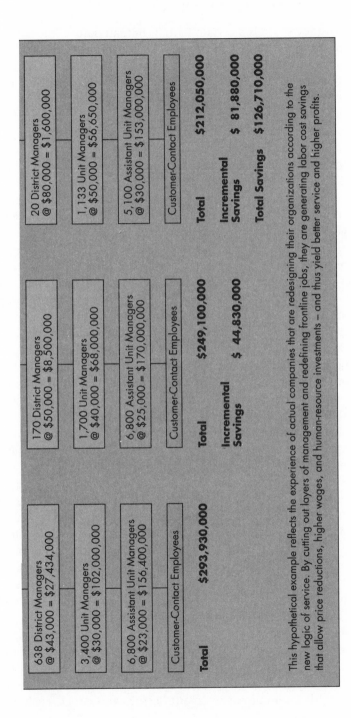

638 District Managers @ $43,000 = $27,434,000	170 District Managers @ $50,000 = $8,500,000	20 District Managers @ $80,000 = $1,600,000
3,400 Unit Managers @ $30,000 = $102,000,000	1,700 Unit Managers @ $40,000 = $68,000,000	1,133 Unit Managers @ $50,000 = $56,650,000
6,800 Assistant Unit Managers @ $23,000 = $156,400,000	6,800 Assistant Unit Managers @ $25,000 = $170,000,000	5,100 Assistant Unit Managers @ $30,000 = $153,000,000
Customer-Contact Employees	Customer-Contact Employees	Customer-Contact Employees
Total $293,930,000	Total $249,100,000	Total $212,050,000
	Incremental Savings $ 44,830,000	Incremental Savings $ 81,880,000
		Total Savings $126,710,000

This hypothetical example reflects the experience of actual companies that are redesigning their organizations according to the new logic of service. By cutting out layers of management and redefining frontline jobs, they are generating labor cost savings that allow price reductions, higher wages, and human-resource investments – and thus yield better service and higher profits.

ice. What they share is a certain faith in human nature, the belief that many people want to do good work. They reject the prevailing notion that "you can't find good people anymore." And they repudiate any suggestion that a positive work ethic can only be assumed if people have the right degrees or skin color or native language. As a result, these companies have consciously set out to develop human resource policies and practices that will make them employers of choice, not just in their industries but in the labor market overall.

Selection and hiring practices are the most obvious way in which these companies differ markedly from their competitors. Take recruitment: whereas most large service companies have to rely on the luck of the draw, these employers tend to have applicants who have come through referrals or because they have heard good things about working for the company. The selection process is also sharply different. In essence, they prefer to interview ten candidates to find the right person for a job rather than hire the first warm body who comes along—and then have to fill the same job ten times over. Moreover, they are able to say, quite specifically, what "right" means in their particular business. Interviewers at Dayton's, for example, favor applicants who see retail sales as a career. Suitable candidates for housekeeping jobs at Fairfield Inn (the Marriott Corporation's new chain of economy inns) are not only dependable people with good work habits and a passion for cleanliness but also people who are willing to be evaluated and compensated on the basis of their performance.

As these examples indicate, hiring decisions at pioneering service companies are based largely on how people think, not on what they are. Those decisions are possible because these employers have carried out careful analyses to determine the characteristics entry-level workers need to be successful in their jobs and the degree to which those characteristics can or cannot be imparted through training. In hiring front-desk clerks, Fairfield Inn will gladly take on a candidate who relates easily to customers but needs to learn how to use a personal computer. Computer whizzes with no interest in people are another matter altogether. As a result, the work forces at these companies can be enormously diverse and still be homogeneous on the one dimension that matters, their ability to provide excellent service.

Training and development is another area in which these employers are breaking new ground in their industries. Increasingly, training is seen as both a means to more competitive performance and as an end in itself. At ServiceMaster, for example, medical professionals regularly talk to entry-level employees about basic health issues, such as how diseases are transmitted from one person to another. The talks contribute to the company's ability to provide good service because they emphasize how crucial it is for everyone to be scrupulous about cleanliness. But they also add to the hospital workers' stock of knowledge as well as to their pride in themselves and the importance of their work.

In addition to educating and motivating employees, training sessions typically provide the context in which employees commit themselves to the company and its service expectations. New sales consultants at Dayton's take part in a two-day "celebration" in which the underlying theme is "It's my company." During the sessions, they work through exercises to identify and improve their attitudes toward service and customers, watch videotapes on the importance of body language, and engage in role playing to build their enthusiasm for the company. Throughout, the focus is on helping the associates think and act like customers instead of on teaching technical skills like using the registers.

Moreover, training pertains to everyone, not just to newcomers. Capital budgeting in these organizations places as much emphasis on people as on money. One prerequisite for making the shift from the old industrial model of service to the new customer-centered model is an intensive investment to train and communicate with existing employees. The rationale for this investment comes partly from the need to set higher performance standards and expectations and partly from the need to convey the information and skills workers will need to meet those expectations. Urging salespeople to "go the extra mile" for customers will not accomplish anything, for example, unless those salespeople also understand why and how things can be done differently. Likewise, managers whose chief responsibility has shifted from supervising workers to coaching and developing workers will need coaching and developing themselves to perform successfully in their new roles.

Ironically, a critical piece of many managers' reeducation is an on-the-job refresher course in service. Today more and more supervisors and managers are spending large portions of their days on the front line. At Dayton's, department managers and even some buyers are on the sales floor 50% of the time. Store managers at Taco Bell typically work out front where they can interact with customers instead of being hidden away in the back room to monitor operations. One advantage of this arrangement is the repeated opportunity it provides for managers to model good service for frontline workers. Another is the fact that it gives managers a steady stream of the richest possible data: firsthand feedback from customers on the quality of their operations. A third (and often double-edged) advantage is that it gives at least some middle managers a productive job to do and so creates a place for them in their companies' newly flattened organization charts.

In virtually every large-scale change effort we have studied, one of the most stubborn problems is resistance from middle managers. Many people call them the concrete layer and tell endless stories of how they get in the way of progress. The plain fact is, in this new service model, they often do get in the way. As spans of control widen, fewer middle managers are needed. Moreover, if they are left in place, the problems of change increase geometrically. Without a lean organization, senior management cannot push operating decisions down to the front line. Without cuts in middle-management head count, it cannot redistribute wages either.

By and large, middle managers understand this (which is why they engage in acts of sabotage if the problem is not addressed—any rational person would do the same). Nevertheless, the unpleasant truth remains: moving to the new service model demands the resizing of middle management's ranks. This means moving some people up, moving some back into expanded unit-manager jobs that can keep good managers close to customers, and moving some out of the organization.

What supports this resizing and makes it possible is the development of new technology to retrieve and transfer the information that middle managers once controlled. With good systems in place, a company can achieve great gains in productivity in ways that assist frontline workers and are not obvious to consumers. But as this suggests, in the new model, technology is almost always viewed as a resource and support and not as a source of competitive advantage in its own right. Sooner or later, new systems and tools become available to everyone. Employees with positive, customer-oriented attitudes are a lot harder to copy or buy.

Becoming a quality service organization is tumultuous; there is no getting around that fact. After the "Performance Plus" program was initiated at Dayton Hudson three years ago, frontline turnover rose as sales consultants decided whether pay-for-performance and other aspects of the new system worked for them. Fears of performance pressure and job insecurities contributed greatly to the success of a union-organizing campaign at the Detroit Hudson's store before the program was even introduced. (Dayton Hudson's management has chosen to make the change incrementally, adding three or four stores to the program each year.) Nevertheless, management has persevered on the strength of conventional financial results (sales gains of up to 25% in individual sales per hour, compensation that averages 20% more, stable—though shifting—operating costs) and on the strength of results that are just as crucial competitively but not yet as easily quantified: significant gains in customer satisfaction.

At Dayton's, as at other service pioneers, the formulas that will show the dollars-and-cents consequences of reversing the cycle of failure are still being derived. But the base for those calculations is growing rapidly as more and more managers start to measure and track the costs associated with keeping and losing customers and employees. In addition, they are sharing that information with employees, through paychecks linked to performance and through "scorecards" from departing guests, mystery shoppers, and random samplings of customers.

Today companies in many service industries and labor markets have chosen to reverse the cycle of failure. The benefits are already apparent in higher profits and higher pay. Further evidence will only become more obvious over time, as the gap widens between these employers of choice and their more traditional competitors. For years, customers had no alternative but to accept the poor performance and limited quality that were designed into almost every service operation. Today they do.

Notes

1. Frederick F. Reichheld and W. Earl Sasser, Jr., "Zero Defections: Quality Comes to Services," *Harvard Business Review*, September–October 1990, p. 105.
2. Dave Ulrich et al., "Employee and Customer Attachment: Synergies for Competitive Advantage," *Human Resources Planning*, vol. 14, no. 3, 1991.
3. J. Douglas Phillips, "The Price Tag on Turnover," *Personnel Journal*, December 1990.

2
The New Productivity Challenge

Peter F. Drucker

The single greatest challenge facing managers in the developed countries of the world is to raise the productivity of knowledge and service workers. This challenge, which will dominate the management agenda for the next several decades, will ultimately determine the competitive performance of companies. Even more important, it will determine the very fabric of society and the quality of life in every industrialized nation.

For the last 120 years, productivity in making and moving things—in manufacturing, farming, mining, construction, and transportation—has risen in developed countries at an annual rate of 3% to 4%, a 45-fold expansion overall. On this explosive growth rest all the gains these nations and their citizens have enjoyed: vast increases in disposable income and purchasing power; ever-wider access to education and health care; and the availability of leisure time, something known only to aristocrats and the "idle rich" before 1914, when everyone else worked at least 3,000 hours a year. (Today even the Japanese work no more than about 2,000 hours each year, while Americans average 1,800 hours and West Germans 1,650.)

Now these gains are unraveling, but not because productivity in making and moving things has fallen. Contrary to popular belief, productivity in these activities is still going up at much the same rate. And it is rising fully as much in the United States as it is in Japan or West Germany. Indeed, the increase in U.S. manufacturing productivity during the 1980s—some 3.9% a year—was actually larger in absolute terms than the corresponding annual increases in Japan and

Germany, while the 4% to 5% annual rise in U.S. agricultural productivity is far and away the largest recorded anywhere at any time.

The productivity revolution is over because there are too few people employed in making and moving things for their productivity to be decisive. All told, they account for no more than one-fifth of the work force in developed economies. Only 30 years ago, they were still a near-majority. Even Japan, which is still manufacturing intensive, can no longer expect increased productivity in that sector to sustain its economic growth. Indeed, the great majority of working people in Japan are knowledge and service workers with productivities as low as those in any other developed country. And when farmers make up only 3% of the employed population, as they do in the United States, Japan, and most of Western Europe, even record increases in their output add virtually nothing to their country's overall productivity and wealth.

The chief *economic* priority for developed countries, therefore, must be to raise the productivity of knowledge and service work. The country that does this first will dominate the twenty-first century economically. The most pressing *social* challenge developed countries face, however, will be to raise the productivity of service work. Unless this challenge is met, the developed world will face increasing social tensions, increasing polarization, increasing radicalization, possibly even class war.

In developed economies, opportunities for careers and promotion are more and more limited to people with advanced schooling, people qualified for knowledge work. But these men and women will always be a minority. They will always be outnumbered by people who lack the qualifications for anything but low-skilled service jobs—people who in their social position are comparable to the "proletarians" of 100 years ago, the poorly educated, unskilled masses who thronged the exploding industrial cities and streamed into their factories.

In the early 1880s, intelligent observers of every political persuasion were obsessed with the specter of class war between the industrial proletariat and the bourgeoisie. Karl Marx was hardly alone in predicting that the "immiserization" of the proletariat would lead inevitably to revolution. Benjamin Disraeli, perhaps the greatest of the nineteenth century conservatives, was equally persuaded of the inevitability of class war. And Henry James, the chronicler of American wealth and European aristocracy, was so frightened by the prospect that he made it the central theme of *The Princess Casamassima*, one of his most haunting novels.

What defeated these prophecies, which seemed eminently reasonable, indeed almost self-evident to contemporaries, was the revolution in productivity set off by Frederick W. Taylor in 1881, when he began to study the way a common laborer shoveled sand. Taylor himself worked in an iron foundry and was deeply shocked by the bitter animosity between the workers and managers. Fearful that this hatred would ultimately lead to class war, he set out to improve the efficiency of industrial work. And his efforts, in turn, sparked the revolution that allowed industrial workers to earn middle-class wages and achieve middle-class status despite their lack of skill and education. By 1930, when according to Marx the revolution of the proletariat should have been a fait accompli, the proletariat had become the bourgeoisie.

Now it is time for another productivity revolution. This time, however, history is on our side. In the past century, we have learned a great deal about productivity and how to raise it—enough to know that we need a revolution, enough to know how to start one.

Knowledge and service workers range from research scientists and cardiac surgeons through draftswomen and store managers to 16-year olds who flip hamburgers in fast-food restaurants on Saturday afternoons. Their ranks also include people whose work makes them "machine operators": dishwashers, janitors, data-entry operators. Yet for all their diversity in knowledge, skill, responsibility, social status, and pay, knowledge and service workers are remarkably alike in two crucial respects: what does not work in raising their productivity and what does.

The first thing we have learned—and it came as a rude shock—is about what does not work. Capital cannot be substituted for labor. Nor will new technology by itself generate higher productivity. In making and moving things, capital and technology are *factors* of production, to use the economist's term. In knowledge and service work, they are *tools* of production. The difference is that a factor can replace labor, while a tool may or may not. Whether tools help productivity or harm it depends on what people do with them, on the purpose to which they are being put, for instance, or on the skill of the user. Thirty years ago, for example, we were sure the efficiency of the computer would lead to massive reductions in clerical and office staff. The promise of greater productivity led to massive investments in data-processing equipment that now rival those in materials-processing technology (that is, in conventional machinery). Yet office and clerical forces have grown at a much faster rate since the introduction of information technology than ever before. And there has been virtually no increase in the productivity of service work.

Hospitals are a telling example. In the late 1940s, they were entirely labor intensive, with little capital investment except in bricks, mortar, and beds. A good many perfectly respectable hospitals had not even invested in readily available, fairly old technologies: they provided neither x-ray departments nor clinical laboratories nor physical therapy. Today hospitals are hugely capital intensive, with enormous sums invested in ultrasound, body scanners, nuclear magnetic imagers, blood and tissue analyzers, clean rooms, and a dozen more new technologies. Each piece of equipment has brought with it the need for more highly paid people but has not reduced the existing staff by a single person. (In fact, the worldwide escalation of health-care costs is largely the result of the hospital's having become a labor-intensive and capital-intensive monstrosity.) But hospitals, at least, have significantly increased their performance capacity. In other areas of knowledge or service work there are only higher costs, more investment, and more people.

Massive increases in productivity are the only way out of this morass. And these increases can only come from what Taylor called "working smarter."[1] Simply, this means working more productively without working harder or longer.

The economist sees capital investment as the key to productivity; the technologist gives star billing to new machines. Nevertheless, the main force behind the productivity explosion has been working smarter. Capital investment and technology were as copious in the developed economies during the first 100 years of the Industrial Revolution as they have been in its second 100 years. It was only with the advent of working smarter that productivity in making and moving things took off on its meteoric rise.

And so it will be for knowledge and service work—with this difference: in manufacturing, working smarter is only one key to increased productivity. In knowledge and service work, working smarter is the only key. What is more, it is a more complex key, one that requires looking closely at work in ways that Taylor never dreamed of.

When Taylor studied the shoveling of sand, the only question that concerned him was, "How is it done?" Almost 50 years later, when Harvard's Elton Mayo set out to demolish Taylor's "scientific management" and replace it with what later came to be called "human relations," he focused on the same question. In his experiments at Western Electric's Hawthorne Works, Mayo asked, "How can wiring telephone equipment best be done?" The point is that in making and moving things, the task is always taken for granted.

In knowledge and service work, however, the first questions in increasing productivity—and working smarter—have to be, "What is the task? What are we trying to accomplish? Why do it at all?" The easiest, but perhaps also the greatest, productivity gains in such work will come from defining the task and especially from eliminating what does not need to be done.[2]

A very old example is still one of the best: mail-order processing at the early Sears, Roebuck. Between 1906 and 1908, Sears eliminated the time-consuming job of counting the money in incoming mail orders. Rather than open the money envelopes enclosed with the orders, Sears weighed them automatically. In those days, virtually all Sears customers paid with coins. If the weight of the envelope tallied with the amount of the order within fairly narrow limits, the envelope went unopened. Similarly, Sears eliminated the even more time-consuming task of recording each incoming order by scheduling order handling and shipping according to the weight of the incoming mail (assuming 40 orders for each pound of mail). Within two years, these steps accounted for a tenfold increase in the productivity of the entire mail-order operation.[3]

A major insurance company recently increased the productivity of its claims-settlement department nearly fivefold—from an average of 15 minutes per claim to 3 minutes—by eliminating detailed checking on all but very large claims. Instead of verifying 30 items as they had always done, the adjusters now check only 4: whether the policy is still in force; whether the face amount matches the amount of the claim; whether the name of the policyholder matches the name on the death certificate; and whether the name of the beneficiary matches the name of the claimant. What provoked the change was asking, "What is the task?" and then answering, "To pay death claims as fast and as cheaply as possible." All that the company now requires to control the process is to work through a 2% sample, that is, every fiftieth claim, the traditional way.

Similarly, a few hospitals have taken most of the labor and expense out of their admissions process by admitting all patients the way they used to admit emergency cases who were brought in unconscious or bleeding and unable to fill out lengthy forms. These hospitals asked, "What is the task?" and answered, "To identify the patient's name, sex, age, address and how to bill"—information found on the insurance identification cards practically all patients carry.

These are both examples of service work. In knowledge work, defining the task and getting rid of what does not need to be done is even more necessary and produces even greater results. Consider how one multinational company redefined its strategic planning.

For many years, a planning staff of 45 brilliant people carefully prepared strategic scenarios in minute detail. The documents were first-class works and made stimulating reading, everybody agreed. But they had a minimal impact on operations. Then a new CEO asked, "What is the task?" and answered, "To give our businesses direction and goals and the strategy to attain these goals." It took four years of hard work and several false starts. But now the planning people (still about the same number) work through only three questions for each of the company's businesses: What market standing does it need to maintain leadership? What innovative performance does it need to support that standing? And what is the minimum rate of return needed to earn the cost of capital? Then the planning people work with the operating executives in each business to map out broad strategic guidelines for achieving these goals under various economic conditions. The results are far simpler and much less elegant, but they have become the "flight plans" that guide the company's businesses and its senior executives.

When people make or move things, they do one task at a time. Taylor's laborer shoveled sand; he did not also stoke the furnace. Mayo's wiring-room women soldered; they did not test finished telephones on the side. The Iowa farmer planting corn does not get off his tractor between rows to attend a meeting. Knowledge and service work, too, require concentration. The surgeon does not take telephone calls in the operating room, nor does the lawyer in consultation with a client.

But in organizations, where most knowledge and service work takes place, splintered attention is more and more the norm. The people at the very top can sometimes concentrate themselves (though far too few even try). But the great majority of engineers, teachers, salespeople, nurses, middle managers, and the like must carry a steadily growing load of busywork, activities that contribute little if any value and that have little if anything to do with what these professionals are qualified and paid for.

The worst case may be that of nurses in U.S. hospitals. We hear a great deal about the shortage of nurses. But how could it possibly be true? The number of graduates entering the profession has gone up steadily for a good many years. At the same time, the number of bed patients has been dropping sharply. The explanation of the paradox: nurses now spend only half their time doing what they have learned and are paid to do—nursing. The other half is eaten up by activities that do not require their skill and knowledge, add neither health-care nor economic value, and have little or nothing to do with patient care and patient well-being. Nurses are preoccupied, of course, with the avalanche of paperwork for Medicare, Medicaid, insurers, the billing office, and the prevention of malpractice suits.

The situation in higher education is not too different. Faculty in colleges and universities spend more and more hours in committee meetings instead of teaching in the classroom, advising students, or doing research. But few of these committees would ever be missed. And they would do a better job in less time if they had three instead of seven members.

Salespeople are just as splintered. In department stores, they now spend so much time serving computers that they have little time for serving customers—the main reason, perhaps, for the steady decline in their productivity as producers of sales and revenues. Field-sales representatives spend up to one-third of their time filling out reports rather than calling on customers. And engineers sit through meeting after meeting when they should be busy at their workstations.

This is not job enrichment; it is job impoverishment. It destroys productivity. It saps motivation and morale. Nurses, every attitude survey shows, bitterly resent not being able to spend more time caring for patients. They also believe, understandably, that they are grossly underpaid for what they are capable of doing, while the hospital administrator, equally understandably, believes that they are grossly overpaid for the unskilled clerical work they are actually doing.

The cure is fairly easy, as a rule. It is to concentrate the work—in this case, nursing—on the task—caring for patients. This is the second step toward working smarter. A few hospitals, for example, have taken the paperwork out of the nurse's job and given it to a floor clerk who also answers telephone calls from relatives and friends and arranges the flowers they send in. The level of patient care and the hours nurses devote to it have risen sharply. Yet the hospitals have also been able to reduce their nursing staffs by one-quarter or one-third and so raise salaries without incurring a higher nursing payroll.

To make these kinds of improvements, we must ask a second set of questions about every knowledge and service job: "What do we pay for? What value is this job supposed to add?" The answer is not always obvious or noncontroversial. One department store looked at its sales force and answered "sales," while another in the same metropolitan area and with much the same clientele answered "customer service." Each answer led to a different restructuring of the jobs on the sales floor. But each store achieved, and fairly fast, substantial growth in the revenues each salesperson and each department generated, that is, gains in both productivity and profitability.

For all its tremendous impact, Taylor's scientific management has had a bad press, especially in academia. Perhaps the main reason is the unrelenting campaign U.S. labor unions waged against it—and against Taylor himself—in the early years of this century. The unions did not oppose Taylor because they thought him antilabor or promanagement. He was neither. His unforgivable sin was his assertion that there is no such thing as "skill" in making and moving things. All such work was the same, Taylor asserted. And all could be analyzed step by step, as a series of unskilled operations that could then be combined into any kind of job. Anyone willing to learn these operations would be a "first-class man," deserving "first-class pay." He could do the most advanced work and do it to perfection.

To the skill-based unions of 1900, this assertion represented a direct attack. And this was especially true for the highly respected, extremely powerful unions that dominated what were then some of the country's most sophisticated manufacturing sites—the army arsenals and navy shipyards where nearly all peacetime production for the military took place until well after World World I. For these unions, each craft was a mystery whose secrets no member could divulge. Their power base was control of an apprenticeship that lasted five or seven years and admitted, as a rule, only relatives of members. And their workers were paid extremely well—more than most physicians of the day and triple what Taylor's first-class man could expect to get. No wonder that Taylor's assertions infuriated these aristocrats of labor.

Belief in the mystery of craft and skill persisted, as did the assumption that long years of apprenticeship were needed to acquire both. Indeed, Hitler went to war with the United States on the strength of that assumption. Convinced that it took five years or more to train optical craftsmen (whose skills are essential to modern warfare), he thought it would be at least that long before America could field an effective army and air force in Europe—and so declared war after the Japanese attack on Pearl Harbor.

We know now Taylor was right. The United States had almost no optical craftsmen in 1941. And modern warfare indeed requires precision optics in large quantities. But by applying Taylor's methods of scientific management, within a few months the United States trained semiskilled workers to turn out more highly advanced optics than even the Germans were producing, and on an assembly line to boot. And by that time, Taylor's first-class men with their increased productivity were also making a great deal more money than any craftsman of 1911 had ever dreamed of.

Eventually, knowledge work and service work may turn out to be like the work of making and moving things—that is, "just work," to use an old scientific management slogan. (At least this is what Taylor's true heirs, the more radical proponents of artificial intelligence, maintain.) But for the time being, we must not treat knowledge and service jobs as "just work." Nor can we assume they are homogeneous. Rather, these jobs can be divided into three distinct categories by looking at what productive performance in a given job actually represents. This process—defining performance—is the third step toward working smarter.

For some knowledge and service jobs, performance means quality. Take scientists in a research lab where quantity—the number of results—is quite secondary to their quality. One new drug that can generate annual sales of $500 million and dominate the market for a decade is infinitely more valuable than 20 "me too" drugs with annual sales of $20 million or $30 million each. The same principle applies to basic policy or strategic decisions, as well as to much less grandiose work, the physician's diagnosis, for example, or packaging design, or editing a magazine. In each of these instances, we do not yet know how to analyze the process that produces quality results. To raise productivity, therefore, we can only ask, "What works?"

The second category includes the majority of knowledge and service work: jobs in which quality and quantity together constitute performance. Department store sales are one example. Producing a "satisfied customer" is just as important as the dollar amount on the sales slip, but it is not so easy to define. Likewise, the quality of an architectural draftswoman's work is an integral part of her performance. But so is the number of drawings she can produce. The same holds true for engineers, sales reps in brokerage offices, medical technologists, branch bank managers, reporters, nurses, claims adjusters, and so on. Raising productivity in these jobs requires asking, "What works?" but also analyzing the process step by step and operation by operation.

Finally, there are a good many service jobs (filing, handling death claims, making hospital beds) in which performance is defined much as it is in making and moving things: that is, largely by quantity (for example, the number of minutes it takes to make up a hospital bed properly). In these "production" jobs, quality is primarily a matter of external criteria rather than an attribute of performance itself. Defining standards and building them into the work process is essential. But once this has been done, real productivity improvements will come through conventional industrial engineering, that is, through analyzing the task and combining the individual simple operations into a complete job.

Defining the task, concentrating work on the task, and defining performance: by themselves, these three steps will produce substantial growth in productivity—perhaps most of what can be attained at any one time. They will need to be worked through again and again, maybe as often as every three or five years and certainly whenever work or its organization changes. But then, according to all the experience we have, the resulting productivity increases will equal, if not exceed, whatever industrial engineering, scientific management, or human relations ever achieved in manufacturing. In other words, they should give us the productivity revolution we need in knowledge and service work.

But on one condition only: that we apply what we have learned since World War II about increasing productivity in making and moving things. The fourth step toward working smarter, then, is for management to form a partnership with the people who hold the jobs, the people who are to become more productive. The goal has to be to build responsibility for productivity and performance into every knowledge and service job regardless of level, difficulty, or skill.

Frederick Taylor has often been criticized for never once asking the workers he studied how they thought their jobs could be improved. He told them. Nor did Elton Mayo ever ask; he also told. But Taylor's (and Mayo's, 40 years later) methodology was simply a product of the times, when the wisdom of the expert prevailed. (Freud, after all, never asked his patients what they thought their problems might be. Nor do we have any record that either Marx or Lenin ever thought of asking the masses.) Taylor considered both workers and managers "dumb oxen." And while Mayo had great respect for managers, he thought workers were "immature" and "maladjusted," deeply in need of the psychologist's expert guidance.

When World War II came, however, we had to ask the workers. We had no choice. U.S. factories had no engineers, psychologists, or foremen. They were all in uniform. To our immense surprise, as I still recollect, we discovered that the workers were neither dumb oxen nor immature nor maladjusted. They knew a great deal about the work they were doing—about its logic and rhythm, its quality, and its tools. Asking them what they thought was the way to address both productivity and quality.[4]

At first, only a few businesses accepted this novel proposition. (IBM was a pioneer and for a long time one of the few large companies to act on this idea.) But in the late 1950s and early 1960s, it was picked up by Japanese industrialists whose earlier attempts to return to prewar autocracy had collapsed in bloody strikes and near-civil war. Now, while still far from being widely practiced, it is at least generally accepted in theory that the workers' knowledge of their job is the starting point for improving productivity, quality, and performance.

In making and moving things, however, partnership with the responsible worker is only the *best* way to increase productivity. After all, Taylor's telling worked too, and quite well. In knowledge and service work, partnership with the responsible worker is the *only* way.

The last component of working smarter is a two-part lesson that neither Taylor nor Mayo knew. First, continuous learning must accompany productivity gains. Redesigning a job and then teaching the worker the new way to do it, which is what Taylor did and taught, cannot by itself sustain ongoing learning. Training is only the beginning of learning. Indeed, as the Japanese can teach us (thanks to their ancient tradition of Zen), the greatest benefit of training comes not from learning something new but from doing better what we already do well.

Equally important is a related insight of the last few years: knowledge workers and service workers learn most when they teach. The best way to improve a star salesperson's productivity is to ask her to present "the secret of my success" at the company sales convention. The best way for the surgeon to improve his performance is to give a talk about it at the county medical society. We often hear it said that in the information age, every enterprise has to become a learning institution. It must become a teaching institution as well.

One hundred years ago, the signs of class conflict were unmistakable. What defused that conflict—and averted class war—was growth in the productivity of the industrial work force, something so unprecedented that even its prime mover, Frederick Taylor, had no term to describe it.

Today we know that productivity is the true source of competitive advantage. But what we must also realize is that it is the key to social stability as well. For that reason, achieving gains in service productivity comparable with those we have already achieved in manufacturing productivity must be a priority for managers throughout the developed world.

It is an economic truth that real incomes cannot be higher than productivity for any extended length of time. Unless the productivity of service workers rapidly improves, both the social and the economic position of that large group of people—whose numbers rival those of manufacturing workers at their peak—must steadily go down. At a minimum, this raises the prospect of economic stagnation; more ominously, it raises the prospect of social tensions unmatched since the early decades of the Industrial Revolution.

Conceivably, service workers could use their numerical strength to get higher wages than their economic contribution justifies. But this would only impoverish all of society, dragging everyone's real income down and sending unemployment up. Alternatively, the income of unskilled and semiskilled service workers could continue to fall in relation to the steadily rising wages of affluent knowledge workers. But this would lead to an even wider gulf between the two groups as well as to increasing polarization. In either case, service workers can only become increasingly bitter, alienated, and ready to see themselves as a class apart.

Fortunately, we are in a much better position than our ancestors were a century ago. We know what Marx and his contemporaries did not know: productivity can be raised. We also know how to raise it. And we know this best for the work where the social need is most urgent: unskilled and semiskilled service work—maintenance jobs in factories, schools, hospitals, and offices; counter jobs in restaurants and supermarkets; clerical jobs in insurance companies, banks, and businesses of all kinds. In essence, this is production work. And what we have learned during the past 100 years about increasing productivity applies to such work with a minimum of adaptation.

Further, a model of sorts exists in the steps some multinational maintenance companies have already taken to improve their employees' productivity. These U.S. and European employers have systematically applied the approach this article discusses to low-skilled service jobs. They have defined the task, concentrated work on it, defined performance, made the employee a partner in productivity improvement and the first source of ideas for it, and built continuous learning and continuing teaching into the job of every employee and work team. As a result, they have raised productivity substantially—in some cases even doubled it—which has allowed them to raise wages. As important, this process has also greatly raised the workers' self-respect and pride.

It is no coincidence that outside contractors achieved these improvements. Obtaining major productivity gains in production-type service work usually requires contracting it out to a company that has no other business, understands this work, respects it, and offers opportunities for low-skilled workers to advance (for example, to become local or regional managers). The organizations in which this work is being done, the hospitals that own the beds, for instance, or the colleges whose students need to be fed, neither understand it nor respect it enough to devote the time and hard work that are required to make it more productive.

The task is known and doable. But the urgency is great. To raise the productivity of service work, we cannot rely on government or on politics altogether. It is the task of managers and executives in businesses and nonprofit organizations. It is, in fact, the first social responsibility of management in the knowledge society.

Notes

1. Among the few attempts to apply working smarter in health care are Roxanne Spitzer's *Nursing Productivity: The Hospital's Key to Survival and Profit* (Chicago: S-N Publications, 1986) and Regina Herzlinger's *Creating New Health Care Ventures* (Gaithersburg, Md.: Aspen Publishers, 1991).

2. See Michael Hammer, "Reengineering Work: Don't Automate, Obliterate," *Harvard Business Review*, July–August 1990, and Peter F. Drucker, "Permanent Cost Cutting," *The Wall Street Journal*, January 11, 1991.

3. See Boris Emmet and John E. Jeucks, *Catalogues and Counters: A History of Sears, Roebuck & Company* (Chicago: University of Chicago Press, 1965).

4. In my 1942 book, *The Future of Industrial Man* (Westport, Conn.: Greenwood, 1978 reprint of original), and my 1950 book, *The New Society* (Greenwood, 1982 reprint), I argued for the "responsible worker" as "part of management." W. Edwards Deming and Joseph M. Juran developed what we now call "quality circles" and "total quality management" as a result of their wartime experiences. Finally, the idea was forcefully presented by Douglas McGregor in his 1960 book, *The Human Side of Enterprise* (New York: McGraw Hill, 1985, twenty-fifth anniversary printing), with its "Theory X" and "Theory Y."

3
Loyalty-Based Management

Frederick F. Reichheld

Despite a flurry of activities aimed at serving customers better, only a few companies have achieved meaningful, measurable improvements in customer loyalty. In manufacturing as well as services, business leaders intuitively know that when customer loyalty goes up, profits do too. Yet few companies have systematically revamped their operations with customer loyalty in mind.

Instead, most companies adopt improvement programs on an ad hoc basis. Hearing about the success of a loyalty leader such as MBNA's credit card business, which loses customers at half the industry rate, companies copy one or two of MBNA's practices. They set up customer-recovery units, for instance, that try to save defecting customers—who, because they are probably less homogeneous than MBNA's customer base, may or may not be profitable. Or they adopt MBNA's policy of delivering employee paychecks in envelopes labeled "Brought to You by the Customer"—while failing to base the bonuses inside those envelopes on incentives that enhance customer value and loyalty. Not surprisingly, payoffs don't materialize.

Building a highly loyal customer base cannot be done as an add-on. It must be integral to a company's basic business strategy. Loyalty leaders like MBNA are successful because they have designed their entire business systems around customer loyalty. They recognize that customer loyalty is earned by consistently delivering superior value. By understanding the economic effects of retention on revenues and costs, loyalty leaders can intelligently reinvest cash flows to acquire and retain high-quality customers and employees. Designing and managing this self-reinforcing system is the key to achieving outstanding customer loyalty.

The economic benefits of high customer loyalty are considerable and, in many industries, explain the differences in profitability among competitors. When a company consistently delivers superior value and wins customer loyalty, market share and revenues go up, and the cost of acquiring and serving customers goes down. Although the additional profits allow the company to invest in new activities that enhance value and increase the appeal to customers, strengthening loyalty generally is not a matter of simply cutting prices or adding product features. The better economics mean the company can pay workers better, which sets off a whole chain of events. Increased pay boosts employee morale and commitment; as employees stay longer, their productivity rises and training costs fall; employees' overall job satisfaction, combined with their knowledge and experience, leads to better service to customers; customers are then more inclined to stay loyal to the company; and as the best customers and employees become part of the loyalty-based system, competitors are inevitably left to survive with less desirable customers and less talented employees.

The forces in a loyalty-based system are cumulative. The longer the cycle continues, the greater the company's financial strength. At MBNA, a 5% increase in retention grows the company's profits by 60% by the fifth year. And at State Farm Insurance Companies, another champion of customer loyalty, small increases in retention create substantial benefits for the company and its policyholders.

Learning how to compete on the basis of loyalty may be complex, but it is not mysterious. It requires, first of all, understanding the relationships between customer retention and the rest of the business and being able to quantify the linkages between loyalty and profits. Only then can daily decisions reflect systematic cost-benefit trade-offs. It involves rethinking four important aspects of the business—customers, product/service offerings, employees, and measurement systems. To get the full benefit of a loyalty-based system, all these facets must be understood and attended to simultaneously because each is essential to the workings of the whole. If any area is overlooked or misunderstood, the system will underperform. When all areas are aligned, they reinforce each other, and the results are outstanding.

The "Right" Customers

Customers are obviously an essential ingredient of a loyalty-based system, and success depends on their staying with the company a long time. But not all customers are equal. Companies should target the "right" customers—not necessarily the easiest to attract or the most profitable in the short term but those who are likely to do business with the company over time. For various reasons, some customers don't ever stay loyal to one company, no matter what value they receive. The challenge is to avoid as many of these people as possible in favor of customers whose loyalty can be developed.

Demographics and previous purchase history give some indication of a customer's inherent loyalty. People who buy because of a personal referral tend to be more loyal than those who buy because of an advertisement. Those who buy at the standard price are more loyal than those who buy on price promotion. Home owners, middle-aged people, and rural populations also tend to be loyal, while highly mobile populations are inherently disloyal because they interrupt their business relations each time they move.

But generalizing about the right customer fails to take into account the fact that a customer who is disloyal and therefore expensive for one company may be valuable for another. USAA, a loyalty leader with a remarkable 98% retention rate in its field of auto insurance, has created a steady client base among military officers, a group known for frequent moves. Military officers are not very profitable for most insurers, but by developing a system tailored to that group's particular needs, USAA has made it possible and economical to keep them.

The heart of USAA's system is a centralized database and telephone-sales force that customers can access from anywhere in the world. The system itself rather than the insurance agent provides continuity with the customer. That continuity works to the customer's and company's advantage. The military officer doesn't have to find a new agent every time he or she is redeployed, and USAA doesn't have to transfer records or create new ones. More important, USAA avoids having to lure a new customer to replace the one it would have lost.

Finding loyal customers requires taking a hard look at what kinds of customers a company can deliver superior value to. If the analysis is done well, that customer segment will be fairly homogeneous, and that homogeneity improves the economics of serving the segment. MBNA, a loyalty leader in the credit card business, provides cards primarily to members of affinity groups such as the American Dental Association or the Georgetown University Alumni Association. Because members in these groups share important qualities, MBNA has been able to understand their common needs and has made adjustments to serve them well. Its data-processing systems are designed so every group can receive customized packages of services. As a result, MBNA keeps its customers once it gets them. When AT&T introduced its Universal Card, other credit card companies lost market share, but MBNA held its ground.

Historical attrition rates can also point the way to the most promising customer segments. Direct marketers such as L.L. Bean have accounting systems that track individual customers year by year. Other companies can get similar information by asking a sample of customers to reconstruct their purchase patterns from various suppliers over the past five years. This will reveal attrition rates and lifetime value for each type of customer.

With knowledge of which customers are likely to be loyal comes knowledge of which customers are not. Companies can then direct resources away from customers who are likely to defect and toward those likely to stay. Special promotions and other kinds of pricing strategies aimed at acquiring new customers often backfire. Companies typically use pricing as a blunt instrument to bring customers in indiscriminately, when instead, they should use pricing to filter out precisely the customers unlikely to be loyal. Cable television companies talk about increasing retention rates but then recruit new customers via price promotions and free sampling—techniques that draw out of the woodwork precisely those customers hardest to keep. Those recruitment efforts merely load the pipeline with people who are inherently disloyal.

Even attempts to recover customers who threaten to leave are often a waste of resources. Investments in service-quality improvements may be counterproductive when they are focused on customers the business actually should get rid of. Auto insurers discovered that certain segments of young drivers were a drag on profits. It took ten years to break even on them, but due to high attrition, only 10% to 15% would stay that long. The industry also realized that it took at least four years before most companies could break even on the average customer, in part because of the high front-end commission paid to salespeople for signing new customers. If the customer didn't stay with the same insurer for four years, the company never recouped those costs.

Lifetime Products and Services

Once a company has identified the customers it *should* keep, it has to go about the business of keeping them. Often that means adding new products and services to meet customers' evolving needs. Companies that fail to use their knowledge of customers to develop the product or service those people will need next are leaving the door open for another company to lure them away. Although it is tempting to use new products to win whole new markets, it almost always makes better sense to stick with existing customer segments. Over time, the company develops intimate knowledge of those people, and then can make good intuitive market judgments. Also, it is easier to build sales volume with customers who already know the company than it is with newcomers. USAA, for example, having come to understand one narrow market segment inside and out, found it relatively easy to go beyond auto insurance to offer mutual funds, life insurance, health insurance, and credit cards.

When Entenmann's of New York, a loyalty leader in specialty bakery products sold through grocery stores, saw its sales leveling off, it monitored customer purchase patterns in each local market. It discovered that as its core customers aged, they were looking for more fat-free and cholesterol-free products. Through direct contact with customers via telephone surveys and focus groups, the company found that consumers would buy those products from Entenmann's if they were available.

So the company had a choice. It could create a new line of products to serve those customers, or it could search for a whole new market segment. Ultimately, the company determined that it was much more economical to develop new fat- and cholesterol-free products than to go with another group of customers. Entenmann's new product line has been highly successful. It addressed the changing needs of the company's core clientele and even attracted new customers.

In yet another industry, Honda has emerged as the loyalty leader in the midpriced U.S. auto market. Life-cycle marketing has helped propel Honda's owner repurchase rate to 65%, versus an industry average of 40%. After the success of the subcompact Civic, Honda's next car, the Accord, was designed to meet the needs of Civic owners, who continued to care about reliability, conservative design, and value as they moved from their early twenties to marriage and family. Honda added the Accord wagon when it noticed customers defecting to other brands as their families grew.

By growing through the repeat purchases of its core customer base, Honda has maintained a relatively simple product line, and its manufacturing economics have benefited from this low product complexity. Honda's dealer and distribution system also benefits from low customer complexity in equally important, if less well-understood, ways.

One of the largest multifranchise dealers in the United States described this advantage as he saw it: "My Honda dealership is my most profitable because the company makes it so simple. There are fewer models and option packages. The key is the customers, who are very similar to one another." His sales and service operations are geared to the "Honda" customer. In contrast, he described his Mitsubishi dealership as a real challenge: "Salespeople have to deal with a lawyer buying a $30,000 Diamonte one minute, a construction worker buying a pickup truck the next." How can one salesperson (or service representative) develop proficiency with such customer complexity?

Curiously, Honda has had a tougher fight in Japan, where it remains a small player. Even though Honda had the same product advantages that resulted in its strong U.S. position, Toyota remains the dominant player in Japan because of its strong dealer network. In Japan, dealers don't have a lot of showrooms but instead rely on a direct sales force. Because sales-force turnover is low (less than 10% per year for Toyota), they get to know customers very well. It is this enduring bond that has outmuscled Honda. In the United States, where car salespeople turn over quickly (60% to 100% annually) and customers have virtually no relationship with the sales force, Honda's product advantage blasted right through to put it out ahead.

Loyal Employees

Many companies diminish their economic potential through human resource policies that ensure high employee turnover, in part because they can't quantify the economics of retaining employees. Executives might say they want to keep employees, but if doing so means raising salaries, their conviction soon fades. They question the wisdom of increasing pay by, say, 25% in order to decrease employee turnover by 5%. Yet the fact is that employee retention is key to customer retention, and customer retention can quickly offset higher salaries and other incentives designed to keep employees from leaving.

The longer employees stay with the company, the more familiar they become with the business, the more they learn, and the more valuable they can be. Those employees who deal directly with customers day after day have a powerful effect on customer loyalty. Long-term employees can serve customers better than newcomers can; after all, a customer's contact with a company is through employees, not the top executives. It is with employees that the customer builds a bond of trust and expectations, and when those people leave, the bond is broken.

Companies wanting to increase customer loyalty often fail because they don't grasp the importance of this point. While conducting customer focus programs, they may be terminating or rotating the people who have the most influence on the customer's experience. While they are reengineering their business processes, they are failing to reengineer career paths, job content, and compensation so that employees will stay with the company long enough to learn the new processes.

Just as it is important to select the right kinds of customers before trying to keep them, a company must find the right kinds of employees before enticing them to stay. That raises the issue of hiring. The goal is not only to fill desks but also to find and hold onto workers who will continue to learn, to become more productive, and to create trusting relationships with customers. State Farm, the loyalty leader among auto insurance companies that sell through agents, has a distinctive agent-appointment strategy. Prospective agents may spend a year or more in a recruiting and selection process. During this time, they are in competition with several other well-qualified candidates. The lengthy process enables the company's field managers to select the best qualified person. State Farm often looks for candidates with roots in the community who are already likely to have long-term relationships with prospective customers.

One way for any company to find new hires who will likely stay is to look at the patterns of their own employees who defected early. Had they found the job at your company through newspaper ads, college recruiting, or personal referrals? Equally important, how long had they stayed with employers before coming to you? In a loyalty-based system, skills and education are important, but not as important as how long a prospective worker is expected to stay and grow with the business.

Although longevity deepens familiarity, some company policies render familiarity useless. Banks, for instance, are notorious for offering branch managers career paths that rotate them through a series of branch offices. Each time managers move, they take with them the knowledge learned at the branch where they put in their time. They have to start over again in each branch, building a network with the customers and the other employees. Their incentives to acquire the right customers and employees are reduced since it is their replacements who will reap the benefits. In a major bank with several hundred branches, branch managers who had been in the system an average of 12 years stayed at a given branch for only 2 years. Only one branch manager had remained in place and, not surprisingly, his office had the highest customer-retention rate in the entire system. It's worth noting that most banks have 50% to 100%-a-year teller turnover, which is also costly. Because most bankers cannot quantify the systems costs of these policies, they cannot justify the investments required to fix the situation.

But not all businesses follow those practices. The highly successful Olive Garden restaurant chain goes against the industry norm of moving successful managers to open new restaurants or to run bigger ones every few years and letting assistants take over. The chain hires local managers whose major asset is that they are known and trusted in the community. These managers are then kept in place so their asset appreciates in value. Learning accumulates as people stay on the job. By becoming intelligent about the business, getting to know customers, and providing the advantages knowledge gives, long-time hires add value to the company.

Leo Burnett Company's strong position in the advertising industry is largely attributable to its slavish devotion to employee retention. Most advertising firms experience high turnover of their creative people, and they make a point of rotating people through various accounts. They also experience constant client churn accompanied by massive layoffs and severe downturns in revenues and profits. At Leo Burnett, in contrast, new staffers are assigned to their first account "for life," in the words of one executive. Layoffs are rare, and customer retention is high.

Even businesses that don't rely on direct relationships between customers and employees can benefit from boosting employee retention. USAA has an information system that lets any employee pull up a customer's records instantly, so customers don't have to speak with the same employee every time. But USAA's employee turnover of around 7%—one-third the industry average—is one of the most important reasons its productivity is the best in the business. The learning unleashed by employee retention helps in other ways. When the marketing department wants to know more about customer needs or reactions to a new product, they can hold a focus group meeting of employees whose daily customer contact provides powerful insight.

Of course, employees won't stay and apply their knowledge unless they have an incentive to do so. All other things being equal, the best people will stay with the company that pays them the most. Loyalty leaders know this, and they share their "loyalty surplus" with employees as well as stockholders. They view their best employees as they do their best customers: once they've got them, they do everything possible to keep them. And they provide incentives in the form of higher salaries or bonuses and commissions that align the employees' self-interest with the interests of the company. Bonuses can be based on aggregate customer retention rates, and commissions can be designed to be small initially but grow the longer the customer stays with the company.

There are many ways reward programs can be structured to recognize loyalty. Olive Garden found that its experienced waiters and waitresses resented the fact that new hires were receiving the same base wage as they did, so management established a slightly higher base wage for employees who had served $25,000 of meals.

If employees are expected to be long-termers, companies can justify investing more in them. It becomes worthwhile to teach employees to do the right thing for the customer, which in turn leads to happier customers and ultimately to increased profits, which can be put toward the higher salaries of long-term employees. And the commitment to creating a loyalty-based system has spillover effects. Employees take pride in delivering value to a customer time and again. Their satisfaction in contributing to a positive goal is another thing that induces their loyalty to the company.

Measures of Loyalty

Even the best designed loyalty-based system will deteriorate unless an effective measurement system is established. Competitors, customer preferences, technologies, and employee capabilities are constantly changing. Measures establish the feedback loops that are the foundation of organizational learning. Only through effective learning can an organization consistently deliver value in an ever-changing world.

Unfortunately, most accounting systems do not measure what drives customer value. They can show the benefits of the one-year magic cure but not of programs and practices that take three to five years or longer to affect profits. Managers who have a year to earn a bonus or two years to turn a business around are forced to think of the usual shortcuts to higher profits: raising prices and cutting costs. Those actions alone rarely create value for customers, and although customers don't all leave at once, if they are not getting the best value, they will eventually turn to a competitor. To make matters worse, the best customers are often the first ones to go.

The first step in developing effective measures is to understand the cause-and-effect relationships in the system. The primary mission of a loyalty-based company is to deliver superior value to customers. Success or failure in this mission can be clearly measured by customer loyalty (best quantified by retention rate or share of purchases or both). Customer loyalty has three second-order effects: (1) revenue grows as a result of repeat purchases and referrals, (2) costs decline as a result of lower acquisition expenses and from the efficiencies of serving experienced customers, and (3) employee retention increases because job pride and satisfaction increase, in turn creating a loop that reinforces customer loyalty and further reducing costs as hiring and training costs shrink and productivity rises.

As costs go down and revenues go up, profits (the third-order effect) increase. Unless managers measure and monitor all of these economic relationships, they will default to their short-term, profit-oriented accounting systems, which tend to focus on only the second- and third-order effects. Focusing on these symptoms—instead of on the primary mission of delivering superior value to customers—often leads to decisions that will eventually reduce value and loyalty.

In the life insurance business, for instance, a five percentage point increase in customer retention lowers costs per policy by 18%. However, very few companies have quantified this relationship, and as a result, they focus their cost-reduction efforts on process reengineering and layoffs, which appear to lower costs but in fact lower employee motivation and retention, leading to lower customer retention, which increases costs!

When life insurers want to grow, they hire more agents, raise commissions, drop prices (to new customers only, if possible) and/or add new products. The result: more inexperienced salespeople (low productivity and high cost) bringing in the wrong kind of customer (disloyal price shoppers) with escalating costs of product-line complexity. The only way to avoid these mistakes in insurance, or any business, is to develop systems that allow employees to track and understand the cash-flow consequences of changing customer loyalty.

It is only the true defection of the target customer that should be of concern because that means something may have gone wrong, and if it has, it's worth a considerable amount of effort to find out what. It could mean that another company has done something innovative that gives customers a better value.

It is important to define customer retention carefully and what it means in a particular industry. In the auto business, for instance, a manufacturer should worry about a customer who switches to another brand—but not about a customer who sells his or her car and takes public transportation. In an industrial setting, customers might shift a percentage of their purchases to competitors, so changes in purchase patterns should be watched as carefully as customer defections.

Customer satisfaction is not a surrogate for customer retention. While it may seem intuitive that increasing customer satisfaction will increase retention and therefore profits, the facts are contrary. Between 65% and 85% of customers who defect say they were satisfied or very satisfied with their former supplier. In the auto industry, satisfaction scores average 85% to 95%, while repurchase rates average only 40%. Current satisfaction measurement systems are simply not designed to provide insight into how many customers stay loyal to the company and for how long.

State Farm's Loyalty-Based System

State Farm insures more than 20% of the nation's households. It has the lowest sales and distribution costs among insurance companies of its type, yet its agents' incomes are generally higher than agents working for the competition. Its focus on customer service has resulted in faster growth than most other mutiple-line insurers, but rather than being consumed by growth, its capital has mushroomed (all through internally generated surplus) to more than $18 billion, representing the largest capital base of any financial services company in North America. Because of careful customer selection and retention, State Farm is able to price below the competition and still build the capital necessary to protect its policyholders in years such as 1992 when they incurred $4.7 billion in catastrophe losses.

These impressive achievements can be traced to State Farm's well-designed loyalty-based system. State Farm began by choosing the right customers. The company was founded more than 70 years ago to serve better than average drivers, first in farming communities and now throughout suburban and urban markets across the United States and in three Canadian provinces. State Farm agents work from neighborhood offices, which allows them to build long-lasting relationships with their customers and provide the personal service that is the basis of the corporate philosophy.

This kind of personal service can start at an early age. Teenagers in State Farm households are usually written while still under the umbrella of their parents' policies. Many State Farm agents routinely sit new drivers down in their offices for a "dutch uncle" speech about the responsibilities of driving and the impact an accident or ticket—particularly for drunken driving—would have on their rates. Also, in an effort to educate all teens on safe driving, agents have available company-produced safe-driving materials for high schools. All these efforts tend to make the young drivers that State Farm insures more careful, and their parents grateful for the interest and help.

When agents are rooted in the community, they often know who the best customers will be. For example, they can scan the local newspaper for the high school honor roll and be sure that their young customers' good grades are recognized with premium discounts. Agents make it their business to get to know the people they insure. The most powerful computer and the brightest underwriter at headquarters simply can't compete with that level of customer insight.

Pricing policies work as a magnet to retain good customers. At the end of three years, accident-free customers get a 5% discount, followed by another 5% decrease three years later. The discounts make customers feel they've earned special status and value, and they create a disincentive to jump to another company, where they might have to start all over again.

State Farm agents not only want to attract and keep good customers, they also have the incentive to do so. Commissions are structured to encourage long-term thinking. Agents receive the same compensation rate on new auto and fire policies as for renewals, thus rewarding agents for serving existing customers, not just for drawing in new business. Unlike organizations that say retention is important while pushing salespeople to find new customers, State Farm consistently conveys the message that both are important.

Remaining focused on its target customers, State Farm provides a full life-cycle product line. Rather than bringing in lots of new customers, the company's marketing efforts encourage existing customers to buy additional products, like home and life insurance. The homogeneity of their market means that one agent can sell and service everything. The full product line preserves the agent's relationship with the customer and allows the agent to learn more about the customer's needs. In addition to benefiting the policyholder and company, this approach serves the agent well, as multiple-line customers are less expensive for the agent to service than are single-line customers. Multiple-line customers have also proven to stay with the agent longer.

State Farm agents are also loyal. According to industry studies, more than 80% of newly appointed agents remain through their fourth year, compared with 20% to 40% for the rest of the industry. And the average agent at State Farm has 13 years of tenure, compared with 6 to 9 years for the industry. This retention advantage can be attributed both to the lengthy recruiting and selection process before appointment and to the fact that State Farm agents are independent contractors who sell and service State Farm products exclusively. Because agents have built and invested in their own businesses, they are more likely to remain with State Farm than their counterparts representing other companies. In return, State Farm is loyal to its agents and distributes its products only through them. The company has built a marketing partnership with its agents and involves them in key decisons that affect them or their customers.

Agent retention and customer retention reinforce one another. The agent who is committed to a long-term relationship with the company, and indeed, to his or her own business, is more likely to build lasting relationships with customers. In addition, loyal customers make life easier for the agents, who spend more time working with people they know and like and far less time chasing new customers. Finally, agents like being part of a system that consistently delivers superior value to customers. Agents' experience, plus the fact that they spend more time servicing and selling to proven customers, raises agents' productivity to 50% above industry norms.

State Farm's business systems support its focus on loyalty. Measures of customer retention and defections are distributed throughout the organization. Agents and employees at all levels know whether the system is working and can adjust their activities. Agents find a list of their nonrenewing customers each morning when they switch on their computers, which they can use to prompt telephone follow-ups to try to retain the account. And management can use the same kind of information as a check against policyholders' satisfaction with the service, product, and price they receive.

State Farm's success in building customer loyalty is reflected in retention rates that exceed 90%, consistently the best performance of all the national insurers that sell through agents. State Farm agents make more money by operating in a business system engineered for superior loyalty. And they are more productive, which makes it possible for them to earn superior compensation (after adjusting for the fact that State Farm agents pay their own expenses) while the company actually pays lower average commission rates. The result is a 10% cost advantage. The company also keeps its costs relatively low because it avoids excessive administrative and claims costs associated with acquiring and servicing a large percentage of new customers. State Farm's system provides outstanding value to its customers, benefits for its agents, and has created a company that is a financial powerhouse.

Managing for Loyalty

The success of State Farm and other loyalty leaders shows the direct linkages between providing value for customers and a superior financial and competitive position. Doing the right thing for customers does not conflict with generating substantial margins. On the contrary, it is the only way to ensure profitability beyond the short term.

Creating a loyalty-based system in any company requires a radical departure from traditional business thinking. It puts creating customer value—not maximizing profits and shareholder value—at the center of business strategy, and it demands significant changes in business practice—redefining target customers, revising employment policies, and redesigning incentives.

Most important, if companies are really serious about delivering value and earning customer loyalty, they must measure it. And while senior executives may be daunted by the time and investment required to engineer an entire business system for high retention, they may have no alternative. Customer loyalty appears to be the only way to achieve sustainably superior profits.

Managing for loyalty serves the best interests of customers, employees, and investors. The only losers are the competitors who get the leftovers: an increasingly poor mix of customers and employees and an increasingly less tenable financial and market position. As loyalty leaders refine their ability to deliver value by more effectively harnessing the economics of loyalty, their advantages will multiply. Competitors must respond, or they will find it increasingly difficult to survive on the leftovers of the marketplace.

4

My Employees Are My Service Guarantee

Timothy W. Firnstahl

I own a chain of four restaurants in and around Seattle, and my company exists for one reason only—to make other people happy. Every time a customer leaves one of our restaurants with a more optimistic view of the world, we've done our job. Every time we fail to raise a customer's spirits with good food, gratifying service, and a soothing atmosphere, we haven't done our job.

To the extent that we satisfy customers, we fulfill our company goal. This observation may seem self-evident and trivial—a useful motto, a business axiom that a lot of businesspeople understandably overlook in the day-to-day flood of details—but I have found it the very key to growth and profits. And after much trial and error, I have come up with a strategy for ensuring customer satisfaction that has worked wonders in our business and can, I'm convinced, work wonders in other businesses as well.

It starts with a guarantee—not that moth-eaten old promise of a cheerful refund—but a guarantee that customers will be satisfied with their whole experience of the company's products and services. It moves on to a system for giving employees complete responsibility and *authority* for making the guarantee stick. It ends with a process for identifying system failures—the problems in organization, training, and other internal programs that cause customer dissatisfaction.

I call the whole thing "ultimate strategy." That may sound pretentious. But because it redefines a company's ultimate reason for being and succeeding, and because it underlines the importance of finding the ultimate causes of every system failure, I think the name is justified.

Service with a Smile and a Seed of Doubt

Ultimate strategy had its origins in the success of a restaurant business I cofounded ten years ago. (I recently started a different restaurant business, but the strategy hasn't changed.) The first restaurant, specializing in steaks and featuring a huge bar, went over so well that we opened another. Five years ago, we had three restaurants, $7.5 million in sales, and moderate profits. Clearly, many of our customers were satisfied.

But I was bothered by what I saw as an unacceptable level of complaints and by our haphazard responses to them. Not that we didn't try. We happily apologized and gave a free dessert to any customer who complained about slow service, and we cheerfully picked up the cleaning bill when one of our employees spilled the soup. Customers who wrote in to complain about reservations mix-ups or rude service got certificates for complimentary meals.

It was just that our procedures for responding seemed all wrong. Giving out that free dessert required approval from a manager. Getting a suit cleaned meant filling out a form and getting a manager to sign it. I also didn't like the idea that people had to write us with their complaints before we made amends. And I wasn't convinced that a free meal was enough.

Moreover, our response to complaints didn't appear to have any effect on the number or type of complaints we received, most of which concerned speed of service and quality of food. And it wasn't the employees' fault. They knew complaints had top priority, but they didn't know how to respond to them. We were all on a treadmill, getting nowhere.

The Guarantee

Then five years ago, when the book *In Search of Excellence* was in vogue, I spent considerable time writing Ten Tenets of Excellence for our organization. We included them in our training manuals and posted them in the restaurants and the offices. One day about a year later, someone asked me what the sixth tenet was, and I couldn't tell her. It came to me that if I couldn't remember the Ten Tenets of Excellence, surely no one else could either. That meant the company had no strategy known to its employees.

So I hit on something simpler and more compelling—the guarantee.

We expressed it as a promise: *Your Enjoyment Guaranteed. Always.* As a company rallying cry, it seemed to work much better than the Tenets of Excellence. Cryptic mission statements, unreviewed strategic plans, the hidden dreams of management: all that gave way to a company game plan—customer satisfaction—that everyone could understand and remember and act on. For the first time, employees and management had a strategy in common.

Your Enjoyment Guaranteed. Always. This promise became our driving force. We included it in all our advertising. We printed it on every menu, letterhead, and guest check. To make it live for our employees, we did a series of internal promotions. We reduced it to an acronym, YEGA, and posted it everywhere for employees to see.

We held a series of meetings, where we found workers receptive to both the acronym and the simplicity of the idea. Each of our 600 employees signed a contract pledging YEGA follow-through. We created a YEGA logo and put it everywhere, on report forms, on training manuals, on wall signs. We started the *YEGA News* and distributed YEGA pins, shirts, name tags, even underwear. We announced that failure to enforce YEGA would be cause for dismissal.

For a year or so, YEGA dominated the company's consciousness. But as time went by, I grew increasingly uncomfortable. Complaints were coming in at the same old rate. I could see the guarantee being implemented here and there, now and then, but not on a regular, companywide basis. I'd run into another brick wall.

Empowering Employees

One evening about two years back as I was driving home from work, the cause of the problem hit me. The guarantee by itself wasn't enough. We had given employees responsibility without giving them authority. The result was that they tried to bury mistakes or blame others. I saw it every time we tried to track down a complaint. The food servers blamed the kitchen for late meals. The kitchen blamed the food servers for placing orders incorrectly.

Problems inevitably crop up in a busy restaurant, and when a customer grumbles the tendency is to gloss over the complaint with pleasantness. Follow-through means fetching the manager or filling out forms or both. Climbing the ladder of hierarchical approvals is simply too frustrating and time-consuming—for customer as well as employee.

For our guarantee to be truly effective, we needed to give workers themselves the power to make good on the promise of the guarantee—at once and on the spot. Eliminate the hassle for the customer and for ourselves. No forms to fill out, no phone calls to make, no 40 questions to answer, just immediate redress by the closest employee.

So I instituted the idea that employees could and should do *anything* to keep the customer happy. In the event of an error or delay, any employee right down to the busboy could provide complimentary wine or desserts, or pick up an entire tab if necessary.

Of course, we provided some guidelines. For instance, when guests have to wait more than 10 minutes beyond their reservation time, but less than 20, we suggest free drinks. If they wait more than 20 minutes, the entire meal might be free. If the bread arrives more than 5 minutes after the guests sit down, we suggest free clam chowder. And so forth, using what we know to be optimum intervals for most orders.

At the same time, we urged employees not to get bogged down in the guidelines. The last thing we wanted was nitpicking: "OK, I got them the bread in five minutes exactly. Do I just apologize, or do they get clam chowder?" Satisfaction does not mean quibbling—it means a contented customer. Different guests respond in different ways, so we told our employees not to feel limited by the guidelines and to do whatever it took to make sure guests enjoyed themselves.

Employees were initially wary of their new authority. Never having had complete control, they were naturally hesitant and skeptical. It was hard to convince them they wouldn't be penalized for giving away free food and drinks.

But once they got used to the idea, employees liked knowing that the company believed so strongly in its products and services that it wholeheartedly stood behind its work—and theirs. They liked working for a restaurant known for its unhesitating commitment to customer satisfaction. Preeminence in any field gives people feelings of self-worth they could never get from just making a buck. Their power as company representatives increased their pride in the business, and that, in turn, increased motivation.

Once our employees overcame their skepticism, they quickly grew creative and aggressive in their approach to the guarantee. In one case, a customer wanted a margarita made the way a competitor made its. So our bartender called the bartender at the other restaurant and, bartender-to-bartender, learned the special recipe. In another case, an elderly woman who had not been in our restaurant for years ordered breakfast, which we no longer served. The waiter and the chef sent someone to the market for bacon and eggs and served the breakfast she wanted.

If the guarantee is really working the way it's supposed to, customers become less inhibited about complaining. Too often, customers hold their peace but vote with their feet by taking their business to the competition. The promise of the guarantee's enforcement stimulates them to help us expose our own failures.

We even asked for their criticism. Once a month, using reservations lists and credit card charges, groups of employees called several hundred customers and asked them to rate their experience. Were the food and service lousy, OK, good, very good, or excellent? If they said "OK," that meant "lousy" to us, and they got a letter of apology, a certificate for a free meal, and a follow-up phone call.

Aside from the data we gathered, the phone calls were great promotion. Most people were amazed and delighted that we took the trouble to phone them, and many developed enormous loyalty to our restaurants.

System-Failure Costs

Customer complaints are company failures and require immediate correction. So far so good. But corrections cost money. Free drinks and meals add up quickly.

Yet, paradoxically, spending money is the goal. Every dollar paid out to offset customer dissatisfaction is a signal that the company must change in some decisive way. The guarantee brings out a true, hard-dollars picture of company failures and forces us to assume full responsibility for our output. The cost of keeping a company's promises is not just the price tag on the guarantee, it is the cost of system failure. The money was spent because the product did not perform, and when the product fails to perform, the system that produced it is at fault.

A somnolent business can be rudely awakened by the magnitude of its system-failure costs. We certainly were. Our previous guarantee expenses doubled. The problems had always been there, hidden. Only the huge cost of the new strategy revealed that they were gutting profits. Suddenly, we had a real incentive to fix the systems that weren't working, since the alternatives—sacrificing profits permanently or restricting the power to enforce the guarantee—were both unacceptable.

Notice that system-failure costs are not the same as employee-failure costs. System-failure costs measure the extent of the confusion in company structure, for which management alone is to blame. By welcoming every guarantee payoff—every system-failure expense—as an otherwise lost insight, you can make every problem pay a dividend. The trick is to reject Band-Aid solutions, to insist on finding the ultimate cause of each problem, and then to demand and expect decisive change. (Another way to sugarcoat the pill of system-failure costs is to think of the free food and drinks as a word-of-mouth advertising budget. No one forgets to mention a free meal to a friend or neighbor.)

Our search for the culprit in a string of complaints about slow food service in one restaurant led first to the kitchen and then to one cook. But pushing the search one step further revealed several unrealistically complex dishes that no one could have prepared swiftly.

In another case, our kitchens were turning out wrong orders at a rate that was costing us thousands of dollars a month in wasted food. The cooks insisted that the food servers were punching incorrect orders into the kitchen printout computer. In times past, we might have ended our search right there, accused the food servers of sloppiness, and asked everyone to be more careful. But now, adhering to the principle of system failure not people failure, we looked beyond the symptoms and found a flaw in our training. We had simply never taught food servers to double-check their orders on the computer screen, and the system offered no reward for doing so. Mistakes plummeted as soon as we started training people properly and handing out awards each month for the fewest ordering errors and posting lists of the worst offenders (no punishments, just names).

Of course, correcting system failures is seldom an easy task. One way to avoid making problems worse is to audition problem solutions with small, quick-hit field tests. For example, we experimented with new service procedures at one station in one restaurant, or we offered new menu items as nonmenu specials, or we borrowed equipment for a test run before leasing or buying it. When we had a problem with coffee quality, we tried using expensive, high-quality vacuum carafes in one restaurant. Quality improved substantially (and waste was cut in half), so we adopted the thermoses in all our restaurants.

When some customers complained about our wine service, we realized that we gave the subject only three pages in our employee manual. So we put together a training and motivation package that included instruction about the characteristics and distinctions of different wines, as well as a system of awards for selling them effectively. We also pointed out to our food servers that selling more wine increases the size of checks and thus of tips.

In short, honoring the guarantee has led to new training procedures, recipe and menu changes, restaurant redesign, equipment purchases, and whatever else it took to put things right and keep them right. In the long run, the guarantee works only if it reduces system-failure costs and increases customer satisfaction.[1]

This kind of problem solving is popular with employees. Since the object of change is always the company, employees don't get blamed for problems beyond their control.

As you find and correct the ultimate causes of your system failures, you can reasonably expect your profits to improve. But you can begin to tell if you're succeeding even before you see it on the bottom line. Remember, costs will go up before they come down, so high system-failure costs and low phone-survey complaint rates probably mean you're on the right track. Conversely, low system-failure costs and a high rate of "lousies" and "OKs" from customers almost certainly indicate that the promise is not being kept, that your expensive system failures are not getting corrected, and that your organization has yet to understand that customer satisfaction is the only reason for the company's existence.

Our own system-failure costs rose to a high of $40,000 a month two years ago and then fell to $10,000 a month. Meanwhile, sales rose 25%, profits doubled, and the cash in the bank grew two-and-a-half times.

Making It Work

It is easier to give someone a bowl of clam chowder than a free CAT scanner or an industry marketing study, so of course the nature of the guarantee will change from business to business. Still, the point is not free food, the point is customer satisfaction. It is always possible to satisfy the customer if the business is sufficiently committed to that goal.

Here are my suggestions for formulating your own ultimate strategy.

1. *Make the guarantee simple and easy to understand.* Think about the company's primary customer benefit and how you achieve it. In our case, the principal benefit is enjoyment. For many, it will be dependability. For others, cost or flexibility.

For the sake of impact, try to develop a guarantee that's memorable, maybe one that reduces to an acronym. The restaurants I now own use WAGS (We Always Guarantee Satisfaction), which I like even better than YEGA. Whatever you do, make it significant, simple, and unconditional. Think of these famous promises that changed whole companies:

"We try harder." (Avis)

"Absolutely Positively Overnight." (Federal Express)

Once you settle on a guarantee, commit to it for the long term. Continual change confuses the public and the organization. Plan to stick with a particular promise for at least five years.

2. *Make sure employees know how to use their new authority.* For most employees, full power and responsibility to put things right will be a new experience. After all, they're used to the old hierarchical approach. So it's up to you to make sure they don't underuse their power. In our training programs, we advise new employees to take action before the guest has to ask for a remedy. We don't want to make customers decide whether they're entitled to get something free—most people find that embarrassing. The food server should find the solution and present it to the guest as a done deal: "I'm sorry your drink wasn't prepared the way you like it. Of course, there will be no charge for that. And please accept these chowders on the house with my apologies."

We also insist that the customer is always right, even when the customer is wrong. Let's say a guest insists that all clam chowder has potatoes. He's wrong, but that's no excuse to make him look stupid. When we say, "The guest is never wrong," we mean a server should never question a guest's judgment and perception. Don't stand and argue about whether a steak is medium-rare or medium. Take it away and get one broiled the way the customer wants it.

The real issues are these: The guest is there to have a good time. The guest is in the employee's care.

Finally, we think that power and responsibility are not enough. Employees must also have rewards. Good thinking and positive action deserve money, praise, the limelight, advancement, and all the other encouragements a company can think of.

We spark employee thought and action by dividing a $10,000 bonus among the employees of each restaurant once its system-failure costs and phone-audit complaint rates drop to 25% of their all-time highs. Every month, we pay thousands of dollars in awards to employees who have helped to find and cure the ultimate causes of system failures. In effect, we commission everyone to change the organization for the better.

3. *Make progress visible.* Stay away from written progress reports—graphs communicate better. A creative in-house accountant can play

with the data until it's readily understandable to everyone. We display our new WAGS graphics throughout the company for everyone to see.

In our experience, system-failure costs go through four phases.

Start: Employees are wary of using their new power and authority. Phone-audit complaint rates are high and system-failure costs are low.

Under way: Employees begin to believe in the organization's commitment to the guarantee. Phone-audit complaint rates are still high; system-failure costs start to rise.

Mid-point: Employees accept and act on the company promise. System-failure costs remain high. Phone-audit complaint rates start dropping as the company starts satisfying customers in earnest.

Success: The company has achieved elemental change and raised itself to a higher level of merit. System-failure costs and phone-audit complaint rates are both low.

In general, there is a roller coaster effect that tells you when ultimate strategy is working. Costs go up. Complaints go down. Sales go up. Costs go down. Profits go up.

One word of caution: you will never perfect your company's system. As long as you offer an absolute guarantee on your products and services, you will incur system-failure costs. There is always more work to do, and a CEO's personal commitment and persistence are often necessary to get it done. But motivated employees are essential.

People often ask us where we find such wonderful employees. While it's true that we screen carefully, I believe our employees are better than most because they have the power and the obligation to solve customer problems on their own and on the spot. Giving them complete discretion about how they do it has also given them pride. Many companies have tried so many different programs and gimmicks that employees have become cynical and indifferent. The people who work for us know we take our guarantee seriously—and expect them to do the same. We use the same ultimate strategy to satisfy both customers and employees.

Note

1. For more on guarantees, see Christopher W.L. Hart, "The Power of Unconditional Service Guarantees," *Harvard Business Review*, July–August 1988, p. 54.

5

Service Comes First: An Interview with USAA's Robert F. McDermott

Thomas Teal

In his 22 years as CEO of the United Services Automobile Association (USAA), Robert F. McDermott has built a company with a reputation for superb service in an industry infamous for its indifference to the customer.

USAA is the nation's fifth largest insurer of privately owned automobiles and homes and is expanding rapidly into the field of financial services. Its 14,000 employees now serve more than 2 million customers and policyholders and manage $20.7 billion in assets. By focusing single-mindedly on service quality—and on its three component parts: customers, work force, and technology—McDermott has revolutionized USAA's approach to its business and to its customers' financial needs.

USAA was formed in 1922 by 25 army officers who wanted to provide one another with reciprocal auto insurance at a time when most local insurance companies saw military personnel as too mobile—and as living lives too full of risk—to be good bets. To this day, most of USAA's policyholders are its military and ex-military member-owners: about 95% of active-duty U.S. military officers are USAA members. To this day, too, the company uses no outside agents but does all its own sales and marketing.

McDermott has expanded USAA's market by taking in his members' children and grandchildren as associate members (with no ownership rights). And by law, the financial services the company sells must be offered to the general public. But the distinctive needs of USAA's military niche have been an important stimulus for the company's service focus.

USAA's origins also shape the company's approach to its work force—emphasizing a quasi-military esprit de corps and the continuous development of human resources. The company has an unmistakable military bearing. Of the 11 people who report to McDermott directly, 8 are ex-military officers. There is a strict dress code, employee performance is carefully measured, and the company's large, open bays allow for little privacy (even McDermott's office has one glass wall).

At the same time, USAA has pioneered progressive employment practices like the four-day workweek, spends $19 million annually on employee training (2.7% of its annual budget and double the industry average), and is a leader in integrating minorities into its work force. The company's 286-acre headquarters complex in San Antonio, Texas includes tennis courts, softball diamonds, jogging trails, three artificial lakes, and 75 classrooms.

The third and final element of USAA's service recipe is technology. At a time when many service companies are discovering that their heavy investments in technology do not translate into productivity gains, USAA has used technology not only to increase productivity but also to improve the quality of service. For example, USAA's state-of-the-art electronic imaging system means that each day some 30,000 pieces of mail never leave the mailroom. Instead, an exact image of the correspondence is placed electronically in the customer's policy service file and, simultaneously, in a sort of electronic in-basket where it will be handled by the first available service representative anywhere in the building.

McDermott is a retired U.S. Air Force brigadier general and former World War II fighter pilot. A graduate of the United States Military Academy and the Harvard Business School, he has taught at West Point and served as the first permanent dean of faculty at the Air Force Academy.

HBR: *USAA limits the sale of its principal financial products to a customer base comprising no more than 2% or 3% of the U.S. population. You do little or no national advertising, you refuse to sell through the thousands of independent insurance agents in this country, and yet your growth and profitability are among the highest in your industry. What's your secret?*

Robert McDermott: The mission and corporate culture of this company are, in one word, service. As a company objective, service comes ahead of either profits or growth.

Now, profits and growth do matter. In 1987, Ernst & Young surveyed 154 CEOs about their top priorities. Profits was first on their list, and growth wasn't far behind. Service came in eleventh. But I submit that it's because service comes first at USAA that profits and growth have been so healthy. We've grown from $200 million to $20.7 billion in total owned and managed assets in 22 years. Our profits are among the highest in the insurance industry. But service comes first.

Is it really as simple as that?

No, not quite. If you want me to describe our mission in several words instead of one, I'd have to say it's service to a particular community of customers and members, because our niche in the market is very important to us. Our members started this company and own it, so this company exists to serve their needs.

Let me give you an example. Whenever a war starts, most insurance companies are quick to invoke the war clause in their life insurance policies so they won't have to pay off on people killed in combat. Since we serve military officers, we have no such clause. So, for example, we're one of only a few companies that didn't invoke a war clause as soon as Desert Storm began. On the contrary, we sold new life insurance to people who'd just been called up.

If an officer had a $100,000 policy with us and he got orders for Desert Storm, we not only kept the full $100,000 in force, we let him increase his insurance. We didn't suggest it, exactly, but we allowed it. We even sold new policies to people who suddenly panicked when they got their orders and realized they might need some protection for their families. We put a $50,000 limit on increases and new policies, but we were the only insurance company I know of that sold those people any new coverage at all.

We also encouraged them to leave a power of attorney with someone at home. And we set up a hotline—the Desert Storm Assistance Center—so that should a member be killed, the survivors could call in and we'd take care of everything: life insurance, bank account, investment management, property insurance—everything with one phone call. When they mobilized, we mobilized. But that's how we see our mission. We insure fighter pilots and tank commanders. We sell life insurance to astronauts. We insured those guys on the moon.

Did you have losses in the Gulf?

Well, of the 263 Americans who died in the course of Desert Storm, 55 were officers, and all of those were USAA members, though not all of them had life insurance. Now, those 55 deaths are a terrible loss in human terms, but in purely financial terms, the loss to the company was not significant—altogether about $800,000.

As a matter of good service, on the auto side, we encouraged members sent to the Gulf to downgrade their insurance and save themselves money. For example, if their cars were just going to sit in garages while they were gone, they wouldn't need liability coverage. And when two-car families had one spouse in the Gulf, we gave them the rates for a single person with two cars, which of course are lower than for a couple with two cars, since one person can't drive two cars at the same time. Moreover, we went out of our way to make sure people understood that we wouldn't cancel their insurance because of late payments due to the war.

How do you justify to member-owners such generosity toward member-policy-holders—even if they are the same people?

In the case of auto insurance, we didn't need much justification. In spite of all our efforts to reduce premiums and save our members money, losses were so much below normal that we declared a 25% dividend—a rebate—on auto insurance for everyone who served in the Desert Storm combat area during hostilities. So everyone came out ahead. In this company, service isn't a matter of generosity, it's our daily bread.

As I understand it, however, service wasn't always USAA's strong suit.

Well, yes and no. I think the company always tried to give good service, it just didn't always succeed.

When I arrived here in 1968, I had six months to look around before I took over as CEO. And what I saw gave me second thoughts. We were good on claims, we were good on price, we were honest and honorable. In most other categories, we fell short.

A lot of our problems were the same ones other bureaucracies face. The company was divided into two divisions: auto and what we called the multiple-line division, which handled all property insurance— homeowners, renters, farm, boat, and so forth. There were also a lot of smaller departments, and these were mostly run by warlords who didn't communicate with one another. They fought perpetual turf battles. Actuarial didn't speak to underwriting, and claims didn't speak to either one. No horizontal communication. No one knew how the whole thing fitted together, they just knew and cared about their own little piece of the company.

There was paper everywhere. We had 650,000 members at that time and 3,000 employees. Every desk in the building was covered with stacks of paper—files, claim forms, applications, correspondence. You can't imagine how much paper. Stacks and piles and trays and baskets of it. And of course a lot of it got lost. On any given day, the chances were only 50-50 that we'd be able to put our hands on any particular file.

In fact, so much of it got lost that, depending on the season, we had from 200 to 300 young people from local colleges who worked here at night finding files, just going around searching people's desks until they found the ones they were looking for. Every night.

When I first started, I would often stay late and go around putting little marks on papers and files, then I'd check the next night to see if they'd been moved. A lot of people moved no paper at all.

Did your members know how bad the situation really was?

We constantly got letters and phone calls about poor service. Most of our members were sticking with us because our premiums were lower than anyone else's and because we were good on claims. It certainly wasn't because of our prompt and dependable service in any other area. Anyway, most of them had auto insurance only. Penetration in the property market was poor.

One old friend told me he'd bought a new car 18 months earlier and insured it with us, but when the insurance didn't come up for renewal a year later, he began to wonder. He discovered that the policy had never been issued. Another old friend said he'd applied for homeowner's insurance, and 90 days later he still hadn't heard anything.

You took over in 1969. What steps did you take to get the company back on track?

By the time I took over, I had already made four basic decisions. First, we were going to automate our policy-writing system.

Second, we were going to reduce the number of employees and do it by means of attrition—we weren't going to fire anyone. Turnover was very, very high at the time, so it wasn't a difficult promise to keep.

Third, we were going to have an education and training program to upgrade employee quality and enrich the jobs. "Enriched" was a word

I'd seen on a loaf of bread, where it meant they'd added something to improve the nutrition. I wanted to add interest and challenge to our jobs.

Fourth, we were going to decentralize. The decisions about how to serve our 650,000 members had to be made on the front line. To get that ball rolling, I divided our policy-writing and servicing people into five groups and assigned each of them a fifth of our members at random, so each group had a cross section geographically and actuarially. Then I put the five groups into competition with one another. Not only was that a good way of motivating people, it was a great way of identifying people with imagination and drive, because competition makes those people stand out like light bulbs.

And did it work? Did service improve?

It worked so well, it changed this company forever. It worked so well, it convinced me that the further down you decentralize, the better run your organization is going to be, provided of course you have the necessary education and training base. "Empowerment" has come to be a buzzword recently. I don't suppose I'd ever heard it in 1969, but it describes what we set about doing almost as soon as I took over. We empowered our employees.

How do you empower people in actual practice?

Well, first of all, we empower them with knowledge. We've got a training and education budget of $19 million, with 211 full-time instructors and 75 classrooms. Before our service representatives start answering phones, they get at least 16 weeks of training and job simulations. We're very proud of the fact that when members or customers ask questions, our service reps know the answers. They don't have to call in the supervisor every time something comes up that's just a little off the beaten track.

We also developed a tuition program. We pay the fees for anybody studying for a business degree or taking a college course relevant to their job, providing they get a grade of C or better, B or better for graduate work. We make it not just possible but easy for people to take courses. For example, this building turns into a college campus at night. We bring teachers here from six local colleges and universities, and on a typical evening, all 75 classrooms are in use. We also introduced training programs for professional designations, of which the insurance industry has quite a few. Today almost 30% of our people are in education and development programs—one of the highest percentages in the country.

Second, we empower them with technology—information, expert systems, image processing—that allows them to serve the customer better than any other insurance company. The image-processing system alone has totally changed the way we do business.

Can you give me an example?

Suppose Colonel Smith has sent us a letter asking for a change in his homeowners insurance, and he calls and wants to know if we've received it. The service representative says, "Yes, sir, I've got it right here." "You do?" he says. "Yes," the rep says, "I have it right in front of me. What can I do for you?"

The colonel's impressed. We received his letter only that morning, but it's already been imaged, so it's instantly available to every service representative in the building.

Now, let's say Colonel Smith calls back the next day with some additional information we've asked him for and talks to a different service rep who *also* has his letter "right here in front of me." Now the colonel's impressed and amazed.

Let's also say that the service rep, who has not only Colonel Smith's letter but his entire file available on the screen, goes on to explain how the change Smith wants to make in his homeowner's coverage may reduce his need for umbrella liability and thus lower the cost of that policy. Now the colonel's impressed and amazed and very pleased. And so are we, because the whole transaction's taken five minutes. And so is the service representative, because serving people better is fulfilling and fun.

And gives people a sense of power.

That's right. The third way we empowered them was in the literal sense of the word—with delegated authority. Our service representatives can make policy changes on the spot, just as a claims representative can authorize certain payments without an inspection and have a check in the mail the same day you phone in the claim. Our people can also invent new improvements to the system. I can't sit here at this level and dream up ways of improving service. It's got to come from the people on the front line.

Let me go back to education and training for a moment. If 30% of your people are involved in training in any given year, that suggests a lot of movement inside the company. Either that, or people get more and more training but stay in the same old jobs.

We don't want anyone to get stuck in a job, especially in a job perceived as repetitive or boring. So we do our best to get people to sign up for training, apply for new positions, learn more jobs—as you say, move around inside the company. Every year, 45% of our people get a promotion, and every year 50% of our people change their jobs. We want people who know what the people in other departments do, we want our managers to have the broadest possible experience of the company, and we want to be able to fill key vacant positions quickly. In other words, we want flexibility, and we want functional integration. A company full of people who've worked in lots of different jobs and divisions has both.

What about the people who didn't want to learn new skills, who wanted to stay in easy jobs?

When I took over, I promised everyone change. That scared some people away. Another group left when the jobs got harder. Of the old warlords who refused to change with the company, most left when I transferred them—at no cut in pay, incidentally—to jobs with less responsibility. All in all, the work force changed a great deal over those first few years.

For example, when I arrived at the company, USAA had a work force that was mostly white female and a management that was mostly white male. But San Antonio was 45% minority—so it didn't make sense. I took steps to make the work force better represent the labor force in our community.

Why? There were no quotas. Why was that important to you?

I'd come from the military, where integration worked. It was shocking to come out of the military and see how poorly it worked in the rest of society.

During World War II, the services limped along with a kind of halfhearted integration—separate black units fighting alongside white ones. But it wasn't fair, it wasn't right, and it didn't work. Truman saw that and ordered full integration, and the military carried it out more quickly and completely than most people expected. After all, the professional officer corps was largely Southern.

But the army had an additional motive on top of the president's order. The military always resists lack of flexibility in the management of its people, and a segregated work force is just one more complication. Military people get occupation specialties so they'll be interchangeable and mobile. The air force can take a hydraulic mechanic at Kelly Field and move him to Japan for a three-year tour, and when he arrives he just goes to work. That was the practical argument that gave traction to the moral argument. Segregation is immoral, but if that's not good enough for you, it's also inefficient.

Did you see gains in efficiency at USAA?

What I discovered when we started hiring minorities was that they were excellent employees and very conscientious. The jobs meant a lot to them. They were hungry for opportunities.

But I also discovered that our merit system wasn't totally objective. So I said, "OK, let's start all over again," because it was clear that there was bias in the system. I put everyone in the same job on the same pay, which meant 25% raises for some people.

But what kept favoritism from simply reasserting itself?

The problem wasn't so much open favoritism as it was the preservation of old inequalities based on seniority and habit. So we did several things. First, we created a forced distribution system. The old way, supervisors could give raises anywhere within a certain range, let's say, 0% to 8%, and they'd often sidestep the issue by giving everyone, say, 4%, which perpetuated earlier inequities—in fact made the actual dollar gaps bigger. We now said they had to identify 20% at the top level, 40% at the next level, and so forth, which forced them to make decisions and encouraged them to give pay for actual performance.

At the same time, we put in a new merit evaluation system and then worked with supervisors until they understood it. It took us about three years to change the system all through the company, a few jobs at a time. [For a fuller discussion of USAA's performance appraisal systems, see "Merit Evaluation and the Family of Measures."]

Merit Evaluation and the Family of Measures

USAA uses several tools to track employee performance. First, supervisors conduct annual evaluations of all individual employees on a range of performance and behavioral skills. They consider such factors as how well employees know their jobs, how they relate to others, the way they organize their work, and they rate qualities like judgment and initiative. For employees whose work is more discretionary, a goal-setting discussion and periodic reviews supplement the annual evaluation scorecard. The company uses all these evaluations to determine performance-based pay increases and to help establish promotion eligibility.

At the same time, USAA has developed a separate tool called the Family of Measures (FOM) to track the quality of individual and unit performance to answer a different basic question: Is this person or group showing improvement, and if not, what areas need training and attention? Because USAA's goal is continuous improvement, FOM's principal function is to measure progress, not to give grades. Individual and group results are compared only with themselves over time, never with other units or individuals.

FOM is based on USAA's belief that judging individual and group performance is an indispensable first step to learning and improvement. The company believes that people want an ongoing picture of how they're doing, that they want to be measured in accordance with standards they themselves have helped to set, and that they value the opportunity to improve performance without direct reference to compensation.

FOM is a flexible, continuous evaluation process rather than a static inventory of numbers such as sales volumes or customer contacts. Its results are not used to determine pay. And workers themselves have developed the grading formulas, determined the relative difficulty of tasks performed, and agreed on how to weight each score in accordance with each individual employee's experience level.

Each monthly FOM report tracks five areas: quality, quantity (of work completed), service timeliness, resource utilization (the percent of available hours that the group actually spends working), and customer satisfaction. The system tracks individual performance in some categories and overall group performance in others. Employees receive an individual report each month showing monthly and year-to-date results.

The FOM for each work unit is developed by a representative group of employees who decide which key aspects of the job they should track and who ask themselves four questions about each potential measure: Is the activity under our control? Is it significant? Does it involve some form of data that we can collect? Can we easily analyze the results? They vote on which measures to include and on their relative weight in the system. Finally, they pass these recommendations along to managers, who do their own fine-tuning before implementation.

To see how FOM operates in practice, we can look at the policy service function for property-and-casualty insurance. (Since USAA has no agents in the field, policy service representatives are the people who deal with customers, by letter or by phone, on all issues not involving claims.) To measure quality, managers audit telephone calls, correspondence, and computerized business transactions in order to identify both exceptional performance and areas of potential improvement. The focus is on communication, accuracy, and knowledge.

FOM defines quantity as the number of telephone and business transactions handled (USAA now does 90% of its business by phone). The different kinds of policies—auto, boat, home, umbrella, and so on—are weighted by difficulty, with the result that umbrella transactions count for five times as much as auto transactions in FOM reports.

These two measures, quality and quantity, are then weighted for the particular unit (policy service weights quality at 60%, quantity at 40%). Individual quantity standards vary by grade level and experience. USAA expects both quality and quantity to improve over time. The company gives special recognition to employees whose performance shows significant improvement and provides coaching and additional training for those who show little or none.

Service timeliness, resource utilization, and customer satisfaction are all monitored and analyzed for the group as a whole. The current measure for timeliness is the percent of calls answered within 20 seconds. Resource utilization measures the ratio of hours worked to hours paid. Customer satisfaction is culled from questionnaires mailed to a random sample of customers after they've dealt with a policy service representative.

And by that time, I suppose, the poorest performers had quit.

Most of them, yes. But there was more to it than that. We weren't making changes just to weed out poor performers. We were also improving management. Another new system we introduced at that time was a thing I call "painting the bridge."

When I was 12 years old, my father took me to visit West Point, and on the way we drove across Bear Mountain Bridge. Part of it was a bluish gray, and part of it was orange, and of course I wanted to know why. My father explained to me how bridges are painted—from one end to the other and then back to the start, which, by then, needs repainting. It's an endless cycle to keep the bridge in working order.

Painting the bridge is the same kind of exercise. An independent team of 14 organizational experts starts at one end of the company and goes through it one division at a time, with an eye to organizational health and organizational development. They look at structures, job content, duplications of effort, inefficiencies, and more. They do a desk-by-desk audit, working from the trenches up.

Most important, they question everything. Does this job need to exist? Does this department need to exist, or could it be merged with another function? Is this work being done the best possible way? Is this piece of infrastructure essential? The team does away with unnecessary work, titles, and fiefdoms. They hold managers' feet to the fire and remember the promises those same managers made the last time the team came through, two years earlier.

It's not a new concept. The air force does the same thing, which is where we got the idea. But we do it better. We're more sensitive to the impact on individual employees. Significant changes have to be discussed with personnel, and if there's no agreement, I have to arbitrate. They're not popular, those 14 people, but they're respected because they keep the company healthy. They keep cutting out the fat. The bridge keeps getting painted. We keep making better managers, and we keep enriching the jobs.

And greater efficiency makes jobs more rewarding?

People don't want to spend their lives doing effortless, pointless work. In that sense, painting the bridge is another way of making sure that jobs have meaning, along with giving people opportunities to educate themselves, to broaden their experience by changing jobs, to become decision makers.

But all those programs aside, the biggest piece of job enrichment was and still is service. Fulfilling the mandate to "love thy neighbor as thyself"—or however you choose to express the golden rule—enriches the job and enriches life.

No matter where we start, you always come back to service. Why is it so important to your work force?

In a military organization, the first thing you worry about is the morale of your troops, and the key to morale is the quality of work life. At USAA, that includes the fitness centers and the softball diamonds and the cafeterias as well as good salaries and benefits, a clean, cheerful place to work, and 52 four-day workweeks every year. It also includes the dress code and high expectations. We give a lot, and we demand a lot. But most of all, the quality of work life here is a matter of our service orientation.

In the military, we found that perhaps the most important factor in esprit de corps is being needed by the other guys in your unit. That's a fairly simple concept in a platoon or on a ship, but it's a little harder in a large corporation. In our case, it's a matter of feeling needed by the membership. I think you'll find that most of the service representatives who answer the 90,000 phone calls we get every day are anxious to help the people on the other end of the line. We know they've got a problem—that's why they're calling. They're reporting an accident, or the body shop didn't fix their car right, or maybe the body shop can't even *find* the car to tow it in. Something's wrong, and they live complicated, busy lives and want to get this thing wrapped up and want our help. Members trust us to help them, and our people know that. I think that makes them feel good. I think they like being needed.

You talk about serving your members as if that were the most important and satisfying assignment in the world. Let me ask an obvious question. What makes them so special?

Well, they're well educated, affluent, and honest. Today 42% have graduate degrees, largely because of the military policy of sending officers to professional schools in addition to an academy or officer training school. The median family income is almost twice the national median.

Moreover, the overwhelming majority are thoroughly honorable people, and of course that's important to an insurance company. When newly commissioned officers tell us they've had this many speeding tickets and this many accidents, we take their word for it. Some companies check every single application, but the money we'd spend would be way out of proportion to the number of misrepresentations we'd find.

The same goes for claims. If one of our members calls us and says, "Somebody stole four hubcaps off my car while I was in a meeting," our operator will punch that into a computer and say, "Okay, that's a 1989 Buick. They run $80 apiece. We'll send you a check for $320." And the check would go out that same day—written, addressed, stuffed, stamped, and sorted by computer. Most companies would go out and look at the car. That costs a lot of money.

So the niche market you have is a good one.

Yes. Exceptionally good.

But when you came to USAA, that niche was not very happy with the company. What was your strategy? Or was it simply better service?

My initial goal was simply to improve service. We had to start taking care of the people we were already supposed to be serving but weren't serving well.

Remember that because of our bylaws, we can't compete with other companies for their customers. But they can compete with us for ours. Any company can take my business away from me—or try to. But we can sell only to our niche. And I don't want to expand those bylaws. I don't want to take on the world. I want us to serve a niche and serve all its personal financial needs as best we can.

At the same time, I did want to penetrate our market better. In the old days, we'd insured only active-duty and retired officers. Those who separated at the end of a tour of duty or left before the end of their 20-year hitch, they were out. USAA changed its bylaws in 1962 to allow separated officers to keep their memberships, but the company had done nothing to bring back the ex-officers who'd left. In 1968, we had 75% of active-duty officers and only a fraction of all those former officers. So we set out to get them back and then hold onto them. Today 95% of all active-duty officers and warrant officers are members, and we've managed to capture several hundred thousand of those separated and retired officers as well.

If I wanted to expand our world further, my next obligation might be to take on enlisted personnel, which would be nine times what we're doing now. But how far do we want to go? Aren't we better off serving the needs of our members and customers and making sure that service, not growth, is the objective?

But many of your employee policies depend on growth. You can't go on promoting 45% of your employees every year unless the company is growing. What if military budgets get cut, there are very few new officers, and your customer base shrinks?

We've taken care of that in two ways. First, it's only our property and casualty insurance—auto and homeowners—that we sell to members only. Anyone at all can use our bank and credit cards or buy our life insurance and mutual funds. Second, we have added one group to our auto and homeowners market. In 1971, we began offering associate membership to the children and grandchildren of members. As associate members, they can buy the insurance, but they have no ownership. Most of our growth today comes from that segment.

Can you do that and maintain the quality of your membership? In terms of education, affluence, self-discipline?

They tend to be chips off the old block. Take education. Something like 42% of their parents did graduate work. Now we see the children getting educations at the same level. We are a little tighter on underwriting on those children, since the culture they've grown up in is not quite the duty-honor-country culture their parents knew. But there's plenty of growth potential there; so far we've penetrated only 40% of that market.

But why don't you broaden your membership? There must be other professional groups that would meet your standards for education, income—even integrity. Why not doctors or architects or airline pilots?

But where do we stop? And do we give them ownership? Our present members get special treatment, and they need special treatment.

If we bring in architects and engineers and doctors, and if the nonmilitary professionals come to outnumber the officers, what happens when the country goes to war? I'm afraid they'd be apt to say, "Let's put in a war clause. I don't want to insure the lives of people when someone's actually trying their best to kill them!"

No, I want to stick to our members. You know, it takes a certain kind of courage to stick to a niche, and I've thought a lot about niche marketing. Instead of skimming the market with a series of gimmicky products that will always attract *someone*, it means forming a bond with your customers, and it means providing for their needs in depth.

I wanted USAA to think about the events in the life of a career officer and then work out ways of helping him get through them. Or "her," though in those days it was pretty much only "him."

Anyway, he gets married, he buys a house, he has children, they learn to drive, they go to college, he retires. All of it on a fairly small, flat income.

So one of the first things I did at USAA was to send our members questionnaires asking if they were interested in life insurance, banking, a car-buying service, car leasing, home mortgages, mutual funds, a whole smorgasbord of offerings. And the answer was yes, they were interested in all of it. On the basis of those replies, I managed to persuade the board to change the bylaws and offer those products.

You wanted to offer them broader services. But didn't that put you into direct competition with financial institutions other than insurance companies?

Right, and we couldn't compete on bonding alone. We would also have to outperform others on price, quality, convenience, and efficiency. We were going to have to offer mutual funds as good as the best. From here in San Antonio, we were going to have to offer banking services to people all over the country and the world. We were going to have to do marketing and servicing by telephone, which was still a fairly innovative concept in 1968.

What it all pointed to was technology. Computers, automation, telecommunications. And that was a new idea—it was certainly new to USAA.

We had two pieces of electronic hardware back then, and we chose people to operate it on the basis of their high-school math grades. It was like buying a piano and then assigning concert duty to anyone who knew what notes looked like. It was a case of the deaf leading the blind. We had no training program and no systems-development people.

The systems were archaic. In auto insurance, every application and letter that came in went through 55 steps. The first person would open the envelope, remove the paper clips, and pass it to the second person, who would check addresses on big Rolodexes and write in corrections with a pen, then pass it to the third person, and the fourth person, and so on—55 steps. There were people who did nothing but staple and people who did nothing but stuff envelopes and people who did nothing but punch their time cards in and out.

And, incidentally, the ones who weren't doing much work weren't having much fun. The average employee stayed with the company for 11 months. We were giving terrible service and boring our employees—and that is a question of cause and effect. No one's happy in a slack, easy job. Working harder makes people happier. Or at least working *better* makes people happier. Technology was going to be our way of doing better work.

How did you go about it?

The first thing I did was to bring in an automated policy-writing system. We didn't have the resources to develop our own, so we bought one from another insurance company and had them come in and train our people. It worked with code sheets and punch cards that were run through in batches at night, very primitive stuff, but we thought it was wonderful.

From there we gradually moved on to a quasi-on-line system for claims that tracked and more or less integrated the entire claims process. It would look pretty old-fashioned today, but at the time—the mid-1970s—it was the Cadillac of the industry. And it was a danger for us.

In what way?

Information technology has to be a strategic competitive weapon—not just a cost center. We'd spent a lot of money and acquired the best automated claims system in the country, probably in the world—so the danger was complacency. We were in danger of resting on our laurels, of using that new system as if it were merely a better machine rather than a new way of doing business.

We had no cause for complacency, because we were still basically reactive. Someone would ask for the automation of some task, some state would pass a new law or regulation, and we would adapt with the latest technology we could find. It was short-term thinking. And I was beginning to see that we needed a broad systems strategy that looked ahead.

The result was a five-year plan. It consisted of 81 projects and had a projected price tag of $100 million. In the end, it took us six years and $130 million. But that wasn't bad, considering that along the way we enlarged the scope of the plan, made a lot of changes, dropped some projects, added others, and incorporated new technology as it came along. More important, we achieved our basic goal, to create an AIE—an automated insurance environment—that includes policy writing, service, claims, billing, customer accounting, everything.

More important yet, it changed the way we think. Now when you want to buy a new car, get it insured, add a driver, and change your coverage and address, you can make one phone call—average time, five minutes—and nothing else is necessary. One-stop, on-line, the policy goes out the door the next morning about 4 a.m. In one five-minute phone call, you and our service representative have done all the work that used to take 55 steps, umpteen people, two weeks, and a lot of money.

That's faster and more efficient, all right, but how does it represent a change in the way you think?

It changes everybody's definition of what's possible, of what we can do, of what they themselves can do. First, it's a radical change in the status of the service representative. Thirty years ago, this was a little bit of a sweatshop. For example, employees were issued pencils one at a time. When you thought you'd used it up, you took it to the pencil lady, and she measured it, and if it was short enough, she gave you a new one. Compare that with the situation today, where technology gives people the direct power and authority to make things happen, to create change. Our employees aren't just agents for the company, they *are* the company.

Second, it's a revolution in the relationship between the company and the customers, who now have instantaneous access to and control over their own financial transactions, no matter whom they're talking to. We've got 14,000 employees, but every time you call, you're talking to someone who's got your file in front of them. Someday, we won't even mail the policies out. You'll trust us to make the changes and keep the policy here.

Third, it means an end to paper—almost. We get about 150,000 pieces of mail every morning, of which 60% to 65% are checks. Of the remainder, less than half ever leaves the mailroom. All of our policy-service correspondence is imaged, indexed, prioritized, and it's then instantly available anywhere in the company. Work management is hugely simplified and leveraged. We can change priorities on the fly, for example. Someone gets sick and her work can be sent to someone else. A supervisor can check a backlog, find out why it's there, change the order and logic of the priorities, and clear it away.

We've only just started building an image system for claims, where there's quite a bit of paper—affidavits, powers of attorney, photographs—but the future there is even greater.

You mean a step beyond paperlessness?

In claims, the next step is the integrated workstation. We're working with IBM to develop a multimedia system that will include imaging, pictures, voice, and video. Say you're discussing a court case with a doctor and a lawyer in Florida. You'll be able to go through the file together—color photographs of injuries, a recording of the original telephoned claim, a video of the damage to the car—all of that on a telephone-integrated desktop workstation.

We're also going to build in knowledge-based systems—expert systems—that will leverage the knowledge of our experts down to a level below them. People will be able to underwrite and approve loans, for example, at a level much higher than their education and experience would otherwise allow.

We ran a little experiment with an expert system to detect fraud, and it worked so well—90% accuracy—that we've kept it.

Don't expert systems lead to de-skilling? How do you get people to internalize an electronic decision tree?

Right now, we have service people who do automobile, homeowners, and renters, including pretty difficult and unusual problems. But there are limitations on how many areas they can cover efficiently. Where we're headed, we hope, is to integrated expert systems that will allow those same people to do mutual funds, life insurance, credit cards, banking services, and other things as well, including some fairly complicated transactions. It's the next challenge, and I think it means an increase in skills, comprehension, and job satisfaction, not a decrease.

The systems we're developing are transparent. You can ask them why, and they'll explain the rules and show you why they did what they did. What's more, if you find a new rule, you can add it to the sequence. So both the operator and the system can learn.

How did you get your people to accept such challenges? How did you get them to accept technology in the first place? A lot of knowledge workers have found it threatening.

We're not interested in technology for its own sake, only if we can turn it into better service and more satisfying jobs. To begin with, we've never laid off a single soul because of technology, and we hope we never have to. We also spend an inordinate amount of time keeping users involved from the moment we begin developing any new program. Consequently, when we finally get the product, it's what they need, want, and like. They can sit down and say, "Yes, this feels right."

We use what we call living laboratories, users who test it and kick it and break it during development. When the product is ready, they become the nucleus that goes out and sells it to the first group that's going to use it. They can say, "You're going to love it, and here's why."

Then, by and by, that first group sells it to the next group, and so on. It takes a lot of planning to make sure it's not threatening, to make sure it will lead to better service and better jobs. We try very hard to think of everything—the productivity effects, the sociological effects, the comfort effects, as well as the bottom-line effects. For us, customers and employees are both precious resources.

So far, the employees have loved it. They can't wait to get the newer applications. So it's worked for the company. Over the last ten years, we've had 35% growth in policies in force, but the growth in service personnel has been zero. And people love these jobs. How did we do that? We did it with technology.

So the ultimate result of a really tenacious dedication to service, job enrichment, and niche marketing turns out to be an exceptional flowering of technology.

The big companies love developing new systems with us because we put a strain on everything they make. If a system can be broken, we'll break it. We're the largest single electronic business site in the country. We do eight million transactions a day, counting one transaction every time somebody hits "enter" on a keyboard.

There's no computer built that can handle our volume alone. We have six IBM 3090s, the biggest thing they build, all lashed together. We also have elaborate backups. Everything we do is written somewhere else on another tape or another disk almost simultaneously.

If we lost our entire center—if an airplane flew right into the building—it would take us from 2 to 11 days to get back in operation, depending on the day of the week. All we'd lose would be the conversations taking place at the moment of the disaster.

And the cost? I know you spent $130 million developing some of these systems, which have come to constitute a virtual core competence of this corporation. But how much does technology cost you annually? And how much do you continue to spend on development?

We don't think of technology as a cost center. It's a strategic weapon. It contributes to service, so cost is not the only or even the primary consideration.

But isn't there a strategic line somewhere between customer service and financial irresponsibility? Isn't there ever a conflict between altruism and profits?

What you need to understand is that what you call core competence and strategy and altruism and mission are all the same thing for USAA. They're all a matter of community. This company has formed a bond with its members, and the members have a natural bond with one another. We're a family, if you like. And our part of the family, the company, provides financial services for the rest of the family, the members. That's the knitting we stick to, that's our strategy, that's our goal. Not the narrow slots of property insurance or life insurance or banking or credit cards or technological leadership or whatever, but the financial security and peace of mind that our family needs and wants.

PART

III

Delivering Quality Service in the Public Sector

1

How I Turned a Critical Public into Useful Consultants

Peter T. Johnson

When I became the head of Bonneville Power Administration in Portland, Oregon, I was no different from lots of other executives, including those in the private sector, where I had spent most of my years. I viewed conflict with people outside the company as an annoyance I'd do almost anything to avoid. I had enough on my plate without environmentalists, politicians, special interests, or the general public second-guessing my decisions and interfering with my operations.

As it turns out, as a public servant, I didn't have a choice. Outsiders had a way of exerting influence whether I liked it or not. I had no sooner arrived at BPA when the agency became the target of political, legal, and even physical threats from people outside the organization who had lost confidence in BPA's ability to act without jeopardizing their interests. Those of us on the inside knew we were capable of making good decisions, and we made every effort to explain our reasoning.

But that was the problem. By first making decisions and then explaining them, we were essentially telling people that we knew what was good for them. Meanwhile, the people affected by our decisions were telling us in any way they could—lobbying to curtail BPA's authority, taking BPA to court, or aiming rifles at BPA surveyors—that the father-knows-best approach to decision making was completely unacceptable.

Just when it began to seem that BPA was doomed to a future of litigation and hostility, we made an important discovery. We found that by inviting the public to participate in our decision-making process, our adversaries helped us make better decisions. When I say we included outsiders in decision making, I'm referring to real involvement, with real changes in decisions based on what we heard. By listening to people's concerns and soliciting their advice on how to reconcile vast differences of opinion and conflicting needs, our operations did not come to a screeching halt. On the contrary, by involving the public in the decision-making process itself, we gained authority and legitimacy, avoided costly lawsuits and political challenges, and arrived at creative solutions to seemingly intractable problems. Overall, our policy-making improved.

BPA's public-involvement program was a big change for the agency and for me personally, one that required letting go of outmoded attitudes, facing up to underlying fears, and hoping that "outsiders" would do the same.

From Chaos to Commitment

When I arrived at BPA in 1981, things seemed to be running smoothly. I thought the agency simply needed some fine-tuning to make it more efficient. A lot I knew. I spent my first few months managing my way through one crisis after another. It seemed that everyone in the Northwest suddenly had a bone to pick with BPA, and there I was in the middle of it. At first I couldn't find a common root in the dissatisfaction various groups were leveling at BPA. The only conclusion I reached was that something important had changed.

BPA had a staff of intelligent, well-trained, and dedicated people who were becoming deeply frustrated. Ever since BPA had been established in 1937, its success at transmitting and marketing electrical power from federal hydroelectric dams in the Pacific Northwest had earned the agency a good reputation, in which employees took pride. By 1981, for instance, BPA had built a premier 15,000-mile electric transmission grid connecting Canada with four Northwestern states and California. Many veteran employees talked fondly of the warm welcome they had received when BPA's construction projects brought jobs and reliable power to communities across the Northwest. As one senior executive remarked, "It was really an honor to be a Bonneville employee, because we did so many good things."

By the early 1980s, despite the staff's competence and hard work, respect for BPA was waning, and in some situations, the agency was even reviled. When BPA set out to build high-voltage transmission lines linking generating plants in eastern Montana to points across the Pacific Northwest, protestors threatened BPA employees and disrupted every public hearing we had. On one occasion, project surveyors examining the proposed right-of-way for the transmission lines were confronted by a rancher aiming a rifle at them. Workers didn't dare identify themselves as BPA employees when they ate in local restaurants or checked into motels. We even had to rush a consignment of unmarked vehicles to Montana to protect them. And then there were the "bolt weevils," who surreptitiously unbolted transmission towers to collapse them.

The reality of my new job left me as frustrated as the staff. For example, just two weeks after I took office, I received a desperate call from the head of the Washington Public Power Supply System (WPPSS, or "Whoops," as Wall Street wags called it when it became the largest public bond default in U.S. history). With electricity demand in the Northwest projected to grow rapidly, BPA had agreed in the early 1970s to purchase the output of three out of five nuclear power plants WPPSS was building, and it had guaranteed the debt of those three plants. Now the man who headed WPPSS was telling me that they were out of money on two of the plants and couldn't even meet their payroll. WPPSS, the organization to which BPA had written a blank check, was on the verge of insolvency. He further informed me that he was being followed by reporters wherever he went, so we would have to hold a clandestine meeting. We met in the basement of a hotel in Seattle to patch together a solution to the immediate crisis.

The collapse of WPPSS damaged BPA's reputation as a leader in energy planning for the Northwest and contributed to the creation of the Northwest Power Planning Council, a deliberative body whose mandate was a direct challenge to the authority of the BPA administrator. The council consisted of eight members, two each appointed by the governors of Washington, Oregon, Idaho, and Montana, and gave these Northwestern states a greater role in shaping energy policy—something their governors had been wanting. There was controversy, and even a Constitutional question, about whether the council could direct the administrator of BPA or merely provide advice and counsel. By 1981, as I came into office, I didn't know whether the newly created council was supposed to be my adviser, my new boss, a competitor, or what. What I did know was that BPA was sailing in hostile and uncertain waters.

Also around the time I came on board, BPA was finishing up the "Role Environmental Impact Statement," which a court injunction had forced BPA to prepare. This document was an evaluation of the environmental and social impacts of BPA's total operations—its "role" in the region. It was a huge undertaking and the first of its kind (until then, BPA had prepared impact statements only for specific projects), and BPA had tried in earnest to cover all the bases. To ensure that the document was objective and independent, we engaged a number of outstanding consultants to prepare it. When it was done, the Role EIS stood seven feet tall. We couldn't even fit it in a wheelbarrow. It was as complex and comprehensive as it could possibly be, full of facts and good analysis.

Yet no one appreciated it. People complained that it was ponderous, that they couldn't find what they wanted in it, that they were bothered by some of the document's findings and analysis. Clearly, fulfilling our legal requirements was a step in the right direction, but it was not enough to please our stakeholders. I started to wonder what was.

The U.S. Congress had already passed legislation compromising some of BPA's authority. The governors were trying to assert their authority through their new council. Public credibility was clearly low. No matter how you looked at it, BPA's wings had been clipped. And I had no reason to believe it would end there.

So I began to think that BPA had to change its ways. But even while I recognized the need for change, I have to admit, I wasn't sure what it should be. When two staffers, Jack Robertson, then my assistant for external affairs, and Donna Geiger, a public-involvement specialist, advised me that we could solve our problem by inviting the public into the decision-making process, all the apprehensions I had accumulated during my 20 years in the private sector began to surface. BPA's attorneys reinforced my fears. They argued that public involvement would force the premature release of important documents and jeopardize the attorney-client privilege, that BPA would forfeit its flexibility and become hostage to its own policies and guidelines, that outsiders would have the leverage to make unreasonable demands, and that BPA would become vulnerable to lawsuits right and left.

The lawyers' arguments were compelling, but Robertson in particular kept working on me. As a former staffer to Republican Senator Mark Hatfield of Oregon, he had seen how well-intended governmental initiatives were frustrated by the political process when a group of people could claim that their interests had been ignored. He warned that the public outcry for BPA to be more accountable was not going to disappear and that attempts to exercise arbitrary authority would get us into trouble. Public involvement, he argued, was the way forward. BPA would have to engage in meaningful consultation with third parties.

As I thought about Robertson's reasoning, I began to realize that while the legal risks the BPA attorneys had pointed to were real, I had to balance those risks against many other risks to the organization. When I was in the private sector, third parties didn't have the power to bring down my business. But in a government agency, political pressure and litigation surely can keep the organization from implementing its programs. That risk had to be taken seriously.

If including people in the decision-making process would prevent political protests and legal challenges, it was worth a try. But not a half-hearted one. Robertson was quick to add that any new approach would fail if we thought of it as something we did when we had political problems. We had to make a rock-solid, ethical commitment to be open and honest, whether or not it was to our presumed, near-term advantage. "I've got to have your credit card," he insisted, which meant I had to trust his expertise, as I would any other professional in the agency. I pulled Geiger and her staff into my own office to centralize public-involvement activities and also to send a message to the whole organization about the importance of public involvement.

Then we began to put our new philosophy into action, starting with the transmission lines in Montana. We decided to invite input from anyone who had an interest in that situation. We arranged dozens of meetings with individuals and groups to identify problems, to listen to their concerns and suggestions, and to respond openly to their questions. I particularly remember one meeting with environmentalists who were bitter about the way we'd selected our right-of-way and upset because no one would listen to them. They came into my cramped motel room, about ten of them, and sat on the bed and the floor. One young woman nursed her infant as she sat on the floor and upbraided me for my lack of sensitivity to the people of the state and its pristine environment.

We took the concerns to heart. As a result of those discussions, we relocated transmission lines off scenic agricultural lowlands and behind forested ridges, and we reduced the visibility of towers with a special treatment that made the lines less prominent. We even found that if we had not already made some investments in our original route, the new routing would have been less expensive. We developed a plan to compensate local communities for things like road maintenance and also contributed several thousand dollars to help fund the state's oversight of our activities.

Pleased with this initial success, I was convinced that the new public-involvement program had taken root. But Donna Geiger knew better. She had made a point of reviewing public-involvement activities in all the agency's offices and had found several pockets of lukewarm acceptance. She recounted a number of instances when one part of the organization would make a decision after consulting the interested parties outside the agency, while another part of the organization would make a decision affecting the same people with little or no consultation. Some staff went out of their way to remind people that the administrator made all final decisions, which was true in a legal sense but sent a clear message that anything anyone said was pointless. This explained why customers had taken me aside and asked, "Which way are you really going? We don't see you acting on the talk." The public clearly was getting whipsawed.

At Geiger's suggestion, we retained consultant James Creighton, the "guru of public involvement," to assess our program. The results were disturbing. Despite the beginning attempts at public involvement, the public saw BPA as "arrogant, insensitive, and uncaring." With such a long way to go, once again the question arose: Were we really committed to public involvement? And more to the point, was I?

There was little time to deliberate. We immediately faced the problem of what to do with the consultant's report. Its mere existence posed a public-relations threat because the press was clamoring for copies. Some people, including our own media-relations department, feared that the media would use the document's harsh findings against us. They advised us to view the report as an internal document. To be honest, I shared the concern. But Jack Robertson reminded me of that credit card I had given him and, along with Donna Geiger, recommended that we give the report, accompanied by a letter outlining steps we were taking to address the findings, to the media and to anyone else who requested it. Robertson and Geiger firmly believed that the media would act responsibly if given full information. I swallowed hard and stepped out of the way.

It was exactly the right move. After releasing the report, BPA immediately won kudos from the press. The *Seattle Post-Intelligencer*, which had been writing critical editorials for months, said, "BPA leadership deserves double credit, despite the scathing report, for commissioning the study of its operations and for accepting the findings unflinchingly. . . . The agency has set a commendable example for other public agencies to follow in examining the need for self-improvement."

Meeting the "Crazies"

Having taken the bold step of releasing the consultant's report, we began the hard work of restoring public confidence. Two tasks lay ahead: to change the attitude at BPA and to develop practical skills in working with the public.

At my insistence, top management added public involvement to the performance requirements of every management position. There was to be no mistaking its importance. Those who did an exceptional job of consulting with the public were recognized in the BPA newsletter and received cash awards.

We also established a requirement that managers prepare a public-involvement plan for all major decisions. Each plan would outline the activities appropriate to that decision, including the number and kind of people to be included in the decision-making process. Employees had little experience with public involvement, and many were terrified at the prospect of confronting our adversaries, so we set up a mandatory training program for employees ranging from top management to first-line supervisors. We taught people how to organize and conduct public meetings, how to listen even when tempers flared, and how to improve their public speaking and writing skills.

I also used one other weapon in my arsenal: an agency policy on public involvement. It occurred to me that by letting the whole organization help shape the policy, I could win support for the new philosophy and create the culture shift BPA needed. Like the public-involvement process itself, inviting employees to help create corporate policy was somewhat risky. It gave employees a chance to fight back—which they did. Each BPA operational office had to sign off on the policy, and many offices registered their resistance to the policy by simply stalling. It took two years to get the policy approved, and even then we had a few holdouts.

At the same time that we were working to create a culture shift within BPA, we were considering what the public would need to play a meaningful role in decision making. My experience in the private sector had given me a firm belief in hard-sell public relations, but I could see that it was no longer appropriate to put the best spin on everything BPA did. The job now was to be open and honest so that people were well informed. Instead of producing documents that were stuffy, bureaucratic, and inaccessible, we began preparing "background-ers," which summarized the important information about a controversial issue, and "issue alerts," which told people about an upcoming decision-making process and how to participate.

It was clear, though, that our worst critics were not getting any closer. Ratepayer advocates and environmental groups opposed to nuclear power were at the top of the list of people who distrusted us; everything we did provoked fresh torrents of criticism from them. Finally, we asked them directly, "What is it you want?" They replied that they wanted to meet with top management, they wanted the right to set the agenda for those meetings, and the meetings could not be costly for them to participate in.

We had been meeting and making good progress with most key interests that would be affected by our decisions, but the idea of going eyeball-to-eyeball with our toughest critics, whom some at BPA referred to as "the crazies," was scary. Still, I agreed to it. And that's when things got really interesting.

We arranged to hold the first few meetings in BPA's conference room with access to an elaborate conference call system for those participants who couldn't afford the trip to Portland, Oregon. We invited virtually every critic not previously consulted, not to resolve any major issues but just to explain how we felt about them. I remember how tough it was to walk into that room the first few times and how tense the interest-group leaders were as they sat in the chairs against the wall. Their whole demeanor said, "Show me!"

I was constantly aware of how easily meetings could degenerate into shouting matches, so I worked hard to guard my reactions, especially when people misinterpreted the facts or said things I didn't agree with. The most important thing was that we be open and forthright.

Over time, as people realized we could have a frank discussion on any subject, the tension dissipated. Both BPA staff and the interest-group leaders began to relax and enjoy the debate. Soon we were able to spot concerns before they became full-blown issues, and fewer disagreements were based on misperceptions and misinformation. Most important, we began to trust and respect each other. People felt comfortable picking up the phone and calling me, where before they'd have gone to the media or formed a coalition against us. The process, while not perfected, was working.

But was it really making a difference? The WPPSS debacle had contributed to a 304% increase in industrial electrical rates between 1980 and 1984, and the Northwest Power Act of 1980 had significantly changed our relationship to utilities in the region, while leaving many other questions about roles and authority highly ambiguous. People who were dissatisfied with what they got from BPA could plead their case to the Power Planning Council created by the new Northwest Power Act or sue BPA. Consequently, few decisions could be counted on until they had been okayed by the Ninth Circuit Court of Appeals, the court the Northwest Power Act specified for resolution of all litigation. Each decision was a battleground.

We weren't sure BPA's public-involvement program could result in any meaningful decisions in such a chaotic and litigious climate. But we soon found that it could. Two early experiences with our new decision-making process not only won over the laggards and completed the culture shift at BPA, but also demonstrated that the process was a practical alternative to litigation and could produce innovative solutions to seemingly intractable problems.

Saving the Aluminum Industry

The rapid rise in electricity rates affected everyone in the Northwest, but the energy-intensive aluminum industry was particularly hard hit. The industry had been located in the Northwest during World War II to take advantage of the cheap electrical power from federal dams. The aluminum companies' presence proved to be advantageous to the region not only in terms of dollars and jobs but also because of the complementary ways the industry and the region use electricity. Aluminum plants operate around the clock and typically schedule production to coincide with releases of vast quantities of water, which reservoirs can't hold during spring runoff. Rather than being spilled over the dams and wasted, this water is run through turbines to generate large amounts of electricity that can be used by the aluminum smelters at times when few other customers need the power. Additionally, aluminum companies are willing to have their production interrupted occasionally, when peak power demands are high in the rest of the region, and for that flexibility, they get special rates.

When the high cost of nuclear power plants drove up electricity rates, the aluminum industry faced rates eight times higher than they had been five years earlier. To make things worse, the price of aluminum on the world market was in free-fall. Aluminum companies in the Northwest were being challenged by other countries with newer, more efficient smelters. Northwestern aluminum smelters that had been among the world's most constant producers were being used as "swing" plants, the first to slow or shut down when world prices drop. By late 1984, one large aluminum plant had shut down completely, two plants were offered for sale, and practically all smelters had reduced production.

The aluminum industry bought 30% of BPA's total output of electricity and represented $640 million of the agency's annual revenues. If it didn't consume that power, rates to other customers would have to rise to cover the high fixed costs of generating electricity. The aluminum industry also employed 9,000 workers in the Northwest, was indirectly responsible for 22,000 more jobs, and produced substantial tax revenues, typically in small communities that had few other sources of revenue. Obviously, BPA had an incentive to help, if it could.

But I felt helpless. The aluminum plants were likely to leave, and the consequences would be severe. I had always thought of myself as a problem solver, but this time I had nothing to bring to the table. The smelter in The Dalles, Oregon, had already closed, and the community was devastated. A group led by their mayor, who was a car dealer with a lot full of unsold cars, implored me to help them. Maybe BPA could lower electrical rates for the plant so that local interests could afford to buy it and reopen it. After describing the impact of the plant closing on local schools, one woman turned to me and said, "There must be something you can do."

As much as we wanted to respond to the people of The Dalles and to other aluminum companies and their communities, we couldn't set new rates without going through the legal rate-making process. Since other customers had also absorbed heavy rate increases, they were unlikely to sympathize with the aluminum industry, and there were sure to be lawsuits.

We needed a creative solution that would not become a battlefield for attorneys, so we turned to our public-involvement process.

We first visited local communities to see if they would join BPA in taking responsibility for the problem. We called meetings in towns where smelters were located and asked what they might be willing or able to do to complement any action we might take. Could they grant tax incentives or make economic development investments to spur employment? But the resources of these local communities were so strained that they were reluctant to take action. We also approached the labor unions, some of which responded by making modest concessions.

We cast the net wider. We decided that we had to initiate a broad study of the problem and that we had to get everyone who had an interest to be directly involved in developing the study. We asked dozens of people to be part of a technical-review committee and ended up with a group of about 75 members representing utilities, local governments, state agencies, public-interest groups, labor unions, aluminum companies, and private citizens.

It became clear that some committee members distrusted BPA's intent. They suspected that the agency was trying to save the aluminum industry at the expense of its other customers. So the first order of business was to convince people of our motives. Then the committee got down to the business of designing the study and developing a computer model that a layperson could use to analyze the economic effects of various approaches.

In the meantime, BPA launched a campaign to educate the public about the problems the aluminum companies were having. We prepared two brochures, one outlining the problem and describing the study and the other explaining the role of the aluminum industry in the regional economy and in BPA's energy system, and we sent them both to about 15,000 people. And in one month, the agency's field staff held more than 50 meetings throughout the region, featuring a 15-minute slide show, a brief address, and a question-and-answer exchange. We also held open forums in The Dalles and other communities where smelters were located.

We were going to every extreme to open the process to outsiders and to consider as many perspectives as possible, and at times it seemed that jangled nerves were our only tangible result. The list of concerns seemed endless, the problems seemed insurmountable, and BPA employees were beginning to lose sight of what we were trying to accomplish.

Finally, at a one-day symposium in April 1985 sponsored jointly by BPA and the League of Women Voters, we made a breakthrough. The symposium had been set up to discuss the options for addressing the aluminum companies' needs, and the turnout was terrific. The hall was packed with key elected officials and with representatives from all the important public-interest groups and all the utilities in the region. On the platform were several experts on the utility industry, including economists who specialized in the aluminum and electric utility industries.

Throughout the day, as various experts presented their opinions, one argument followed another. But by late that afternoon, we had actually made some progress. The day ended with an unspoken consensus that helping the aluminum industry would help everyone in the room. It was a momentous occasion. We had finally moved beyond arguing; we had agreed that there was a problem, and we were ready to talk solutions.

In the months that followed, the BPA staff drafted a paper outlining a number of options, and we scheduled 13 public meetings to take comments. Some 4,600 people attended those meetings—from 10 in Burley, Idaho, to 3,200 in Columbia Falls, Montana. We invited our 75-member technical-review committee to submit written comments. And we received and answered more than 1,100 letters on the study, including hundreds from school children in towns where smelters were located, begging me not to take away their parents' jobs.

The idea that had the broadest support was to tie the price of electricity to the world price of aluminum ingot—in other words, to make it a variable rate. Most people liked the idea, although they suggested ways to set upper and lower limits. I had previously dismissed this proposal as unlikely to be acceptable to our non-aluminum industry customers. But now they were giving me the go-ahead. We were as close to a consensus as we could expect to get on an issue as controversial as this one.

BPA announced the decision to propose the variable rate, and the formal rate hearing moved expeditiously to a decision. When the variable rate went into effect, there were no lawsuits. Although some parties were disappointed with the choice, they had sufficient respect for the openness, thoroughness, and objectivity of the public-involvement process that they did not challenge the decision.

From an economic standpoint, the decision has proven wise for both the aluminum industry and BPA. No smelters closed permanently, and due to a rise in the world price of aluminum, all were soon operating. The agency reaped more than $200 million in revenues it would otherwise not have received. In 1991, when aluminum prices again dropped, the variable rate kicked in to encourage smelters to continue operating.

Public involvement had given BPA a new-found legitimacy to act. From that point on, we knew it was possible to make decisions that would count.

Reconciliation on Nuclear Power

In 1983, BPA was caught between two formidable opponents, and the public-involvement process once again led the way out. At that time, two of the three nuclear power plants BPA had backed financially were incomplete. Only one, WNP-2, was running; the other two, WNP-1 and WNP-3, had been mothballed for two years. BPA had guaranteed all the indebtedness for WNP-1 but only 70% of the indebtedness for WNP-3. The other 30% of WNP-3 was owned by four investor-owned utility companies (IOUs) that planned to use the power to service their own areas.

The shared ownership arrangement was a problem. With WNP-3 two-thirds complete, both BPA and the IOUs had sunk a lot of money into it. Now BPA had to decide whether to complete WNP-3 or leave it mothballed. For the IOUs, the answer to this question was obvious. Their regulators did not permit them to include in the rates they charged customers the costs of any plant that was not actually generating electricity. That, of course, meant that until WNP-3 was complete, the IOUs had no way of servicing the hundreds of millions of dollars of debt on the plant except out of shareholder profits. Needless to say, they were anxious to complete construction on the plant.

But the IOUs were not the only ones that had a stake in BPA's decision on WNP-3. BPA and the publicly owned utilities that bought its power were not subject to the same regulations as the IOUs and were already including in their rates the costs of the unfinished plants. Also, many jobs in the communities where the plants were located depended on completing the plants. On the other hand, there were many in the Northwest who opposed nuclear power on principle and were ready to fight long and hard to keep any nuclear power plant from being finished.

After an extensive series of public meetings and detailed technical analysis, I concluded that it was cheaper for the region to keep the plants on ice. This was true in part because the region now had a surplus of power. But also, newer and cheaper sources of power were emerging as alternatives. So we chose to preserve WNP-1 and WNP-3 as future options.

That decision left the IOUs in a real bind, and it was unclear how they would survive. With their financial well-being in jeopardy, they sued BPA for $2.5 billion, saying we had breached our agreements on the project. Meanwhile, the CEOs of some of the region's largest IOUs called my boss, Donald Hodel, then secretary of energy, and demanded my resignation. Hodel didn't take sides but made a point of telling me, in front of the CEOs, to find a way to reduce the tensions.

We wanted to work something out with the IOUs for practical reasons. Although we knew we had a strong legal position, litigation would drag on for years, and the uncertainty would affect BPA's credit.

All in all, we thought it best to work out some sort of compromise. Now Hodel was turning up the pressure.

I had to be careful, though, not to give the impression that I was going too far to accommodate the IOUs. Under the law, BPA's first obligation was to the publicly owned utilities. People were watching to make sure I didn't sell out to the IOUs—a move many people suspected because of my background in the private sector.

I had to get the IOUs, the public-power organizations, as well as the senators, governors, industrial groups, and public-interest groups to buy into an agreement. And the agreement not only had to be fair but also look fair. The only way out, I concluded, was to have an open public process. We decided to begin by having BPA meet separately with the IOUs and the public-power group. Subsequently, we would hold open public meetings. This strategy pleased no one, particularly the IOU community. The chief executive of a California utility phoned me to inquire whether I'd gone mad to try to settle a giant and bitter lawsuit in a glass house.

We went ahead with the process. At our first meeting, the IOUs' lawyers expressed their outrage at the prospect of public consultation. I explained why BPA was proceeding with public involvement and told them that the agency staff and I were meeting the very next day with representatives of more than 100 public-utility customers to seek their input. At that point, the most intransigent fellow in the group blew up. "I knew it!" he exclaimed. "You have no intention of settling."

The meeting with the representatives of public power was equally tense. More than 100 people were there, at least half of them lawyers. I took a deep breath before entering the room and was greeted with hoots and hollers. They were convinced that I was the guy who was going to sell them out. Charges and countercharges flew. When Bob Ratcliffe, BPA's deputy administrator and a longtime advocate of public power, tried to present an idea, there were so many interruptions that few people understood what he was saying.

We had a long way to go. When we reported back to the IOUs the tenor of the meeting with the public utilities, one CEO was more convinced than ever that it would be impossible to reconcile the differences. It took a real act of faith not to argue with his conclusion. Still, I refused to give up on the process.

As BPA staff, which included our general counsel and the chief lawyer representing the Department of Justice, and I shuttled back and forth from one group to the other over a period of months, people gradually began to understand that there were intelligent people with good ideas on both sides of the public power-private power divide. Reconciliation seemed a less remote possibility. Admittedly, the willingness to reach a resolution was partly attributable to the fact that if we didn't reach an agreement, I was going to take my own proposal to the public. The two factions would have little control over the process from then on. If they wanted the public to review a settlement that they found acceptable, they had to reach a tentative agreement.

By early 1985, after about a dozen meetings, a settlement package looked feasible. The proposal stipulated that BPA would agree to exchange surplus hydropower in the spring for output from the IOUs' combustion turbines, which were frequently idle. That way, both parties would get something of value at little cost.

Then it was time to expand our process to reach out to the general public. We began by issuing a press release that explained the lawsuit, the settlement, and the decision-making process. Then BPA staff contacted hundreds of people who would be interested in the outcome, including four governors. We kept a written record of each contact and made that information public. We also conducted monthly teleconferences with various interest groups.

We thought we were on the home stretch, but we began to hear complaints that the public-power constituency had not been part of the face-to-face negotiations. It was true, although a key part of the proposed settlement—a plan to link the rate for hydropower BPA would supply to the IOUs to the average price of three comparable nuclear plants elsewhere in the country—had come from meetings with the publicly owned utilities. With some trepidation, the four private utilities agreed to meet face-to-face with representatives from the public utilities.

By the time the settlement documents were signed in September 1985, BPA's investment in public involvement had paid off handsomely. The utilities, public and private, were satisfied. The politicians were satisfied, as were their constituents. We had saved the investor utilities from serious financial stress, and we had avoided wasteful legal battles.

Making Controversy Constructive

With these victories, BPA was again strong enough to play its important role in the region, and my tenure was coming to an end. But before I left the organization, I had one loose end to tie up. The formal public-involvement policy had still not completed its rounds at BPA. I discovered that a close assistant had managed to keep it bottled up in different parts of the organization. Finally, I marched into his office and told him I wouldn't leave until it was signed. Apparently that was enough of a threat. The policy was complete within a few weeks, which meant that BPA's commitment to public participation would not disappear when I walked out the door.

In fact, that commitment has grown stronger, and it has been formally recognized. Senator Mark Hatfield praised BPA in the *Congressional Record* for its approach to solving the Northwest's energy problems. And BPA received an award from the Natural Resources Defense Council—once an outspoken critic of BPA—as an outstanding utility in North America, a model for both public and private systems.

Having seen BPA's many victories, I am more convinced than ever that public involvement is a tool that today's managers in both public and private institutions must understand. With external stakeholders now exerting substantial influence on organizations in every sector, conflict is inevitable. The only choice is whether to dodge the controversy or learn to harness it.

Those who harness it by including third parties rather than trying to vanquish them will have the opportunity to consider new possibilities and to test out new ideas in the heat of dialogue. While others are mired in disputes and litigation, astute practitioners of public involvement will have hammered out an agreement and gotten on with the project. In short, they will have made better decisions and found a new source of competitive advantage.

2

Crime and Management: An Interview with New York City Police Commissioner Lee P. Brown

Alan M. Webber

As commissioner of the New York City Police Department, Lee P. Brown faces two enormous challenges. The first is crime. In 1989 in New York City, 712,419 crimes were reported, including 1,905 murders, 93,377 robberies, and 3,254 rapes. As Brown is quick to point out, the situation has grown so severe that people in cities are afraid. It is, Brown says, comparable to a national health emergency, with causes deeply rooted in U.S. social and economic systems and with solutions beyond the capacity of the police to provide alone.

Brown's second challenge is management. The New York City Police Department consists of 26,756 uniformed and 9,483 nonuniformed personnel and is more than twice the size of the Chicago Police Department, the nation's next largest. Its assets include more than 2,000 police cars, 625 scooters, 83 motorcycles, 10 boats, 5 helicopters, 107 horses, 26 dogs, and 4 robots. Its 1990 budget was $1.6 billion, 94% of which went directly into salaries and personnel services.

Lee Brown has determined to combine these two challenges by totally redefining the mission and operating style of the department. According to Brown, "traditional" policing—where officers respond to 911 calls and patrol in cars—is both inadequate to the challenge of crime and a mismanagement of police resources.

Instead, Brown advocates a new approach—"community policing." The concept is simple in some respects, a throwback to the days of the cop on the beat. But in practice, Brown's shift to community policing represents as ambitious—and risky—an undertaking as any major corporate turnaround or restructuring effort. The move to community policing requires a change in operations—cops walking beats, getting to know people in the community, and solving problems rather than riding in patrol cars and responding to 911 calls. But more fundamentally, it entails the creation of a new culture for the police department, new human resource practices, including hiring, promotion, recognition, and extensive training and retraining of officers and managers. It will mean a change in the command-and-control, paramilitary model of police management and the forging of a new partnership between the police and the people in the neighborhoods they protect, the private sector, and other departments in the city government.

Lee Brown comes to the challenge with a master's degree in sociology, a doctorate in criminology, and a record of accomplishment in police administration and teaching. Prior to his appointment in January 1990 by New York City Mayor David Dinkins, Brown had served as public safety commissioner in Atlanta, Georgia, chief of police in Houston, Texas, and director of the department of justice services in Multnomah County, Oregon. He is currently president of the International Association of Chiefs of Police.

HBR: *How do you assess the performance of police departments in U.S. cities today?*

Lee P. Brown: Our traditional role is to arrest and incarcerate people, and we are very good at that. We're arresting people in record numbers. In fact, prison overcrowding is the biggest problem in most states. In New York City, we arrest over 300,000 people a year. A few years ago, the New York City jail system had a capacity of 6,000 inmates. Today we have over 21,000 inmates in our jails and more than 55,000 in our state prisons.

The fact is, crime is higher now than ever before, and the police know that things aren't working. If you ask police officers around America, "Are you happy with what you're doing?" anyone who's honest will answer, "no." The marketplace knows it too. If we were a business, you'd have to say that our market share is declining. People who can afford it are hiring private security; there are more private security personnel today than there are public-sector police. The reason is simple. People are not satisfied with the police service they're receiving.

Any logical, thinking person would tell you that traditional approaches are not solving the problem. Our legacy should not be more prisons. We must look at the underlying factors that produce crime. And if we're serious, we must make a commitment to deal with them.

That means meaningful employment for all Americans. That means an educational system that produces people who can read and write, so they can get a job. Education is critical, and yet a large number of our young people are estranged and alienated from the school system. We're still educating people with a mass-production mentality. But the United States is not a mass-production society anymore.

If we don't address the causes of crime, I fully expect that 20 years from now we will still have a major problem. We'll still have prison overcrowding. People will still be losing their lives. And not to the levels that we have reached with those problems now, but worse.

You say that you're losing market share. How does the public, your customer, look at the crime situation?

Fear of crime is a huge problem in America today. In the large cities, people are afraid. They're afraid to walk the streets. Twenty years ago, if you talked to businesspeople about what concerned them, they'd say internal theft. Now they're concerned about the safety of their employees on the way to work, at work, and on the way home.

Why have things deteriorated so badly?

We are abandoning our cities to the truly disadvantaged. The unemployment rate for young blacks is still twice that of whites. And that's deeply related to our serious crime problem. The leading cause of death of young black males between the ages of 15 and 24 is homicide. The Centers for Disease Control has called it an epidemic. Young black males are more likely to be killed than our soldiers were during a tour of duty in the Vietnam War.

Over 2,000 homicides occurred in New York City last year. Over 20,000 homicides in America. If that many people lost their lives to a single disease in one year, we'd consider it an emergency, a national health problem. We would start to examine the factors behind the statistics to isolate them and find a solution. For example, what the mosquito was to malaria, the gun and the young black man's environment are to homicide. Now, you don't just keep swatting the mosquito, you drain the swamp. We need to drain the swamp of guns. We need to teach conflict resolution in our schools. We need to use city emergency wards to intervene early in the lives of regular victims of violence and abuse.

Why isn't this simply a police problem?

This country's social problems are well beyond the ability of the police to deal with on their own. In the United States, we don't have a full employment policy where every American willing and able to work can get a job. In fact, as a matter of policy this country believes that it's necessary always to have a certain percentage of unemployed. As a result, we have an underclass in our cities that is generally made up of minorities.

In addition, we've suffered a moral decline as a result of fundamental changes in the U.S. family structure. Today the home is more like a dormitory. You come in, you eat, you sleep, and you go about your own way.

In the United States, we deal with social failures by using the criminal justice system to sweep the debris under the rug. We sweep the debris into jail. We imprison more of our citizens than any other country in the world. But that only makes the problem more difficult to solve. Social problems are the real causes of crime that we all must work on if we are concerned about our future.

You are currently the president of the International Association of Chiefs of Police. How does the United States compare with the rest of the world?

There's an enormous difference between crime and violence in the United States and in other countries. Other countries don't create an underclass. In Japan, for example, the private sector cushions the callousness of the marketplace. You don't have the kind of unemployment in Japan that we see in the United States. The government takes care of people in Scandinavian countries.

I was in Japan. They had not seen crack cocaine in the whole country. The homicide rate for Tokyo was .8 per 100,000 in 1989 compared with 22.7 per 100,000 in New York City. There are more murders each year in New York than in all of Japan. Guns are not available. In their culture, people obey the law. Their family structure is still intact.

You don't have to go to Japan to see national differences. Go to Toronto. Go to Germany. Their educational systems are much more advanced and, again, you don't see the proliferation of guns or the link between drugs and violence that we experience.

What do you think makes the difference?

The United States has three serious problems. First, in most large cities, 40% to 50% of those who start school never finish. Of those who do finish, 25% are functional illiterates. They can't read, they can't write. Second, the workplace is changing. We have a significant decline in manufacturing jobs. Some 80% of Americans earn their living at a service occupation, often linked to high tech. When you tie these two points together, you get an educational system that is not producing people with the knowledge and skills to enter the new workplace. Third, we have an epidemic of drugs in America. Drugs are America's number one domestic problem. Unless we get a handle on the drug problem, it will continue to change America as we know it today.

What is the impact of drugs?

Drugs have changed the complexion of crime in America. We are developing a culture that tolerates violence. We have a society that is increasingly insensitive to violence in the minority community. The public is aroused when violence affects the middle class directly.

The crack epidemic has precipitated an explosion of violent crime, unlike anything we've ever experienced. We have a proliferation of illegal guns on the streets. In New York City, we confiscated over 17,000 illegal guns last year. Now we even have small children terrified, seriously injured, and losing their lives.

But the future implications of widespread crack use are even more frightening. In New York City, for example, 50% of crack users today are female. They're having babies, and those babies are now entering the school system. We don't know all the implications for the health and education of these children. But we do know that they are born smaller than other babies, the circumference of their heads is smaller, their brains are smaller. We don't know just how far the damage is going to go.

What will it take to get a handle on the drug problem? Is it a question of hiring more police officers?

Yes, we do need adequately staffed police departments, but we need much more. We must do no less in addressing the crime problem than we have done in winning the war in the Middle East. We must commit all the resources necessary to make a difference. But it isn't feasible or desirable to think about continually increasing the number of police officers. First, we couldn't afford it. We simply don't have the money. No matter how many officers you had, you could never have enough to use traditional policing techniques to deter crime.

Why do you think that traditional policing won't get the job done?

You have to understand the two key tenets of traditional policing. The first is to put police officers in patrol cars and have them respond to incidents, to 911 calls. The second is to have officers randomly patrol their beats so that the potential criminals never know where the officers will show up. That is supposed to act as a deterrent to crime.

What really happens is quite different. First, we end up with police officers being managed by the telephone. They only respond to incidents, rather than taking action to solve the underlying problems. Police officers are always under pressure to get back into their cars, to be available for another call. As a result, a small percentage of the population, the people who keep making 911 calls, consumes a vast majority of police resources.

Second, random patrol only produces random results. It's logical: if you don't have a police officer to cover every part of the city all the time, the chance of an officer on patrol coming across a crime in progress is very small. Research supports this conclusion. There are several decades of studies that show that random patrol makes no difference. The most dramatic is a Kansas City study that analyzed three areas of the city. In one area, they intensified the patrol. In another, they used the regular level of patrol. In the third, they did no patrolling at all. There was no difference in terms of the actual crime level or the perception of crime by the residents of the three areas.

But 911 was supposed to provide better service. Why are 911 calls a problem now?

Unfortunately, 911 has become the public's access point to all government services, not just true emergencies. The assumption in most cities is that there should be a rapid response to every 911 call. Now police officers in regular patrol cars spend 90% of their time just responding to 911 calls. In 1989 in New York City, we took nearly 8.3 million 911 calls. That turned into almost 4.3 million radio runs for our officers to make, or more than 11,700 runs per day. And the public has begun to exaggerate the problems they report, thinking it will get a cop there faster. If they want an officer because there's a loud argument in the apartment next door, they'll call 911 and report a shooting, thinking that makes us come faster. The result of all these calls is that the police have no time to do anything else, to get to know people in their area, to solve problems. But there are actually very few calls that need a rapid response; a life-threatening situation, for example, or if there's the potential to catch someone when a crime is in progress.

If this approach to policing isn't working and won't work, how has it become accepted in every U.S. city?

When we first started having police in America, we actually had more of a community-oriented policing style, exemplified by the old cop on the beat who knew people. He was an integral part of the community. He was able to maintain order, and most parts of the community respected him. Perhaps not in the black community, where the police were part of a system of discrimination and segregation, but in most parts of the community, the cop was respected.

That changed because of corruption, because politicians interfered in the operations of the police, and because of mobilization, putting cops in cars. We adopted the professional model of policing, an approach that intentionally detached the police from the community. It's the old "Dragnet" mentality that you used to see on television: "All we want are the facts, ma'am, just the facts." We don't want to know anything about you. We just pulled up in our cars, and we only want the facts. Along with that mentality came a move toward management based on command-and-control, a paramilitary approach to management.

How does the command-and-control approach operate in policing?

Managers in companies know all about organizational pyramids and rigid lines of reporting. As paramilitary organizations, police departments follow that same model but to an even greater extent. The command-and-control culture of the police department doesn't treat officers as intelligent, creative, and trustworthy people. It allows them very little discretion. It's designed to make sure that they don't get into trouble, don't embarrass the department, and don't get their supervisors into trouble.

I remember when I was a cop on the beat back in the 1960s. I was so frustrated, I even wrote an article called "College-Educated Police Officers: An Unforeseen Problem." Here I was, a college-educated person, a pretty intelligent person, and I thought I had a lot to offer. But there was no opportunity for me to use any of it. Anything I did was prescribed for me. I couldn't use my training in any meaningful way. That's the paramilitary model. Everything should be predictable. We need rules and regulations that cover everything. And if a police officer violates one, then the system catches him or her. It's an approach that doesn't allow officers to be creative, to use their intelligence, or to take a risk in solving problems.

What do you advocate as an alternative management approach?

I look at the police mission in a context broader than what the textbooks say about protecting life and property by making arrests. The police are a service organization for the city that doesn't close at 5:00 P.M. We have 24-hour-a-day, 7-day-a-week service. So my mission is to use the resources of the department to improve the quality of life of the citizens of this city. To me that means community policing. It means a cop back on the beat, the way it used to be.

There are two major tenets to community policing. The first is problem solving. It's the same principle that companies are using, empowering workers. Officers are trained and empowered to solve problems, rather than merely responding to incidents over and over again. The second is citizens' involvement, expanding the resource that the police have at their disposal. Again, just as companies are finding new ways for customers to participate in improvement, we have a virtually untapped resource of community groups, the private sector, and other city agencies, all of which can help us do community problem solving.

People today are more concerned about what happens in the neighborhoods and, at the same time, relying less on government and doing more themselves to improve the quality of life. They realize that crime is a community problem, not just a police problem. And if crime is a community problem, then it's logical that the whole community has a responsibility to address it.

So far, what's been the experience with community policing around the country?

Community policing has never been tried, not the way we're trying it. Not many police chiefs have tried to change the culture of their organization. Most of them are products of their own departments. Success is based on their ability to conform. So change has not been a top priority. In fact, coming in as an outsider, I think I have a better chance to succeed with community policing. I have more experience with other police departments. I know what a police agency should be and what's been tried elsewhere. And I don't have any baggage. I can protect the operational integrity of the department from political interference. One of the good things about the police commissioner's job in New York is that it is an independent position. The mayor does not try to interfere in running the department, and nobody else can. Regardless of what anyone may think, there's no politician who can reassign an officer, discipline an officer, promote an officer. Officers should never have to worry about the politics of doing their jobs.

Haven't there been experiments to implement community policing?

Up to now, community policing has been viewed as a program. A few years back, New York tried "team policing." Under it, a small number of people were doing community policing. But the whole rest of the organization went about its business, doing everything else exactly the way it had been done before. We've also had "Park, Walk, and Talk," where officers park their cars, get out, and walk and talk with people. We've also initiated a program we call "Cops Block," where each officer is assigned one or more blocks.

But like any change program in any company, you can't keep the same training system, evaluation system, reward system, and expect to change the way you police the city. My goal is to change all those systems to be supportive of community policing and not supportive of our traditional way of doing business.

What would you point to if you wanted people to have some idea of what community policing looks like and how it works?

The Community Patrol Officer Program, or CPOP, has come the closest to community policing. It was first tried out in 1984 in one precinct, and when I got here every precinct had 10 CPOP officers. CPOP is viewed as a foot patrol program.

Now, I don't intend to take CPOP as it is and say that is community policing. I want every officer in this department to operate under the concept of community policing, not just those on patrol. That means detectives, it means Narcotics. It means abandoning and eliminating many of the specialized units. In fact, by reassigning people from special units and restructuring the entire patrol force, we will increase the number of officers engaged in community policing by more than 30 times from where it was when I started.

Have you got a plan for implementing community policing in New York?

We recently completed a staffing plan that calls for 17,400 officers and 3,999 detectives to provide services with community policing as our dominant style. But we won't reach that level for four years, and I don't intend to wait four years to implement community policing. For that reason, I initiated a strategic planning process and in January produced a report entitled "Policing New York City in the 1990s: The Strategy for Community Policing."

Our plan is to take one precinct—the 72nd, which is located in the Sunset Park section of the Bronx, and make it a model precinct. It's where we started the pilot project of CPOP, so we'll just go back to where we started. We'll staff it up to the level that we will have citywide in four years and fully implement community policing in that precinct. That means training, new roles, and looking at different performance evaluation systems. That means a new reward system. That means integrating everything in the precinct into the community policing philosophy and getting a snapshot now of what the whole thing will look like in four years. In the other 74 precincts, we will implement all aspects of community policing possible with existing resources.

There really is no manual that describes how to implement community policing. We're writing the manual here in New York. We're changing everything, from the role of the police officer to the role of the commissioner.

The police culture is a very powerful one that places a premium on making arrests. How do you answer the criticism leveled by some officers that community policing isn't "real" police work?

Community policing is not soft on crime. Community policing is tougher on crime than traditional policing because it's smarter. A good community police officer will make more arrests than the regular beat officer because he or she will get more information.

Let me give you an example from Houston. We had an officer who tried community policing in a neighborhood where there wasn't even a sense of community. He pulled people together so successfully that they even gave their neighborhood a name. In a way, he created the community.

In this area, there was a rash of break-ins where the burglars were armed and showed no hesitancy to shoot. Under traditional policing, the neighborhood would have blamed the police: "What's wrong with you? Why can't you catch these guys?" Instead, the community organized itself. People handed out flyers describing the pattern of the crimes and what to look for. As a result, one citizen called in because of some suspicious circumstances, and we caught the burglars. Instead of blaming the police, the citizens joined the police.

That would never have happened under traditional policing. Under traditional policing, there would have been a lot of scared people, a lot of finger pointing, but no progress toward solving the problem. Community policing is based on the realization that most crimes are solved with information that comes from people. The better your relationship with the people, the more information you'll get.

Where do you begin the process of moving to community policing?

In policing, as in business, change always starts with a vision. My vision is community policing as our dominant style. Then, we must change our culture to match our vision. Values play an important role in that. Every organization has values. In police agencies, they usually develop without any managerial input. I want everyone in our organization to understand what our values are. So I'll be writing them down and distributing them throughout the department. They'll become the basis for everything that follows.

After that, we'll start at the top to make these changes. You can't expect cops on the beat to be successful if their supervisors and managers don't understand and support the change. So my strategy has been to start with my executive staff, to change its mind-set. Each member of my executive staff has responsibility for a piece of the organization. One has patrol, another Narcotics, another detectives, another human resources. I want them all to have a corporate mind-set, so they will be responsible for the well-being of the whole department, not just their particular area.

For example, when I became commissioner, I called them all together for weekly meetings of the executive staff. It was the first time
they regularly met as a group. As we implement community policing,
they will keep their areas of responsibility, but already they're beginning to ask how new initiatives in any area will fit in with the depart-
mentwide shift to community policing.

What's the next step in the change process?

We have to change our recruiting system. We hire today by elimi-
nation. We don't select; we eliminate. We put people through tests
designed to eliminate candidates. At the end, whoever's left, we hire.
I want to change that so we select people who have characteristics that
fit with community policing.

I want to bring in people who are better educated, people who are
better equipped to deal with problems that often defy easy solutions.
Someone who understands sociology can understand the dynamics of
groups and community problems. Someone who understands psychology is better able to understand the complexities of the human mind.
Those skills are good for police work. I also want to bring in people
who come to policing more with the spirit of service and less with the
spirit of adventure. We are not looking for people who are simply
looking for action.

Do you intend to change the makeup of the force?

The composition of the police should reflect the ethnic composition
of the community. Any citizen should be able to look at the police
department and say, "That reflects me." That should be true in the
ranks and all the way up. And it should be true for Hispanics, Asians,
blacks, Jews, women; there should be wide diversity. We don't have
that now. One of my goals is to bring people in who historically have
not been sought after. Another goal is to make sure that every New
York police officer has the ability to work anyplace in the city. To do
that, we must provide cultural training and sensitivity training. We
can't expect that someone who comes from upper New York State,
grew up in an all white neighborhood, and went to an all white school
will understand what it's like to live in Harlem. We have to give them
the training they need to do their job.

How do you respond to the concern expressed by some that standards may suffer in an attempt to bring more minorities into the department?

I reject absolutely the notion that you have to lower standards to get minorities. In fact, if you look at the education levels of our people, the minorities are better educated than the whites. The real question is, how do you raise standards for everyone? Can I say that everyone who enters the New York City Police Department must have a four-year degree? Probably not. But I can probably say that anyone who wants to be a New York City police officer must have two years of college.

My goal is to create a continuous flow of people going through the college system here in New York and going on to become police officers. We have a cadet program that hires young college students and gives them a stipend so that when they finish college they can become police officers. I want to expand that to two-year college programs where there are more minorities and increase the number of students in the program from a couple of hundred to 1,000. I'm also supporting federal legislation that gives students loans for college. After four years of service as police officers, the loan is forgiven.

In addition to hiring changes, do you plan other personnel shifts as a part of community policing?

We have to change completely how we train people, both at the entrance level and also in-service. One of my first moves was to bring in a new director of training because as we move to community policing, training is critical. We have to unprogram people from where they are and reprogram them to where we're going. The cops are doing now what we've taught them to do, what we've trained them to do. They don't know anything different. Under our traditional training, we spend 90% of our time training officers to do what they spend 15% of their time doing, that is, making arrests, enforcing the law.

We don't teach young officers the techniques of problem analysis, of identifying and coming up with strategies to solve problems. We don't teach them how to organize a neighborhood in order to deal with neighborhood problems. We don't teach officers how to help neighborhoods develop their own capacity to improve the quality of life.

We have to make this part of everyone's training. I'm going to every one of our 75 precincts to explain community policing. I'm regularly sending out videotapes that will be played at every roll call, explaining different aspects of community policing. I'm talking to every new class that enters the Police Academy. When officers are promoted to sergeant, I talk to the sergeants' class. When they are promoted to lieutenant, I talk to the lieutenants' class. When they're promoted to captain, I talk to the captains' class. As we implement community policing, we'll use the people who are actually doing it as advocates and experts. They're the ones who know that it works. They're the ones who will spread the message. They are the ones who will improve our current understanding of how to do it.

If the change is top down, how will you carry it down into the ranks?

We will take it down into the ranks by intensive training. I am running executive sessions where we bring in people from all ranks to assist in the process. We're doing this right now to design a training program. We bring in the cop on the beat. We bring in his or her supervisor, the manager, and my executive staff, and we ask, "What knowledge, skills, and abilities does one need to serve as a police officer in this department under our new style of policing?" When we have an answer, we'll give it to our training people to use in revising the curriculum. Ultimately, everybody will be trained in community policing.

You've talked about hiring and training. Are there other fundamental changes in the management of the department?

We also have to change the reward system. In most police agencies, rewards are based on valor. If you're in a shootout, if you're shot or you shoot someone else, if you capture a dangerous person, you get special recognition. Usually a lot of danger and excitement go along with achieving a reward.

What about rewarding people for thinking and being creative? We recently gave an award to an officer who made a suggestion about licensing unlicensed livery cabs that will save the city a few million dollars in the short run. That officer didn't have to do that. But he was a thinking, creative person. He saw a problem and came up with a solution. Our reward system should recognize people who solve problems, who use their minds, who think.

We will also change our entire performance evaluation system. Under our traditional system, we evaluate officers on how many arrests they make, how many summonses they issue. But the ultimate evaluation should not be the arrests but the absence of arrests, when there's no crime. If you have no crime on your beat, then you are doing the job you should be doing. There's peace of mind in the community.

Under community policing, what kind of a cop do you want?

I want officers who are generalists, who will be responsible for a small area of the city. Everything possible should be handled at this neighborhood level. Even detectives should be assigned neighborhood responsibilities, rather than just to special units. The police officer becomes a manager of an area. And the role of the first-line supervisor all the way up to the commissioner is to make sure that police officers have the resources to solve the problems in their areas.

That means we're going to minimize the number of layers between the officer on the beat and the commissioner. We're going to cut down on bureaucracy and specialization. We don't want a lot of bureaucratic layers that only hamper us from getting the job done. Overall, our emphasis will be on enhancing the role of the officers out there on the beat, giving them responsibility and authority, allowing them to take risks, and not punishing them for making innocent mistakes.

You talked earlier about the command-and-control management style. Will that change under community policing?

We have to trust our cops. We hire intelligent people, people who are creative. But we don't give them the ability to use that creativity and initiative because of our great concern for command-and-control. We have to give them the opportunity to do the right thing and at the same time understand that they will sometimes make mistakes. But there are two different kinds of mistakes—mistakes of the mind and mistakes of the heart. If you're doing something out of malice, then you've got a problem with me. But if you're trying to do your job and you make an innocent mistake that may violate a rule, the entire circumstance should be taken into account. If we want people to take risks, we have to tolerate mistakes. Ultimately, we want our officers to recognize that they are professionals, and we want the organization to treat them as professionals.

What would you say is the central focus of all these changes?

Community policing empowers the officer on patrol. Under community policing, the officer becomes the most important person in the neighborhood. The cop on the beat is the chief of police for each neighborhood. I see the cop on the beat as a manager, not just answering calls, not just walking the beat, but being able to do problem analysis, knowing the people, being accessible. It means taking ownership of the area.

The backbone of the police department is out there in patrol. Yet today everyone wants to get out of patrol. All the perks come from other places, in special assignments, in detectives. To get monetary rewards, you have to get promoted. Under community policing, we will enhance the patrol officer's status to make it equal to any other in the department. There will be a career path in patrol so that people can spend whole careers in patrol.

How do you expect your customers, the people of New York City, to respond to these changes and to community policing?

People in neighborhoods like community policing because they get to know their police officers. They see something happen. There's a different level of accountability. The officer is not only accountable to the police department but also to the community. Officers will be responsible for knowing the quality-of-life issues and crime problems of a specific area or neighborhood and accountable for doing something about them and reporting back to the people what they've done. The community will be able to see an actual difference in terms of problem solving, rather than being confronted with the same problems over and over again.

How will patrol officers know what problems the community wants them to go after?

Historically, when the police have tried to define what people are concerned about, we've missed the boat. Police think that citizens are exclusively preoccupied with serious crime, like murders, rapes, and robberies. They are concerned about those crimes, but they are also concerned about quality-of-life issues. The drug dealing in the park, noisy kids hanging out on the street corner, the problems of homeless people in the neighborhood. These things can be signs of crime, they can create the incivility that exists on the street corners of the city, they can make people feel unsafe. These are the things that are important to people.

Now if we were to make the judgment, we would miss the mark. We've always missed the mark. That's why we have to empower the people to help us define what's important and to define how to deal with it. Who knows more about what's going on in the community than the people who live there? They not only know what causes the crimes, but they probably know who commits them as well.

Why can't you just use data, such as the official crime statistics, to determine police priorities?

Just as businesses today are looking for new measurements of performance, the Uniform Crime Reports don't have much meaning for a police department. All they tell us is how many crimes were reported. Two or three times more crimes are probably committed than are ever reported. In reality, the Uniform Crime Reports measure the degree to which the people in a city respect their police and criminal justice system. Take the example of Portland, Oregon and Newark, New Jersey. It used to be that Portland always reported much more crime than Newark. But all that meant was that there was a much higher level of confidence in Portland about its police and criminal justice system. More people believed that it mattered if they actually reported crimes that were committed. In fact, victimization studies that ask people if they have been victims of a crime give a much more accurate picture. But again, you have to go to people and ask them, rather than simply relying on internally generated numbers.

How do you think community policing should be evaluated?

Crime is clearly important, but I don't want the police department to be judged solely on crime. To begin with, we don't control the factors that produce criminal behavior. As we implement community policing, with different neighborhoods having different needs, different priorities, and different problems, customer satisfaction will depend on how well we deliver our services to match the characteristics of each neighborhood. Ultimately, if we want to measure customer satisfaction with the police, we will have to create new measurements.

What is your toughest management challenge in implementing community policing?

The police, more than any other agency, have always looked at themselves as being an independent entity. In some cities, they don't even consider themselves part of government. I believe that the police are an integral part of government, a resource that the taxpayers pay for, a resource that should be used for the larger benefit of the community.

That doesn't mean that police officers become social workers. It does mean that police officers need to deal with solving problems. It does mean that we need to make sure that police officers can become advocates for neighborhoods and help them develop their own ability to deal with their problems. It does mean that we expand the role of the police beyond the narrow focus of simply responding to calls and making arrests. It does mean that we empower people to work with us.

What is your own measure of success?

At some point in the future, I want everybody in New York to know who their police officer is. Literally, to be able to say, "Officer Jones is my police officer. He's responsible for taking care of me." I want people, when they see a police officer, whether he or she is in a car, on a motor scooter, or on foot, to look to see if that's their police officer. And I want every police officer to develop an ownership of his or her community. I want them to say, "I'm not going to let something happen to this neighborhood. I'm responsible for it." I want ownership both ways. Once that happens, everything else will fall into place.

Appendix

FOUR HOURS ON THE WEST SIDE: LISTENING TO THE RANK AND FILE

One rainy evening last January, I spent four hours in a New York City police patrol car, listening to the radio call out jobs, responding to 911 calls, and mostly listening to two officers talk about policing. Also, I had the chance to listen to small groups of officers as they talked among themselves about their work, both within the station house and informally outside it. Like the work force of a solid company, the cops I met were good guys and good cops. They cared deeply about their work and their city—and were deeply pessimistic about their capacity to reclaim the city from the criminals. They were interested in Commissioner Lee Brown's idea of community policing—and were cynically streetwise about its chances of success. They constantly exercised their own judgment and discretion in deciding what activities on the street to respond to, what to ignore, and how to respond appropriately—and were angry to the point of paranoia in watching out for supervisors who might be following them to try to catch them violating some minor rule.

We were on the west side of Manhattan in an area that the cops described as an average precinct. It has its share of expensive apartments bordering Central Park, but it also has housing projects. It has a school, and it has a park that has been taken over by crack addicts, at least at night. It has its share of auto theft, drug dealing, and disturbances. And it has its share of average New Yorkers, getting along with their lives.

For the record, in our four hours of patrolling, we were involved with only three incidents worth reporting. In the first, we arrived at a supermarket where a young black male had been apprehended for attempting to shoplift $70 worth of instant coffee. We were one of three cars, each with two cops, that converged on the store. The suspect, in handcuffs, standing in the supermarket aisle, seemed genuinely astonished that he could attract so much attention over so few jars of instant coffee. The cops' judgment: he was stealing the coffee to sell to bodegas for drug money.

Our second 9111 call was to respond to an EDP—an "emotionally disturbed person"—who was calling the police for help because he was feeling suicidal. We found the young white male, still holding on to the telephone on the street corner, and I listened while the two cops gently and considerately explained to him that they were going to get him to a hospital where he could get some help. Again, before he could be transported to the hospital, two more cars on patrol arrived on the scene.

The third 911 call took us to a small vest-pocket park where a young black male had been apprehended for snatching a $5 bill out of the hand of a black woman standing in a grocery line. By the time we got there, he had already been caught and was being searched for the $5. There were six police officers in the park, which was littered with the debris of drugs—empty crack vials scattered all over the ground. Again, the cops' judgment: a drug-related theft.

It turned out to be a slow night for 911 calls, so we took advantage of the time to talk about the problems of policing New York City. The views of the cops I talked with, both black and white, are summarized as follows:

The dominance of the civil service mentality. Cops know that if they make too many arrests, it will look to their supervisors as if they are simply trying to log overtime, since arrests invariably translate into expensive, time-consuming court appearances. On the other hand, if they bring in too few, it will look as if they aren't doing their job. The key to being a successful cop: don't stand out.

It's all politics. To the cop on the beat, one explanation covers virtually every situation: politics. Any decision that involves any degree of controversy is chalked up to politics. In particular, cops complain that they are constantly undermined by political concessions to neighborhood and minority groups, particularly when the cops have had to use force—sometimes deadly force—and the community turns up the political heat.

The city has gone downhill. It used to be that there were certain parts of New York that looked seedy and run-down. Now, say the cops, every borough has a section that looks like that. The police are even wondering if the deterioration has gone so far that it is hopeless to think about bringing the city back.

"It's going to work." Ideas come down from headquarters. Civilianization will mean that uniformed police can move out of clerical and other support jobs and be replaced by civilians who will do the job at less expense with the same quality. The response of the worldly wise cops: "It's going to work." In other words, once again we have to deny our own reality-tested beliefs and accept what headquarters wants to believe is true—even if all our experience on the street tells us it isn't true and it isn't going to work.

Standards have fallen. According to the cops, the emphasis on recruiting women and minorities has led to lower standards. They said that women are both weaker physically and less likely to respond to situations involving danger. In the case of minorities, both black and white cops felt that the department had lowered its overall standards to attract more minority candidates.

Drugs are the difference. Throughout the ride-along, the one constant theme was the prevalence of drugs and the change drugs had made in the neighborhood and in crime. Both the shoplifting and $5-bill incident were attributed to drugs. All night long, as we cruised the precinct, both cops talked about the drug dealers who were standing on the street corners. The cops looked at the drug dealers; the drug dealers looked at the cops. Each knew what the other was doing. But the cops couldn't touch the drug dealers since they were smart enough not to have drugs on them.

Cops in the middle. The prevailing sense of the cops was that they are caught in the middle and can't please anyone. They are concerned about allegations of improper behavior from other cops, from citizens, and from supervisors. "There are lots of ways to take the wind out of a cop's sails," they told me. "You can't please everyone." Cops are open to allegations of wrongdoing from criminals, which are investigated with the same diligence as a complaint from an average citizen. The result is that cops end up feeling that, when it comes to serving the public, they are "spitting into the wind."

"CPOP isn't real police work." The Community Patrol Officer Program is a nice idea, but you'll still need someone to answer the radio. People are addicted to 911. And CPOP will be expensive to implement. CPOP also blurs the line between social work and policing. Real police work entails responding to 911 calls and being in on arrests. It means earning your living by the level of activity in your precinct. On the other hand, most of the cops who had ever been assigned to CPOP remembered it with a certain fondness, and expressed a desire to "get away from the damned radio."

Good cops know how to handle people. Cops know what it takes to be a good cop. Cops know who is and who is not a good cop. There are cops, I was told, who can give the same guy three summonses and leave him smiling. And there are cops with Napoleonic complexes who will cause a riot over a single traffic ticket.

It will take support from above to make community policing work. The cops were willing to give the idea of community policing a chance. But they were clear on one point: if it is going to work, cops on patrol must have support from their supervisors. They need to feel that, if they go out and try to work with the community and if something goes wrong, headquarters will back them up. Otherwise, the cops will once again feel like they are caught in the middle.

3

The New Old-Fashioned Banking

Ronald Grzywinski

Fifteen minutes south of Chicago's Loop, the inner-city neighborhood of South Shore has an old-fashioned bank with a radical twist. For those of us at South Shore Bank, banking means knowing the borrower, the neighborhood, property values, and the economic environment. It means tough credit standards, cautious qualification of borrowers, and close monitoring of the projects and businesses we lend to. So while 20% of our community's population is below the poverty line, our bank's rate of loan failure is well below the national average.

Yet we also see banking as a philosophical return to the days when a bank was the pillar of its community and saw its role as investing in the community's future. And there's the twist, because for us, investing in the future also means banking as a force for economic development, banking as a way of restoring community self-confidence, banking that extends credit to hard-working people who have never known its power.

South Shore Bank is a throwback, almost literally, to the original precepts of the banking business. We believe in geographic service areas. In fact, we believe in both parts of that concept—that banks have local areas and that they owe those areas service.

We also believe that those ideas may be key to solving many poverty-related problems that plague society. Taking advantage of the legal powers granted bank holding companies in 1970, we have spent 18 years putting the principles of old-fashioned banking to work on a social agenda in South Shore. (To see how we've applied these ideas elsewhere, see "Spinning Off Development to Arkansas and Poland.")

Ironically, while we've run our bank on radical values and conservative principles, many banks have done just the opposite. They have grown larger and less community oriented. Banks that began as local institutions grew to national, even global proportions and came to focus more and more on the size, variety, and yield of their transactions, in some cases with dire results. The communities they originally served have changed very little; the banks themselves have changed enormously.

Spinning Off Development to Arkansas and Poland

There are three keys to successful community development. The most critical is some mechanism for releasing the energies of local residents, since they will contribute most of the necessary work and talent. In our experience, one excellent mechanism is credit.

The second key is for the development institution to control the resources needed for a comprehensive development program. A bank holding company not only controls the needed capital but can also set up subsidiaries to help with real-estate development, community organizing, small-business startup capital, and technical assistance to entrepreneurs.

The third key is for the institution and the process to be self-sustaining. Long-term community development cannot succeed when it depends on unreliable government funding or variable foundation grants.

These three factors point directly to the conclusion on which we have built our bank: the best way to achieve a community development agenda is with the hard discipline of business.

Over the past ten years, the Shorebank model has spread. Beginning in 1986, Shorebank began a community development program in Austin, another Chicago neighborhood suffering from disinvestment. Austin is what South Shore might have become if its decline had proceeded unchecked for another 20 years. In its worst sections, the buildings had all been abandoned, burned out, or bulldozed, and living conditions were sometimes sickening. A combination of local groups, the bank, and the bank's affiliates (City Lands and The Neighborhood Institute)—working with Austin entrepreneurs—have concentrated on housing rehab but have also done small-business training and job placement.

In 1987, we embarked on a physically much larger project in rural Arkansas. At the request of the Winthrop Rockefeller Foundation, we began putting together the Southern Development Bancorporation to accelerate the pace of economic activity in a 32-county area of southwestern Arkansas. Southern (as it is called) is a regulated bank holding company owned by a group of philanthropically motivated individuals, charitable foundations, and business corporations whose primary goal is to foster economic development, not to earn a substantial return on equity.

In 1988, Southern created the Opportunity Lands Corporation—a community development company focusing on industrial and commercial properties and residential housing low- and moderate-income residents—and the Arkansas Enterprise Group—a not-for-profit affiliate that owns and operates Southern Ventures Inc. (a for-profit Small Business Administration-licensed investment corporation) along with two other programs. The first is the Good Faith Fund, which makes short-term microloans (some as small as $250) to rural residents, and the second is Arkansas Manufacturing Services, which provides financing, marketing, and accounting services to small businesses. At the same time, Southern bought the Elk Horn Bank and Trust Company in Arkadelphia, to do full-service commercial banking and provide the unsubsidized credit that residents can use to exploit their own skills and create their own wealth.

Arkadelphia, the headquarters of our target area, is a town of 10,000 people, two colleges, and at least four major employers that moved away in the mid to late 1980s, taking with them more than 1,000 jobs. It's a common story in Arkansas. Twenty years ago, the state made aggressive use of its low labor costs to attract industry. But for the same reason that companies built plants in Arkansas in the 1960s, they've now moved those plants offshore, where labor is cheaper still. Arkansas has suffered badly for its lack of a truly indigenous economy. It is that local economy, those local market forces, that we would like to restore.

We're pursuing that same goal on the upper peninsula of Michigan, where we've gone into partnership with the Northern Economic Initiatives Center of Northern Michigan University. With funding from the state of Michigan and additional capital to be raised from foundations, individuals, and corporations, we intend to open a loan-production office to work with local banks and to create an integrated financing and business-support organization that will reduce the local economy's dependence on natural-resource extraction and help develop products for export out of the region.

Our most unusual undertaking is in Poland. In 1989, the U.S. Congress set up the Polish-American Enterprise Fund (PAEF), a quasi-public agency charged to try to jump start private enterprise in Poland with $240 million in public funds. To my delight, PAEF turned to Shorebank to implement two of its projects.

The first goal was to open small loan "windows" in eight existing Polish state banks. These windows are making loans of up to $20,000 to small, privately owned businesses, using $13 million of PAEF funds.

The second project is the establishment, in cooperation with local interests, of up to three private banks in Poland to provide loans primarily to small, private businesses and development projects. The first of these banks, the Poznan Market Bank, has existed since 1990—on a very small scale—and expects to greatly increase its deposit base and lending activities on the basis of a $3 million capital investment by PAEF.

Shorebank has overall responsibility for the management of these two projects, including personnel training in the United States and Poland, establishment of lending operations and policies, and the administration of lending programs.

The founding of South Shore Bank owes much to the principle of a bank and its service area. In the late 1960s, Mary Houghton, Milton Davis, Jim Fletcher, and I, who now make up the management team at the bank and its holding company, Shorebank Corporation, were all about 30 years old. During the day, we worked together doing successful minority lending at a bank in the Hyde Park section of Chicago. Most nights, we did volunteer work in community organizations, addressing things like better housing, crime prevention, child care—the whole litany of neighborhood needs. On Friday nights, however, we'd go to the Eagle Bar and talk about inner cities and what to do about them.

We were products of our times, inspired by the civil rights movement and the kind of idealism that John F. Kennedy espoused. We were also frustrated. We saw that community organizations had identified the right issues but lacked the capital and the technical competency to make a real difference. As keen observers of Lyndon Johnson's Great Society programs, we watched the federal government throw money at the cities—and then watched the cities fight over political control of the programs the money funded.

As bankers and community volunteers, we decided that the answer to rebuilding neighborhoods had to be some kind of business. It had to be self-sustaining; it had to have the independence of a capital base and the discipline of the profit motive. What we were imagining was a development bank—a bank that could be tough-minded about loans, qualify borrowers according to strict standards, satisfy the most demanding federal bank examiners, make a profit, and still transform an inner-city neighborhood without driving out those who lived there. We also imagined that such an institution already existed, and all we had to do was to find and copy it. As it happened, we've spent years working to create it.

While we were trying to picture the form this business would take, Congress and the Federal Reserve Board took two important steps that gave the business definition. First, Congress passed a measure known technically as the 1970 amendments to the Bank Holding Company Act. Those amendments directed the board of governors of the Fed to define permissible activities for bank holding companies. Then, one year later, the Fed came up with a list of activities that it defined as being closely related to the business of banking. The final one permitted bank holding companies to invest in community development corporations, provided the primary purpose was community development for the benefit of low- and moderate-income people.

That prompted us to ask two questions. First, if the Fed was willing to let bank holding companies invest in community development corporations, would it allow a bank holding company to *be* a community development corporation? Second, could we design a special bank holding company that would have a real-estate-oriented, community development subsidiary and a not-for-profit affiliate for job training and low-income housing instead of the usual credit-card and finance-company subsidiaries?

The answer to the second question, we found, was yes. It took us about a year to draw up what is still the basic structure of the Shore-bank Corporation and to incorporate. (See Exhibit I.)

Meanwhile, the Fed issued an interpretation of its own regulations, observing that bank holding companies possessed "a unique combination of financial and managerial resources, making them particularly suited for a meaningful and substantial role in remedying [the nation's] social ills." That answered question number one.

Oddly enough, the concept of a bank service area was what helped us find South Shore. While we were looking for a bank to buy, we saw a newspaper article about the sale of South Shore National Bank (as it then was) to a group of investors—the purchase conditional, however, on the bank getting permission from the federal Comptroller of the Currency to close its South Shore office and relocate in downtown Chicago. The investors argued that the neighborhood's racial transformation (in 1960 it was 100% white; by 1970, it was 70% black) had caused it to deteriorate economically and that as a result, the bank could no longer survive in South Shore.

People in the neighborhood decided to fight. They roused the com-

Exhibit I.

Shorebank Corporation

The South Shore Bank of Chicago. A full-service commercial bank and a 99% owned subsidiary of Shorebank. Offers commercial and neighborhood development loans and services.	City Lands Corporation. A real-estate development company. Develops and manages residential and commercial real estate for the benefit of low- and moderate-income residents.	The Neighborhood Fund. An SBA-licensed Minority Enterprise Small Business Investment Corporation. Finances business with equity investments and long-term subordinated debt.	The Neighborhood Institute. A 501(c)(3) tax-exempt affiliate. Operates economic- and social-development programs for low-income residents.	Shorebank Advisory Services. A consulting firm. Offers technical assistance on development banking and other community economic development strategies.
			TNI Development Corporation. A for-profit subsidiary of The Neighborhood Institute. Develops rental and cooperative housing for low-income residents.	

The Shorebank Corporation (known until 1986 as the Illinois Neighborhood Development Corporation) was incorporated in 1972. To make use of changes in the law enabling bank holding companies to take, in the Fed's words, "an active role in the quest for solutions to the nation's social problems," the company was designed to include, in addition to the bank, a real-estate development subsidiary, a small-business investment subsidiary, and a low-income assistance affiliate. Shorebank Advisory Services and the TNI Development Corporation were added later.

Source: Shorebank Corporation Annual Report, 1989.

munity, got some free legal assistance, and enlisted the help of Texas Congressman Wright Patman, then chairman of the House Banking Committee and a banking populist. Two hearings were held, the bank made some blunders in its case, and the application was turned down. In announcing his decision, the Comptroller of the Currency said the bank had "failed to show a persuasive reason for abandoning its service area."

Three days later, I asked if the bank was still for sale. It was, and for book value, which the Comptroller of the Currency agreed to reduce by cutting the capitalization in half, from $6.4 million to $3.2 million. We started to raise capital.

We were seeking $3.2 million in units of $160,000 to purchase a failing bank in a declining neighborhood in the Chicago metropolitan area to test a radical and perhaps unworkable idea. Our investors would have to be patient. They would have to tolerate a high degree of risk. They would have to have a strong desire to see a new kind of bank take shape. The money did not pour in.

Over the next few months, we raised only $800,000—from two individuals, several foundations, and the United Church of Christ Board of Homeland Ministries. Vastly undercapitalized and overleveraged, we walked into South Shore Bank on August 23, 1973 and took over as managers.

Communities are living things, which means they're involved in a constant process of building up and tearing down. Buildings deteriorate and businesses close; new buildings are built and new businesses open. In a prosperous, growing suburb, the building and growing are more rapid than the tearing down and wearing out. In a slum, the opposite is true.

Communities compete for everything—resources, businesses, people, and skills. Prosperous suburbs, with level upon level of buying power, wealth, knowledge, political connections, and corporate influence, get their pick of the richest, best educated residents, the best shops, and the best public servants. Poor inner-city communities have none of these advantages.

The community of South Shore has been both. In the 1940s and 1950s, it was considered the most attractive, most livable neighborhood inside the Chicago city limits. Brokers and bankers lived here, and, I'm told, the president of the Illinois Central Railroad. Our own 71st Street was the most prestigious shopping strip outside of Michigan Avenue, and at the Lake Michigan end of that strip was the South Shore Country Club, with its grand entrance hall, elegant dining rooms, and regal ballrooms.

Then in the course of a single decade, all those people left and a new population of 80,000 people moved in. The first blacks were escaping the slums. They rented apartments or bought small, single-family houses in the least affluent area of South Shore. They had middle-class incomes and aspirations, and they wanted a middle-class community to live in. But white flight took over, and South Shore went from lily white and middle class to overwhelmingly black and working class. More important, the equilibrium vanished, and the community went from growth to a spiral of decline. The flow of capital reversed direction; people stopped upgrading their homes; landlords stopped maintaining their apartment buildings; store owners stopped improving their businesses and began to close them or move them to other parts of Chicago.

Self-confidence disappeared, and the bank was contributing to the demoralization. In fact, all the institutions in South Shore—the civic organizations, the chamber of commerce, even the schools and churches—were sending the same message: South Shore cannot escape abandonment. But the bank was somehow the worst. People put such faith in the wisdom of bankers. When bankers stop investing in a neighborhood, people think they know something that lesser mortals don't.

Our view was simple: *we're* bankers, and we're here to tell the community that this is still a good neighborhood. It's not going down; it's going to get better. We're going to invest in it; they should too.

As we saw it, one of our chief purposes was to restore South Shore's competitiveness by rebuilding the market forces disinvestment had destroyed. The neighborhood was far from hopeless. A lot of storefronts were boarded up, but far from all. A dozen apartment buildings had been abandoned, but not more. The trouble was, every bank and savings-and-loan in town had red-lined South Shore, including the bank chartered to serve it—South Shore National Bank. In the year before we bought the bank, it had made exactly two conventional home-mortgage loans for a total of $59,000.

Of course, everyone believed we would fail. The first four or five years, we couldn't hire anyone with banking experience because no one believed a job with us had a future. Like the four of us years earlier, the people we ended up hiring came from nonbanking backgrounds but learned fast. Most of us were doing half a dozen different jobs at any given time. For example, Mary Houghton (now president of Shorebank Corporation), was in charge of recruitment, loan policy, loan-reject review, new accounts, new deposit programs, personnel development, and innovative small-business lending.

We tried hard to increase deposits, which had fallen from a peak of $80 million to about $42 million on the day we bought the bank. Like good, traditional bankers, we believed in the sanctity of the small savings account. We reasoned that deposits would climb again if we offered South Shore residents a chance to see their growing deposits put to use in their own community. To help make things easier for customers, we extended our hours, reduced the minimum balance to $1, cut service fees, and eliminated most of the paperwork involved in opening a new account.

We did our best to make the bank more friendly. After a couple of holdup attempts, the previous bank management had rearranged the lobby desks so that all the officers faced the teller lines. They hoped this arrangement would help discourage robbers. But when customers entered the bank, they came in behind the lobby officers and saw nothing but their backs, which was not the warmest welcome. We turned the desks around, and we tried to convince our employees that our customers were friends, not enemies.

We made improvements to the building, which had gone without upkeep for years. We also knocked down some buildings across the street and put in a parking lot with trees. Two blocks away, we tore down a burned-out grocery store and built a landscaped drive-in teller facility.

We worked hard to alter loan policy. We had inherited most of our loan officers from the old bank, and while they knew single-family and small-business lending, the old management had been unwilling to approve any lending in South Shore—except to a handful of white businesspeople who had not yet fled. The only loans the bank was making were in other parts of Chicago.

We went to those loan officers and reassured them. They should continue to make the loans they had been making under the loan programs they had in place. But when it came to loans in South Shore, we were reversing what had been the old procedure. From now on, we said, before they could *turn down* a loan application from someone who lived in South Shore or wanted to buy a home or start a business here, they had to bring it to one of us to approve the rejection.

Then we went out into the community to try to reverse the neighborhood's psychology. Two or three nights a week, Milton Davis—then president, now chairman of the bank—and I went to neighborhood meetings, to PTAs and block clubs, church basements and potluck suppers, committing the bank to the community. We told people who we were and what we intended to do, and we invited them to tell us what they considered to be the community's greatest needs. For months we talked and listened, and if nothing else, we learned a great deal.

Not everything worked the way we'd intended. For one thing, we encountered unexpected resistance to some of our building efforts. The people who lived near the new drive-in teller. facility disliked it, for example. They complained about the increased traffic. And the landscaping we thought spruced up the neighborhood, they saw as shubbery for muggers to hide in. (We fixed that problem by adding a guard, whose putative function was to direct traffic and answer questions.)

For another, we never succeeded in truly converting the old loan officers. They couldn't really buy our new philosophy. So for two or three years, we ran two loan committees, practically two separate banks.

On a larger scale, we eventually had to admit that the solution to diminishing deposits was not more small savers. We did get more accounts, but the costs soared. One problem was that the new small accounts were simply too small. Another was that some people used their savings accounts like jam jars—every Saturday they'd come in and add or withdraw small amounts of cash. On top of that, our relaxed policies attracted more than our share of attempted fraud, as bunco artists and thieves deposited forged or stolen checks and tried to draw on them immediately. It got so bad at one point we simply gave the mail-fraud inspector his own desk in our lobby.

Most discouraging for us was the discovery that South Shore residents had more than $90 million on deposit at the big banks in the Loop. They seemed to enjoy having their money in huge glass palaces that they could then visit and do business in.

In the end, we made the only decision we could: we raised fees enough to cover costs, which meant discouraging some small savers. But that move helped us recognize a change in our thinking that had actually occurred years earlier. Early on, we questioned the principle of community financial self-reliance, a principle to which many advocates of inner-city revitalization were paying tribute in the 1960s. It certainly wasn't the way wealthy communities worked. In such areas, money flowed in from outside—some of it from poor neighborhoods like South Shore. Why should South Shore have to fund its redevelopment from its own meager resources? If South Shore had once been red-lined, we planned to "green-line" it and bring in money from outside.

Most communities like South Shore—and there are hundreds like it all over America—experience a net outflow of residents' savings. People make deposits at their local bank or savings-and-loan, the institution puts a good deal of the money into securities to improve its liquidity, then it lends the rest outside the neighborhood in areas where it believes it has a lower risk. Essentially, the savings of poor communities flow out to more affluent communities.

South Shore Bank's innovation was to reverse the direction of that flow.

I often meet bankers who believe that South Shore Bank operates with various kinds of "funny money"—interest-free deposits, below-market CDs, foundation grants, special government funds, and other forms of charity. There are just two grains of truth in their suspicions.

First, Shorebank Corporation's *nonbank* subsidiaries routinely find government subsidies for projects, and our affiliate, The Neighborhood Institute and Dorris Pickens, its president, are masters at seeking out grants and fitting odd funding into integrated packages.

The second grain of truth is that, since 1986, South Shore Bank has invited customers from all over the country to invest in a product we call Rehab CDs—below-market certificates of deposit dedicated to rehabbing especially blighted apartment buildings and to keeping rents affordable. Rehab CDs draw an average interest rate two points below the market, and they make up 4.1% of our deposits—$7.4 million of $181 million in total bank deposits.

With the single exception of Rehab CDs, however, the bank pays a competitive rate of interest on all its deposits. Where we differ from other banks is in soliciting market-rate deposits from outside our primary service area. Every year, we mail out several thousand letters and brochures promoting and explaining social investing in the form of "Development Deposits," a name we've service marked.

Development Deposits have conventional, competitive yields and liquidity, and, like most bank deposits, they're insured by the FDIC. They can take a dozen different forms—savings accounts, money market accounts, IRAs, CDs, even checking and NOW accounts. Two things make them different. First, they come from outside our service area. Second, depositors know how their money is used—to renovate unlivable apartments, to start small businesses, to help young people get an education. Ever since 1974, we've produced an annual report that details the community-based purposes of all our lending activity.

By 1982, we'd raised $20 million in these outside deposits. Since then, our Development Deposits section and its director, Joan Shapiro, have increased the amount to $94 million—about 52% of total deposits. We have $5 million from an institutional investor in New York, and we have a forest worker in the Pacific Northwest who sends us a small monthly sum for his account. There is only one reason these people choose to put their money in a midsize bank on the south side of Chicago—because they care deeply about the way their money is used.

Another important early discovery was that small-business lending in South Shore was extraordinarily difficult. With the critical exception of housing entrepreneurs, this is still the case. There are three fundamental reasons. First, South Shore is a bedroom community, not a business or retailing center. Second, it does seem to be the case, as has often been claimed, that people in a black community prefer to shop outside it. Many of them believe, clearly with some historical justification, that merchants send inferior goods to black neighborhoods and then charge more for them.

The third and most important reason, however, is that Americans now shop at malls, which means that rejuvenating neighborhood commercial strips is an all but impossible task. We made many loans to black entrepreneurs, and our loss rate on those loans was very low. But too many of the entrepreneurs ultimately failed, usually for lack of a critical mass of attractive retail stores in a single block or area. In the late 1970s, we persuaded the city to spend $750,000 for new paving and trees on 71st Street, but there were still too many abandoned storefronts and whole neglected blocks that kept shoppers away.

Still, small-business lending was what we thought we knew best, and it absorbed our energies and talents for several years as we looked for the key we couldn't seem to find. Gradually, it occurred to us that while we were lavishing attention on this small-business problem, we were also beginning to do a great deal of small-business lending that we called by another name. In fact, we created a mom-and-pop industry in South Shore that has become the key to its prosperity and economic equilibrium.

This key is residential housing. When we speak of small business and small-business lending, we usually mean retailing, light manufacturing, or store-front service businesses. But as a residential community, the principal small business of South Shore was quite simply housing.

We never gave up on other kinds of small business. We finally addressed the mall question by building our own mall right on 71st Street. A range of 22 tenants including Radio Shack, Ace Hardware, and, most important, a huge Dominick's supermarket moved in last winter and appear to be doing well—the first thriving, large-scale commercial activity on that street in 25 years. We've also set up a small-business incubator where fledgling entrepreneurs in service and light manufacturing can share services and pay modest rents while they get themselves ready to fly on their own. But it was multifamily housing that became South Shore Bank's particular focus and expertise.

Despite several large areas of single-family homes, South Shore is one of the most densely built multifamily neighborhoods in Chicago. Between 70% and 75% of the housing units are apartments. Many are in large buildings with 30 to 40 units, but even more of the apartments in South Shore are in 3-story buildings of 6 to 24 units each. It was precisely the combination of rapid racial change and these older, walk-up buildings that had led to abandonment and demolition in other parts of Chicago.

Once a community is ready for the bulldozers, only a colossal investment can rebuild it. You can't take rubble out of the ground and build new housing at today's prices for people earning $15,000 to $18,000 a year—at least not without deep subsidies. But if you can catch such buildings early, when the bricks and mortar, the heating systems, copper pipes, and radiators are still in place, the difference in economics is dramatic. The difference in South Shore was that in 1970, most of the housing was still retrievable.

I've said earlier that one of our principal objectives in South Shore was to rebuild the confidence that the community had lost. A second objective was to get market forces functioning again, to counteract the disequilibrium in which risk overwhelms any potential for reward. In wealthier areas, well-capitalized, experienced, and self-confident business people assume some risk in exchange for the promise of profit. In South Shore, the invisible hand needed overt help. Indeed, we had to orchestrate a massive, focused combination of capital, credit, talent, and enterprise in order to restore the normal forces of investment and entrepreneurialism. The strategy for doing this evolved gradually.

We realized early on that rehabilitating multifamily buildings had to have a high priority in our redevelopment plan, despite other bankers' warnings against it. None of those bankers had ever succeeded at multifamily lending; and some had written off huge amounts of bad loans. In their eyes, the problem was that declining neighborhoods of multifamily housing simply never did turn around but always continued to decline. We believed they misperceived the problem.

To begin with, we understood that we had to target development in such a way that individual loans and projects would support one another. There is a synergy in neighborhoods. Each building that gets improved improves the general economic environment and the quality of all the loans in the area. In the largest sense, this meant we targeted South Shore and refused to make loans beyond its borders. More parochially, it meant we hoped to target specific subneighborhoods in South Shore.

We also understood that the kind of bank holding company sketched out by the Fed had potential that no bank alone could match. Thus we designed our own parent corporation to include a real-estate development company (City Lands Corporation) to buy, renovate, and then operate or resell multifamily buildings at a profit. We believed—

rightly, as it turned out—that the success of our own development company would in time attract others.

Our plan also called for establishment of an activist, not-for-profit organization (The Neighborhood Institute) to mobilize the community, act as an advocate for the least advantaged, and aggressively secure the foundation and federal grant resources that a for-profit institution like the bank could not legally seek or accept. Unfortunately, we didn't have the capital we needed at this early stage—the bank itself was still overleveraged—so the subsidiaries had to wait for better times.

A third piece of the plan was our insistence on rehabilitation. As we began very cautiously making multifamily loans in the mid-1970s— first on a few six-unit buildings, then on slightly larger ones—we refused any borrower who wouldn't renovate. It was an easy policy to enforce. When prospective borrowers balked, we told them politely they'd have to go to some other bank, knowing full well there was no other bank to go to. We knew the policy was good for the community and for the bank, so we insisted it was good for borrowers too, however much they might complain.

In the early days, we also insisted on owner occupancy, at least for the smaller buildings. Later we dropped that requirement, but we've always had a preference for local ownership. We'd known from the day we started our planning at the Eagle Bar that we had to combine social and business goals, and experience taught us again and again that no group of people better combines the social and business agendas than local residents with both a social and financial stake in the neighborhood. As time went by, it was local residents—the mom-and-pop housing entrepreneurs—who became the fourth key element, and the backbone, of our housing strategy.

We had a piece of good luck in 1974. A former resident of South Shore had recently become director of RESCORP (the Renewal Effort Service Corporation), a consortium, at that time, of 57 savings-and-loans formed to invest in inner-city rehabilitation, and RESCORP was looking for its first project. We used all our powers of persuasion, pulled every string we could find, and, in a kind of photo finish, lured RESCORP away from a tempting project on the north side of Chicago and into a 24-block section of South Shore called O'Keeffe, which consisted almost entirely of 3-story, walk-up apartment buildings.

Over the next three years, RESCORP spent almost $8 million renovating 302 apartments in 11 buildings in O'Keeffe, all of them within a 4-block area. In the course of the project, we began to make separate purchase-and-rehab loans to other buildings in the target area but unconnected to the RESCORP project itself. We were very conservative, making 80% purchase loans combined with federally guaranteed renovation loans that went as high as 100% of the rehab cost.

The rehabbing in O'Keeffe was our introduction to the technique of combining dissimilar sources of funding. Grants and conventional loans, subsidized and market-rate rents, a large subsidized developer, one state agency, our commercial bank, and any number of private entrepreneurs—all worked together to leverage maximum benefit from the money being spent. South Shore Bank's housing-activist affiliates, City Lands and The Neighborhood Institute, did not yet exist, but in time, they would become so adept at piecing together dozens of different kinds of financing—from below-market-rate loans to equity syndications using historic tax credits—that their ingenious funding now counts as a fifth critical element in our overall housing strategy.

O'Keeffe was also our first practical experience with a development project that targeted a specific area. Our goal was to lift the standards, appearance, and self-confidence of an entire disinvested neighborhood with a highly visible inner core of well-renovated housing. We didn't yet know that such a strategy would work, but it certainly seemed to hold more promise than the scattergun approach that had failed to work everywhere else.

I remember the Mother's Day weekend when the first of the RESCORP buildings came on the market. The building had 36 one- and two-bedroom units and a newly fenced courtyard with a gate that residents had to buzz guests through. More than 300 people signed up to rent the apartments. It was the first moment of genuine comfort we'd had in the realm of multifamily lending.

Those moments multiplied. The O'Keeffe project spread in concentric circles around the RESCORP core. There were 30 buildings in that central 4-block area, and RESCORP renovated 10. In 1978, we finally capitalized and set up City Lands, and it eventually did another 3 buildings. Housing entrepreneurs rehabbed the remaining 17 with market-rate loans from South Shore Bank (or, in a few cases, other banks).

As the wave of renovation spread to the surrounding area, and as we, our subsidiaries, and the neighborhood gained confidence and skill, these percentages changed. To date, more than half of all the multifamily housing in O'Keeffe has been rehabilitated—some 75 buildings altogether. The bank has provided purchase and rehab financing for about 65% of those renovations, City Lands and The Neighborhood Institute have pieced together deals to buy and rehab another 10%, while the final 25% of the money has come from banks outside South Shore.

South Shore's other multifamily neighborhoods show the same recurring patterns. In the late 1970s in Parkside—only a four-block area but the most severely blighted subsection of South Shore and the one that continued to deteriorate even after other areas were beginning to upgrade—we put together a complicated partnership that included RESCORP, City Lands, The Neighborhood Institute (which was capitalized along with City Lands in 1978 with Jim Fletcher, now president of the bank, as its first chairman), a community-development subsidiary of the First National Bank of Chicago, tax-exempt bond financing by the Illinois Housing Development Authority, community development block grants from the city of Chicago, Section 8 rental assistance from the federal government, equity syndication through the National Housing Partnership, and a lot more. Different organizations took on different pieces of the problem, which included 22 buildings, of which 2 had to be demolished. The ultimate result was 446 completely rebuilt, subsidized apartments in 20 buildings, about a third of all the rental housing in Parkside.

At the same time—and this, again, is perhaps the most critical feature of all such projects—South Shore Bank was there to leverage this public subsidy by making dozens of loans to the small housing entrepreneurs who appeared from nowhere, it seemed, to buy and rehab their own buildings—without subsidies—and take advantage of the sudden new atmosphere of optimism, rejuvenation, and stability. This sixth element of our housing strategy—the presence of a commercial bank to make disciplined, ordinary, conventionally financed loans to private entrepreneurs—yields four or five units of unsubsidized renovated housing for every unit of subsidized rehab, a good deal for taxpayers as well as the community.

And a good deal for the bank. Even though other banks have long since stopped red-lining South Shore, South Shore Bank still makes 75% of all the multifamily loans. In our total loan portfolio of $125 million, real-estate loans account for $75 million, including $55 million in multifamily buildings. Our average yield is 11.25%, slightly above market; our delinquency rate (loan payments 30 days or more past due) averages 1% to 2%, as opposed to a national average of 3% to 5%; and our real-estate losses ran one-tenth of 1% ($79,000) in 1990, which was well below average.

Had we conducted a market survey in 1973 to get a sense of how many potential entrepreneurs we had in the community to buy, rehab, and then manage apartment buildings as small businesses, the answer would have been "none." In fact, they were all around us. Some of them were handymen and janitors, working on other people's buildings. Some of them just lived in the neighborhood and had nothing to do with housing at that time.

One of our most successful housing entrepreneurs managed a dry-cleaning business on the north side in 1973. Urged on by an uncle who had fixed up buildings and resold them, he found a small apartment building in fair condition, bought it with money we lent him (on the strength of his savings, income, projected cash flow, and our judgment of his character), fixed it up, rented it, and made regular payments on his loan. So we helped him buy a second building, and a third. When he'd acquired about 50 units, he quit his job and began to do housing full time. He's now worked on more than a dozen buildings, and has served as a model for at least half a dozen other people who have used his skills and methods to get into the housing business.

We've found literally scores of such people, including about 200 black couples who renovate one apartment house, then buy a second, third, and fourth. They make up a body of small-business people that no market survey could possibly have identified. They were invisible, and now they're an industry—the core of South Shore's recovery. With the bank's help, and without concessionary rates, they've rehabilitated more than 6,000 units of rental housing.

I once heard a presentation by two professors from the Massachusetts Institute of Technology about manufacturing networks in Italy, where thousands of small producers work together to make a world-class industry. At the end, I asked one of them what it was that distinguished these Italian entrepreneurs from others. "There are three things," he said. "They understand machinery, they know how to husband a small amount of capital, and they know how to cooperate and compete with one another at the same time."

If we substitute buildings for machinery, these are precisely the characteristics that distinguish our mom-and-pop housing entrepreneurs in South Shore from the landlords in many other communities. They know how to get steam from a boiler to a cold register 100 yards away by adjusting a few valves. They know how to squeeze a quarter's worth of rehab out of a nickel. And they work hard, share their skills, teach their secrets, and help each other renovate—even as they compete on rents.

South Shore has a second, smaller, but important group of housing entrepreneurs made up of Croatian janitors. There's an older Croatian immigrant who runs a sort of dormitory and soccer club for young Croatian men a few miles from South Shore. They come to the States without their families, he gets them jobs as janitors, and eventually he helps them find a building to buy and brings them to us for a loan.

Over the years, maybe 30 of those young men have qualified for loans, and they've all built successful apartment businesses. Part of the reason is that Jim Bringley, our head of real-estate lending, is such a wonderful judge of character, but another part of the reason is that same Italian recipe—expertise, financial resourcefulness, and the combination of competition and cooperation. Maybe they learn it on the soccer field. Maybe it's the immigrant work ethic. In any case, they help each other fix up their buildings, and then they compete for tenants.

The black entrepreneurs and Croatian janitors of South Shore made up an enormous storehouse of enterprise waiting to be tapped. The bank unleashed their energies by importing the resources they needed for development and by giving them access to credit. Similar wellsprings of entrepreneurialism exist in thousands of disinvested neighborhoods and rural areas all over the country, but they represent an opportunity that most bankers and other members of the middle class have a hard time seeing. We come to places like South Shore with the preconception that low- and moderate-income people, who don't dress or talk or write the way we do, don't have ideas. We believe they aren't as smart as we are or as able to operate in the marketplace.

South Shore demonstrates the opposite. Deliberate, disciplined development banking in a disinvested community can revive a local economy, rekindle the imagination of its people, and restore market forces to their normal health and interdependency.

When we first came to South Shore, normal market forces hardly existed, not in housing, retailing, banking—not in anything. Multifamily housing provides a good example of a restored, complex marketplace in action.

In the early days, when we found people who looked like good credit risks, we did not have to compete with other banks for their business. Among other things, this made our renovation policy easy to enforce. Today, however, a person can buy an apartment building and get a loan from a bank that has no rehab requirement.

Yet an interesting thing has happened in the meantime. Today, unless building owners improve their property, they're not going to get good tenants. So buyers, if they know anything about the market, are looking for a rehab loan to combine with the purchase loan. The market, not South Shore Bank, is telling them to renovate. What we had to do in the beginning is now done for us by forces that we helped to restore.

When the Comptroller of the Currency refused to let the old South Shore National Bank relocate, he said it had "failed to show a persuasive reason for abandoning its service area." For me, those words are compelling, because the idea that banks have an area to which they owe service is still old-fashioned.

The Bank of America is a good example. A. P. Giannini founded it as the Bank of Italy to see to the financial needs of what he called "the little fellow," and on the day after the San Francisco earthquake and fire of 1906, his bank in ashes, Giannini set up a counter on the waterfront and lent out $80,000 he had saved from the fire. "Go home and get that house fixed," he told his customers. That human touch was what his bank was known for.

But the bank became regional, national, and then international in scope. It discovered economies of scale, and in its search for greater volumes and higher yields, it became almost exclusively transaction oriented. It began lending to countries as well as to people. It found it could make more money financing LBOs and gigantic commercial developments than lending to individuals and small businesses.

When Giannini's daughter Claire resigned from the board of directors in 1985, her stated reason was that Bank of America had strayed from her father's values, among them, his "willingness to place the human needs of ordinary people above private ambition" and his insistence that the bank was "a corporate trustee of great public purpose."

To serve almost any geographical or social community we might name, banks must either be small or at the very least maintain a local focus, and they must commit themselves to community development. These two pieces are essential. I am not saying that Bank of America has some sacred obligation to preserve Giannini's management style. What I am saying is that we should encourage Bank of America and all the other banks in the United States to do the kind of local development banking Giannini created his Bank of Italy to carry out.

The fact is that even most small commercial banks do little effective development work. Of a bank's three primary responsibilities—to protect deposits, to earn a reasonable return on invested capital, and, by recycling the savings of the community, to contribute to its economic growth and vitality—bankers in general do a good job on the first and second and a poor job on the third.

Small-town bankers are no different. They are relatively comfortable people. They earn enough money to satisfy their shareholders. The FDIC protects the depositors. There is simply not enough reward for taking the extra risk of putting people into business who've not been in business before.

As a matter of public policy, we should grant the new privileges that bankers are seeking for themselves—mutual fund management, interstate banking, securities underwriting, and more—only to those banks that demonstrate the most exemplary performance in meeting the credit needs of their community service areas. Indeed, these privileges should go only to banks that actively apply their "unique combination of financial and managerial resources" to help remedy the nation's social ills.

In other words, we should link banking privileges to each bank's performance in achieving broader domestic public-policy objectives. The bankers who achieve the best results in community development should be rewarded with competitive advantage in the marketplace—the opportunity to expand and to offer profitable but otherwise prohibited services. (This would have the added public-policy benefit of slowing down to a manageable pace an otherwise headlong rush by bank holding companies to exploit all the new powers that might be granted. The cautionary example to bear in mind is what happened to the thrift industry when it was granted new powers in the early 1980s.)

The Shorebank Corporation proves that the Fed was right 20 years ago. At relatively low cost to the public purse, the nation should now repeat our positive experience by promoting the establishment of permanent urban and rural development organizations with adequate staying power and resources. In the same way that earlier generations learned the necessity of permanent, self-sustaining hospitals, colleges, and museums, this generation must recognize the need for permanent development institutions.

The public policy that governs bank holding companies should benefit all citizens directly—especially people of modest means trying to improve the conditions of their lives—and not just the owners and managers of banks.

4

Profits with a Purpose: An Interview with Tom Chapman

Nancy A. Nichols

Greater Southeast Community Hospital is a 494-bed acute care facility located in southeast Washington, D.C. With revenues of $145 million and 2,650 employees, it is both the largest private employer and the only medical facility in a troubled and isolated community called Anacostia. Nearly a quarter of the area's residents live below the poverty line, and almost half have not graduated from high school. The low level of education and unrelenting poverty of area residents have combined to give Anacostia the highest rates of infant mortality, cancer, and coronary disease in the entire D.C. area.

Yet unlike so many inner-city hospitals that are faltering because of the tremendous needs of the communities surrounding them, Greater Southeast is thriving. Strengthened by the leadership of a 47-year-old executive named Tom Chapman, Greater Southeast now sits at the center of Anacostia and offers a wide range of social services that at first glance have little in common with traditional health care. Under Chapman's leadership, the hospital has renovated housing, started day care programs for children and the elderly, developed stay-in-school programs, and created adult literacy programs. Both Chapman and the hospital have received national awards for their outstanding work in the community.

Chapman, who grew up in a housing project in New Haven, Connecticut brings to his job an innate understanding of inner-city problems. After attending St. Anselm's College in Manchester, New Hampshire on a basketball scholarship, he turned down an offer to try out with the New York Knicks, seeking instead "to make a difference" in communities like the one in which he was raised. In 1971, Chapman received a master's degree in hospital administration and public health from Yale University. After working both as a consultant and an administrator at several health care facilities, he joined Greater Southeast as president in 1984.

Last year, Chapman was promoted into his current position as CEO of the Greater Southeast Health Care System, where he is responsible for the operation of two hospitals, three nursing homes, a physician care network, and over 50 community programs. Chapman's greatest challenge is to keep his inner-city hospital viable while also pouring services into the surrounding community.

HBR: *What was the biggest challenge you faced when you joined Greater Southeast in 1984?*

Tom Chapman: At that time, the hospital was giving away about 11% of its care to people who were uninsured—or about $11.5 million worth of medical services. We couldn't keep giving away that amount of services and still keep the hospital solvent. It was eroding whatever profits we had. I knew that I had to get behind those numbers early on and try to reduce that amount, but I also knew that I had to do it in a way that was consistent with the history of the hospital.

Greater Southeast has always had strong links with the community it serves. Community residents raised the money to build it, they sit on our board, and, most important, they support the hospital by patronizing it. So we couldn't fix our problem by just turning our backs on the community and trying to find patients who were better insured. But in the long run, if we kept giving away that amount of free care, there wouldn't be a hospital here to serve the community anymore.

Working with our trustees and the financial department, we reached the conclusion that we couldn't devote any more than 7% of our revenues to free care and still keep the hospital operating profitably. Since we weren't about to start turning people away, we needed to try to correct some of the problems that had propelled us to offer free care in the first place.

Therefore, it was our attempt to solve a narrowly defined business problem that forced us to define our mission broadly. We now care for the physical, social, and mental well-being of our patients. At Greater Southeast, we don't just treat the illnesses our patients bring to us; we try to treat the diseases that are racking our community—poverty, illiteracy, drugs, and violence.

But in a community that needs everything, where do you begin?

Our task is huge, but our focus is clear: we are driven by the needs of the patients. Whether we are working inside the hospital with an individual patient or working outside with community groups, we are always conscious of the needs of our customers who, taken together, form the community we serve. Let me give you an example. We don't perform open heart surgery at Greater Southeast, but that's OK. It isn't part of our mission. On the other hand, we have a state-of-the-art kidney dialysis unit because so many of our patients suffer from diseases that call for dialysis.

Beyond that, we've tried to make serving children our top priority. When we can, we try to structure our services around their needs. We have a grant from the Robert Wood Johnson Foundation to create a network of child health services. This involves dozens of community-based organizations involved in health education and social services. In fact, we've recently completed renovating 50 units of a 155-unit apartment complex across the street that includes a day care center in the basement that can serve 70 children.

What makes constructing affordable housing the work of the hospital?

During the winter, we often treat children with pneumonia, which is a common and treatable disease. Then, after that child is well, we send him home to an apartment without heat. Now what sense does that make? We claim to be treating diseases, but what we are really treating are the symptoms of larger social problems. We can take care of the symptoms surprisingly well. We sew up gunshot wounds and administer antibiotics, but we aren't dealing with violence on the streets or the fact that we have to discharge a child to a cold apartment. Those are the real diseases that are racking our community.

Our health care costs will continue to skyrocket until we start to deal with these problems. Our hospital does a miraculous job of keeping very sick, fragile infants alive. Yet most of that incredibly expensive care should be unnecessary. With good nutrition, proper prenatal care, decent housing, and a little bit of education, most deliveries can be low-cost, joyous events.

You have to think beyond the walls of the hospital and get beyond technology and what it can do. Simply staying in the shop and providing good emergency care without thinking about what happens before our patients arrive and after they leave is a tremendous waste of resources. For instance, by saving low-weight and drug-addicted babies, we may actually be adding to society's problems. Those kids are going to have complicated and expensive needs throughout their lives. Ironically, by performing many of these technological miracles, we may not be doing society a service after all. In fact, we are probably doing a disservice.

Certainly, we are wreaking havoc with our hospital budgets. Many of these complicated births are drug related. Usually the mother is on Medicaid. At Greater Southeast, we receive a flat fee of $4,000 from the government for each delivery we make. If we spend more than that, and we almost always do during a complicated delivery, we eat the difference. In some extreme cases, mothers will abandon the child to us altogether. At times, children have been with us upstairs in pediatrics for over a year. A hospital is a very expensive place to warehouse a child. It is also a totally unacceptable place to spend your first year of life.

Are you suggesting that the hospital's margins are inextricably linked to its mission?

Absolutely. At Greater Southeast, we want to provide medical care to people at the point at which it can be delivered most effectively, and that, incidentally, happens to be the cheapest point too. One of the major problems we face is that people in poor communities often can't and don't seek care unless the situation is extreme. There is such social and psychological apathy around any sense of future in this and many other inner-city communities. If people feel as if they're never going to be employed or they're never going to have decent housing or they're never going to have enough food, why should they care about good health care?

As a result, they often access the health care system at the most expensive point possible: the emergency room. About 40% of the children in our emergency room are there for nonemergency treatments. A woman who works all day long will come home to find her child has a temperature of 103°. She may not have a pediatrician, so she brings the child in to our emergency room. It costs $50 just to pass through the doors, before we've even touched the patient. It probably would have cost only $20 or $30 to treat the child in a doctor's office.

How do you solve this problem?

In part, it is just making things more convenient for people. In the past, health care services have been organized around providers' needs, not patients'. For instance, there is a city-run health clinic down the street that isn't open on weekends or after 5:00 P.M. We need to change that if we are going to offer quality care that people can access in a cost-effective manner.

One of the ways Greater Southeast has approached this problem is by forming a public-private partnership with the city of Washington, D.C. In 1989, we opened a health clinic in the local high school, and we will soon begin working in the middle schools. At the clinics, we can both monitor students for major diseases and treat minor problems that would otherwise end up in our emergency room. More important, we can also do a lot of health education and promotion that can lead to good habits and better life-styles.

School clinics are a simple solution, but they can be difficult to implement because the barriers between public health providers and private hospitals are huge and often insurmountable. For example, in the past, we had no links with the city clinic in Anacostia. So if a pregnant woman received prenatal care at the clinic and showed up here eight months later to deliver, we wouldn't have copies of a single medical report. Today we're trying to establish better record coordination and other links with the clinic. As a business, we can't afford to disassociate the community's public health needs from its emergency needs. In the end, it is all the same group of people with the same set of health problems. Sooner or later, we're going to have to deal with them. If we don't address it at one step, we are going to see it at another. There is no escaping it, and the longer we wait, the more expensive the problem becomes.

If the benefits of preventive care are so obvious, why do we see so little of it in our country today?

The incentives in health insurance programs are all built around the most intensive use of medical resources to address the short-term needs of specific patients and diagnostic groups. There is no incentive, from either private insurers or government programs, to provide preventive care or to make the best use of society's health care dollars overall. For example, Medicare will pay us $30,000 for a hospital stay for a patient with advanced hypertensive disease, but it won't reimburse us for a screening program to test for high blood pressure.

Left untreated, high blood pressure can lead to strokes, kidney failure, heart disease, and, in the most severe cases, death. It was a factor in 30% of all the deaths of our black patients. Yet it is a treatable and preventable illness if it is caught early. So we've pinpointed this as one area where we need to be proactive.

Working with the Southeast Vicariate Cluster, a group of local black churches, we've organized volunteers to screen for high blood pressure after Sunday services in 24 churches. We've screened 8,000 people since 1984 and found 3,000 elevated readings. All of those patients have been referred to a physician.

In a community like this, if you sit and wait, the hospital will end up with patients whose conditions have advanced so far that it is impossible to treat them either effectively or efficiently. A recent study sponsored by the D.C. Hospital Association confirmed what we already knew: poor people are admitted to the hospital more often than rich people for conditions that are easily treated and, in some cases, preventable. Our admission rate for hypertension, or high blood pressure, is four times higher than the average.

So for Greater Southeast, the preventive medicine program is a cost-cutting move?

There is a right reason and a real reason to do everything. The right reason to provide preventive care is to keep people healthy. The real reason or, I should say, the organizational reason Greater Southeast provides preventive care is because it is more cost-effective to treat patients this way than it is to wait until they have had a stroke. The hospital's entire blood pressure program costs, at a maximum, $20,000 to $30,000 a year to administer. It is probably the lowest cost health prevention program available. If you contrast that with the $30,000 it can routinely cost to treat just one stroke victim, you can see where the savings come from.

Yet the government will not reimburse us for these prevention programs. And the more aggressively and efficiently we pursue these efforts, the more we slowly shrink our market share. That's the great irony: we need to keep the occupancy rate of the hospital up because that is how we fund all of our outreach programs. Yet the goal of these outreach programs is to keep people out of the hospital. So we're stuck.

Are you saying that the hospital is caught in a paradox: either do good or make good?

All health care institutions are caught in that bind. We are all trying to provide a social good in an environment that is full of conflicts. The economic incentives in the health care system not only drive you away from preventive care but they also discourage caring for low-income populations. For instance, federal regulations for Medicare and Medicaid, introduced in 1983, put an economic value on every diagnosis. Hospitals went from a fee-for-service program, under which they were paid for each day the patient was admitted, to a system that reimbursed them at a flat rate for each diagnosis.

As a result, some patients are now a lot more lucrative than others. In general, it is now more profitable to have healthier and wealthier patients than others. Say the government will reimburse a hospital for 12 inpatient days for a given procedure. If a patient recovers in 8 days, the government lets you keep the difference. Under these rules, the hospital has an incentive to compete for the healthiest individuals with the least complicated problems because they have the greatest chance of getting in and out of the hospital the fastest.

That puts us at a tremendous disadvantage. Many of our patients are elderly people who have lacked proper health care most of their lives. They arrive under emergency conditions with all sorts of unknown problems. On average, black Medicare patients stay 50% longer than other Medicare patients. Often they stay from three to six months beyond what's required because they have no family to go home to and nursing homes don't want government-sponsored patients.

Have you tried to attract wealthier patients as many other hospitals have done?

It's true that, faced with these regulations, some hospitals simply have abandoned unprofitable patients or markets. The changes in reimbursement just intensified the whole business of trying to find the best patients so as to generate the maximum amount of profit to buy the best technology, which would, in turn, attract the best doctors—who, of course, bring in the best patients. The entire hospital industry got stuck on a treadmill, and it just couldn't get off.

At Greater Southeast, we made a conscious effort not to get stuck on that treadmill. We understand the importance of technology to modern medicine, but we've purchased our technology judiciously. So, in that respect, we aren't driven by the technology; we're driven by the needs of our patients. We aren't going out to try to get the latest technology to attract the best insured patients; what we are trying to do is meet the needs of the patients we have. In business terms, we aren't supply driven, we're demand driven. We attempt to serve the market, not just market to our service area in an attempt to skim off the most profitable patients.

Is that key to your strategy? Always having some purpose to your profit?

Remember, we are a nonprofit hospital. At a for-profit hospital, there is a purpose to your profit. You have stockholders, you have specific responsibilities, and you've declared your purposes and profit intentions in the beginning of the year. If you're Greater Southeast Community Hospital, you ought to have some clear societal purpose to your profit, and it shouldn't just be to buy a few more technological gadgets. It should be used to reinvest and redeploy assets into the community. We have maintained operating profits averaging $4.5 million each year for ten years and invested most of that back into the community.

What are some of the investments Greater Southeast has made?

Over the last two decades, we've expanded from a single, acute care hospital into a network of community-based entities. We now operate two hospitals, three nursing homes, and a multitude of ambulatory programs for elderly people, children, and their families. We try to create services that are relevant to the needs of the people. In business, this might be called being close to the customer. In health care, we call it responding to the needs of the community.

For instance, there is a senior citizen apartment complex right across the street from the hospital. Years ago, we found that a lot of residents would come and sit for hours in our lobby. Maybe they were waiting for the bus, maybe they were lonely, or maybe they just thought the hospital was an exciting place to be. Eventually we gave them a room at the back of the emergency ward, and gradually our staff started some arts and crafts activities on a volunteer basis. After working with the elderly for a while, Gloria Anderson, who was then a social worker at the hospital, recognized a need for elderly day care. Using the basement of one of our buildings, she started our community's first senior day care center.

So what led you from day care to nursing homes?

It was a logical next step. When our elderly patients could no longer stay at home, we saw them shipped off to a nursing home on the other side of the river, where they were isolated from this community. Working with Gloria, we made the decision to build a nursing home here in Anacostia so they wouldn't have to leave the community.

Today, through our center for the aging, we operate three nursing homes in the District of Columbia and Maryland, and we have purchased a van called "The Dr. Feel Good Van" to provide home visits for seniors who can't travel—and Gloria is in charge of the whole operation.

Is that typical of the way programs get started at your hospital?

If you can't find more financially attractive patients, you have to find more attractive and cost-efficient ways to treat the patients you have. That is our basic approach. In fact, one of our employees, Lester Scheuermann, has just won a national award for doing that. He created a program called Serving Spoons using a Freedom Grant, which we give out to employees who have a novel idea. Each year, we give out a few Freedom Grants of up to $5,000 to help employees create programs that solve an identified problem in our delivery system.

From his work as a social worker, Lester knew that elderly hospitalized patients often have trouble feeding themselves. They can't swallow or they aspirate, taking food down into their lungs. This can be dangerous for a number of reasons: the patient can choke or get pneumonia.

To avoid this problem, we had been tube-feeding many of our elderly and frail patients. Yet the tube feeding also had its drawbacks. The patients hated the tubes and often tried to dislodge them. Then they had to be restrained, which caused them further physical and mental problems. In addition, there is an increased risk of infection from tube feeding. Infections mean lengthier stays and, since the hospital is reimbursed by Medicare on a flat basis, we can't afford to have extended stays. They aren't good for us, and they aren't good for our patients either.

Seeing this problem, Lester began a program where employees would feed the elderly on their lunch hours and before and after work. At first, a lot of people around here doubted whether employees would choose to spend their lunch hours doing extra work. But we've found that clerical employees, who are detached from the caring mission of the hospital, like being involved in this nursing activity. They find it fulfilling. From the hospital's perspective, the program saves both time and money. We don't have to pay a highly trained nurse to perform a routine feeding, and we don't have lengthened stays brought on by infections resulting from the feeding tubes. The patients also benefit physically and mentally from the added nutrition and from the extra social contact.

How do you create an environment that encourages employees to develop programs like that?

The Freedom Grants certainly help. But they are just part of our program. Every three to four weeks, I meet with a randomly selected group of employees. The only rule I have for this "coffee break" is that if an employee brings up a problem, he or she has to have an idea for solving it. That sends a message: it isn't enough just to complain. Our employees are expected to take responsibility for solving the problems we have in this hospital, and we take their ideas seriously. One of the first things I did when I got here was oversee the renovation of each of eight nursing stations, one on each floor of the hospital. I gave each nursing team the responsibility of designing its area. The nurses loved it, and as we went up floor by floor, each renovation became more cost-effective—because they were learning from each other as the process went on.

Historically, hospitals have been doctor-driven hierarchies where the executive administrators served as a sort of privileged class. I've tried to change that here. One of my first jobs after I left graduate school was to work as an "administrative resident" at a hospital in Boston. Back then, the administrative wing was sealed off from the rest of the hospital by a big glass door leading to a long silent hallway. Talk about barriers. When you walked in there, you sank into six inches of plush carpeting. The design created a psychological and social separation between the administrators and the healing work of the hospital.

How have you made sure that barriers like that don't exist at Greater South-east?

One of the ways we do it is by working in teams that are focused on the patient. For example, each elderly patient is treated by a geri-atric team that includes a doctor, a nurse, a social worker, a dietician, and a physical therapist. In effect, the patient picks the team leader. If the patient's most critical needs are emotional, then the social worker leads the team—not the doctor. That, of course, turns the traditional hierarchy of a hospital upside down. It also allows for an integrated approach to health care. We recently had an elderly patient who refused to eat. The nutritionist, using her expertise, was trying to make the patient's diet more appealing. But it wasn't until a team meeting that the dietician found out from a social worker that the patient's daughter had just died. Her lack of appetite was caused by an emotional problem, not a physical one. But without seeing the patient within the context of her whole life, it was impossible to really help her. What makes us unique at Greater Southeast is a shared mind-set that says working together we can solve these problems, whether it is the problem of one patient or the whole community.

How do you find employees who share this unique mind-set?

Fifty-five percent of the employees we hire at Greater Southeast are recommended by people who already work here. So we have people who have already bought into the mission recommending people who they think will fit into the system, and it is a natural marriage. Another 29% applied because they were in this hospital, either visiting patients or receiving services themselves. So over 80% of our employees have some knowledge about us before coming here, and once we've infected them with our spirit, we try not to let them go.

We have a very low turnover rate—as low as 4.5% in difficult-to-fill nursing positions. One of the reasons for that low rate is that we are committed to our employees and continue to invest in their professional development. My vice president of human resources, Jo Ann Kurtz, says her goal is to hire only entry-level workers and promote from within for all our other positions. That's a goal I fully support.

What kinds of programs do you offer for employee development?

Jo Ann has set up a full complement of educational and career development services. Employees are eligible for literacy training, college and graduate equivalency degree courses, all the way up to specialized training in nursing and physical therapy. We have a tuition assistance program for college programs, and GED students are paid for one-half of the course time.

When we first started the GED program, you had to be an employee or an immediate family member to qualify. We used to laugh about how many immediate family members the human resources staff had. If somebody came in and said, "So-and-so doesn't work here but she wants to take your GED course," a staff person, in order to make sure she was eligible to be enrolled, would say, "Fine, she's my sister." Now we've opened those programs to the community as well.

Why open it up to the community?

We are the biggest private employer in our area, and if one of our goals is to combat poverty in the community, then an obvious solution is to hire people from the neighborhood. That, however, has proved more difficult than it would seem. A few years ago, we realized that the high schools in our area were turning out graduates who could barely read or write and could do mathematics only at the fifth grade level. We had two choices: stop hiring those kids and recruit elsewhere or train them in-house. We chose to train them in-house. If we were a private for-profit hospital, we would probably have acted differently, but we're a community hospital. And in order to be a community hospital, you have to be willing to tie your fate to the community. We now have a program where high school students attend classes here at the hospital after school and work in different areas of the hospital. Then if we have openings, we hire them. We are getting good employees, and the kids are getting training in a field that is growing: health care.

What you are describing sounds like an informal partnership. Is that how you see it?

Everyone needs partners—on an individual and an organizational level. When I look back on my own journey out of the projects, I can remember several people who were willing to reach out and help me—a coach, a teacher, a counselor. One of the things I see nowadays is that adults are too threatened by teenagers to get involved. That's one reason we want to start a mentoring program to get these two groups together. We've recently received a grant from the Commonwealth Fund to start a school-to-work transition program, a sort of mentoring program for 50 high school students. The program will pair high school students with individuals, not necessarily hospital employees, who would work with them for a period of four years and be concerned about their homework and behavior at school. We plan to develop a business sponsorship that would come from outside the hospital. That is, to get not only the partner in the law firm or the executive to be a mentor but also to get the companies to provide young people with employment, advanced training, or financial support for college.

I want to create a network of participants, stringing together various organizations and players, each of whom have something special to contribute to urban problems. After all, a community is nothing more than a set of relationships. If you reach out and create a lot of partnerships, what you are really doing is creating a community.

PART

IV

Linking Service and Profit

1
Putting the Service-Profit Chain to Work

James L. Heskett, Thomas O. Jones, Gary W. Loveman, W. Earl Sasser, Jr., and Leonard A. Schlesinger

Top-level executives of outstanding service organizations spend little time setting profit goals or focusing on market share, the management mantra of the 1970s and 1980s. Instead, they understand that in the new economics of service, frontline workers and customers need to be the center of management concern. Successful service managers pay attention to the factors that drive profitability in this new service paradigm: investment in people, technology that supports frontline workers, revamped recruiting and training practices, and compensation linked to performance for employees at every level. And they express a vision of leadership in terms rarely heard in corporate America: an organization's "patina of spirituality," the "importance of the mundane."

A growing number of companies that includes Banc One, Intuit Corporation, Southwest Airlines, ServiceMaster, USAA, Taco Bell, and MCI know that when they make employees and customers paramount, a radical shift occurs in the way they manage and measure success. The new economics of service requires innovative measurement techniques. These techniques calibrate the impact of employee satisfaction, loyalty, and productivity on the value of products and services delivered so that managers can build customer satisfaction and loyalty and assess the corresponding impact on profitability and growth. In fact, the lifetime value of a loyal customer can be astronomical, especially when referrals are added to the economics of customer retention and repeat purchases of related products. For example, the lifetime revenue stream from a loyal pizza eater can be $8,000, a

Cadillac owner $332,000, and a corporate purchaser of commercial aircraft literally billions of dollars.

The service-profit chain, developed from analyses of successful service organizations, puts "hard" values on "soft" measures. It helps managers target new investments to develop service and satisfaction levels for maximum competitive impact, widening the gap between service leaders and their merely good competitors.

The Service-Profit Chain

The service-profit chain establishes relationships between profitability, customer loyalty, and employee satisfaction, loyalty, and productivity. The links in the chain (which should be regarded as propositions) are as follows: Profit and growth are stimulated primarily by customer loyalty. Loyalty is a direct result of customer satisfaction. Satisfaction is largely influenced by the value of services provided to customers. Value is created by satisfied, loyal, and productive employees. Employee satisfaction, in turn, results primarily from high-quality support services and policies that enable employees to deliver results to customers. (See Exhibit I.)

The service-profit chain is also defined by a special kind of leadership. CEOs of exemplary service companies emphasize the importance of each employee and customer. For these CEOs, the focus on customers and employees is no empty slogan tailored to an annual management meeting. For example, Herbert Kelleher, CEO of Southwest Airlines, can be found aboard airplanes, on tarmacs, and in terminals, interacting with employees and customers. Kelleher believes that hiring employees that have the right attitude is so important that the hiring process takes on a "patina of spirituality." In addition, he believes that "anyone who looks at things solely in terms of factors that can easily be quantified is missing the heart of business, which is people." William Pollard, the chairman of ServiceMaster, continually underscores the importance of "teacher-learner" managers, who have what he calls "a servant's heart." And John McCoy, CEO of Banc One, stresses the "uncommon partnership," a system of support that provides maximum latitude to individual bank presidents while supplying information systems and common measurements of customer satisfaction and financial measures.

A closer look at each link reveals how the service-profit chain functions as a whole.

Exhibit I.

The Links in the Service-Profit Chain

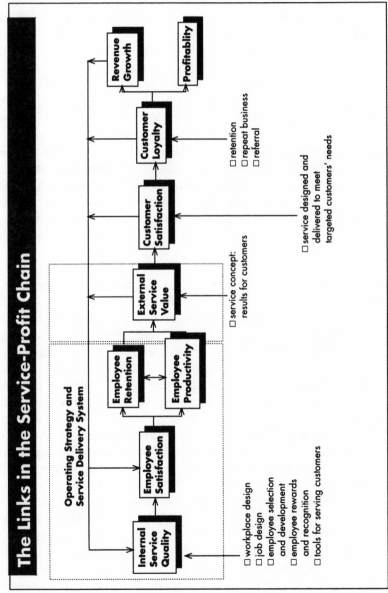

Operating Strategy and Service Delivery System

Internal Service Quality → Employee Satisfaction → Employee Retention / Employee Productivity → External Service Value → Customer Satisfaction → Customer Loyalty → Revenue Growth / Profitability

□ workplace design
□ job design
□ employee selection and development
□ employee rewards and recognition
□ tools for serving customers

□ service concept: results for customers

□ service designed and delivered to meet targeted customers' needs

□ retention
□ repeat business
□ referral

CUSTOMER LOYALTY DRIVES PROFITABILITY AND GROWTH

To maximize profit, managers have pursued the Holy Grail of becoming number-one or -two in their industries for nearly two decades. Recently, however, new measures of service industries like software and banking suggest that customer loyalty is a more important determinant of profit.[1] Reichheld and Sasser estimate that a 5% increase in customer loyalty can produce profit increases from 25% to 85%. They conclude that *quality* of market share, measured in terms of customer loyalty, deserves as much attention as *quantity* of share.

Banc One, based in Columbus, Ohio, has developed a sophisticated system to track several factors involved in customer loyalty and satisfaction. Once driven strictly by financial measures, Banc One now conducts quarterly measures of customer retention; the number of services used by each customer, or *depth of relationship*; and the level of customer satisfaction. The strategies derived from this information help explain why Banc One has achieved a return on assets more than double that of its competitors in recent years.

CUSTOMER SATISFACTION DRIVES CUSTOMER LOYALTY

Leading service companies are currently trying to quantify customer satisfaction. For example, for several years, Xerox has polled 480,000 customers per year regarding product and service satisfaction using a five-point scale from 5 (high) to 1 (low). Until two years ago, Xerox's goal was to achieve 100% 4s (satisfied) and 5s (very satisfied) by the end of 1993. But in 1991, an analysis of customers who gave Xerox 4s and 5s on satisfaction found that the relationships between the scores and actual loyalty differed greatly depending on whether the customers were very satisfied or satisfied. Customers giving Xerox 5s were six times more likely to repurchase Xerox equipment than those giving 4s.

This analysis led Xerox to extend its efforts to create *apostles*—a term coined by Scott D. Cook, CEO of software producer and distributor, Intuit Corporation, describing customers so satisfied that they convert the uninitiated to a product or service. Xerox's management currently wants to achieve 100% apostles, or 5s, by the end of 1996 by upgrading service levels and guaranteeing customer satisfaction. But just as important for Xerox's profitability is to avoid creating *terrorists*: customers so unhappy that they speak out against a poorly delivered service at every opportunity. Terrorists can reach hundreds of potential customers. In some instances, they can even discourage acquaintances from trying a service or product. (See Exhibit II.)

VALUE DRIVES CUSTOMER SATISFACTION

Customers today are strongly value oriented. But just what does that mean? Customers tell us that value means the results they receive in relation to the total costs (both the price and other costs to customers incurred in acquiring the service). The insurance company, Progressive Corporation, is creating just this kind of value for its customers by processing and paying claims quickly and with little policyholder effort. Members of the company's CAT (catastrophe) team fly to the scene of major accidents, providing support services like transportation and housing and handling claims rapidly. By reducing legal costs and actually placing more money in the hands of the injured parties, the CAT team more than makes up for the added expenses the organization incurs by maintaining the team. In addition, the CAT team delivers value to customers, which helps explain why Progressive has one of the highest margins in the property-and-casualty insurance industry.

EMPLOYEE PRODUCTIVITY DRIVES VALUE

At Southwest Airlines, the seventh-largest U.S. domestic carrier, an astonishing story of employee productivity occurs daily. Eighty-six percent of the company's 14,000 employees are unionized. Positions are designed so that employees can perform several jobs if necessary. Schedules, routes, and company practices—such as open seating and the use of simple, color-coded, reusable boarding passes—enable the boarding of three and four times more passengers per day than competing airlines. In fact, Southwest deplanes and reloads two-thirds of its flights in 15 minutes or less. Because of aircraft availability and short-haul routes that don't require long layovers for flight crews, Southwest has roughly 40% more pilot and aircraft utilization than its major competitors: its pilots fly on average 70 hours per month versus 50 hours at other airlines. These factors explain how the company can

Exhibit II.

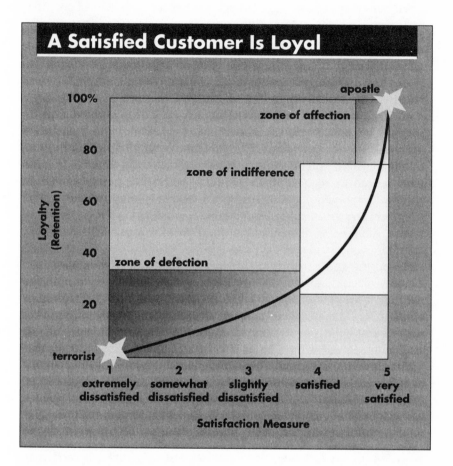

A Satisfied Customer Is Loyal

charge fares from 60% to 70% lower than existing fares in markets it enters.

At Southwest, customer perceptions of value are very high, even though the airline does not assign seats, offer meals, or integrate its reservation system with other airlines. Customers place high value on Southwest's frequent departures, on-time service, friendly employees, and very low fares. Southwest's management knows this because its major marketing research unit—its 14,000 employees—is in daily contact with customers and reports its findings back to management. In addition, the Federal Aviation Administration's performance measures show that Southwest, of all the major airlines, regularly achieves the highest level of on-time arrivals, the lowest number of complaints, and the fewest lost-baggage claims per 1,000 passengers. When combined with Southwest's low fares per seat-mile, these indicators show the higher value delivered by Southwest's employees compared with most domestic competitors. Southwest has been profitable for 21 consecutive years and was the only major airline to realize a profit in 1992. (See Exhibit III.)

EMPLOYEE LOYALTY DRIVES PRODUCTIVITY

Traditional measures of the losses incurred by employee turnover concentrate only on the cost of recruiting, hiring, and training replacements. In most service jobs, the real cost of turnover is the loss of productivity and decreased customer satisfaction. One recent study of an automobile dealer's sales personnel by Abt Associates concluded that the average monthly cost of replacing a sales representative who had five to eight years of experience with an employee who had less than one year of experience was as much as $36,000 in sales. And the costs of losing a valued broker at a securities firm can be still more dire. Conservatively estimated, it takes nearly five years for a broker to rebuild relationships with customers that can return $1 million per year in commissions to the brokerage house—a cumulative loss of at least $2.5 million in commissions.

EMPLOYEE SATISFACTION DRIVES LOYALTY

In one 1991 proprietary study of a property-and-casualty insurance company's employees, 30% of all dissatisfied employees registered an intention to leave the company, a potential turnover rate three times higher than that for satisfied employees. In this same case, low employee turnover was found to be linked closely to high customer satisfaction. In contrast, Southwest Airlines, recently named one of the country's ten best places to work, experiences the highest rate of employee retention in the airline industry. Satisfaction levels are so high that at some of its operating locations, employee turnover rates are less than 5% per year. USAA, a major provider of insurance and other financial services by direct mail and phone, also achieves low levels of employee turnover by ensuring that its employees are highly

Exhibit III.

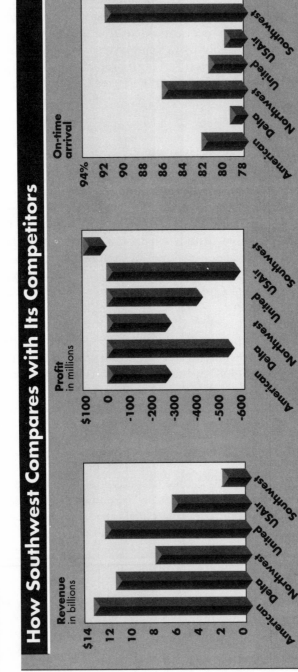

How Southwest Compares with Its Competitors

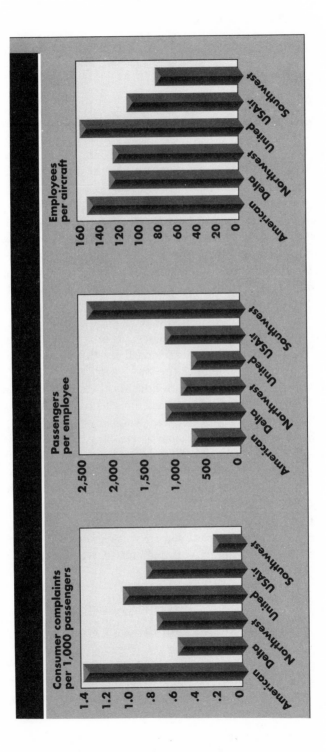

Consumer complaints per 1,000 passengers

Passengers per employee

Employees per aircraft

satisfied. But what drives employee satisfaction? Is it compensation, perks, or plush workplaces?

INTERNAL QUALITY DRIVES EMPLOYEE SATISFACTION

What we call the *internal quality* of a working environment contributes most to employee satisfaction. Internal quality is measured by the feelings that employees have toward their jobs, colleagues, and companies. What do service employees value most on the job? Although our data are preliminary at best, they point increasingly to the ability and authority of service workers to achieve results for customers. At USAA, for example, telephone sales and service representatives are backed by a sophisticated information system that puts complete customer information files at their fingertips the instant they receive a customer's call. In addition, state-of-the-art, job-related training is made available to USAA employees. And the curriculum goes still further, with 200 courses in 75 classrooms on a wide range of subjects.

Internal quality is also characterized by the attitudes that people have toward one another and the way people serve each other inside the organization. For example, ServiceMaster, a provider of a range of cleaning and maintenance services, aims to maximize the dignity of the individual service worker. Each year, it analyzes in depth a part of the maintenance process, such as cleaning a floor, in order to reduce the time and effort needed to complete the task. The "importance of the mundane" is stressed repeatedly in ServiceMaster's management training—for example, in the seven-step process devised for cleaning a hospital room: from the first step, greeting the patient, to the last step, asking patients whether or not they need anything else done. Using this process, service workers develop communication skills and learn to interact with patients in ways that add depth and dimension to their jobs.

LEADERSHIP UNDERLIES THE CHAIN'S SUCCESS

Leaders who understand the service-profit chain develop and maintain a corporate culture centered around service to customers and fellow employees. They display a willingness and ability to listen.

Successful CEOs like John Martin of Taco Bell, John McCoy of Banc One, Herb Kelleher of Southwest, and Bill Pollard of ServiceMaster spend a great deal of time with customers and employees, experiencing their companies' service processes while listening to employees for suggestions for improvement. They care about their employees and spend a great deal of time selecting, tracking, and recognizing them.

For example, Brigadier General Robert McDermott, until recently chairman and CEO of USAA, reflected, "Public recognition of outstanding employees flows naturally from our corporate culture. That culture is talked about all the time, and we live it." According to Scott Cook at Intuit, "Most people take culture as a given. It is around you, the thinking goes, and you can't do anything about it. However, when you run a company, you have the opportunity to determine the culture. I find that when you champion the most noble values—including service, analysis, and database decision making—employees rise to the challenge, and you forever change their lives."

RELATING LINKS IN THE CHAIN FOR MANAGEMENT ACTION

While many organizations are beginning to measure relationships between individual links in the service-profit chain, only a few have related the links in meaningful ways—ways that can lead to comprehensive strategies for achieving lasting competitive advantage.

The 1991 proprietary study of a property-and-casualty insurance company, cited earlier, not only identified the links between employee satisfaction and loyalty but also established that a primary source of job satisfaction was the service workers' perceptions of their ability to meet customer needs. Those who felt they did meet customer needs registered job satisfaction levels more than twice as high as those who felt they didn't. But even more important, the same study found that when a service worker left the company, customer satisfaction levels dropped sharply from 75% to 55%. As a result of this analysis, management is trying to reduce turnover among customer-contact employees and to enhance their job skills.

Similarly, in a study of its seven telephone customer service centers, MCI found clear relationships between employees' perceptions of the quality of MCI service and employee satisfaction. The study also linked employee satisfaction directly to customer satisfaction and intentions to continue to use MCI services. Identifying these relationships motivated MCI's management to probe deeper and determine what affected job satisfaction at the service centers. The factors they uncovered, in order of importance, were satisfaction with the job itself, training, pay, advancement fairness, treatment with respect and dignity, teamwork, and the company's interest in employee's well-being. Armed with this information, MCI's management began examining its policies concerning those items valued most by employees at its service centers. MCI has incorporated information about its service capabilities into training and communications efforts and television advertising.

No organization has made a more comprehensive effort to measure relationships in the service-profit chain and fashion a strategy around them than the fast-food company, Taco Bell, a subsidiary of PepsiCo. Taco Bell's management tracks profits daily by unit, market manager, zone, and country. By integrating this information with the results of exit interviews that Taco Bell conducts with 800,000 customers annually, management has found that stores in the top quadrant of customer satisfaction ratings outperform the other stores by all measures. As a result, Taco Bell has linked operations managers' compensation in company-owned stores to customer satisfaction, realizing a subsequent increase in both customer satisfaction ratings and profits.

However, Taco Bell's efforts don't stop there. By examining employee turnover records for individual stores, Taco Bell has discovered that the 20% of the stores with the lowest turnover rates enjoy double the sales and 55% higher profits than the 20% of stores with the highest employee turnover rates. As a result of this self-examination, Taco Bell has instituted financial and other incentives in order to reverse the cycle of failure that is associated with poor employee selection, subpar training, low pay, and high turnover.

In addition, Taco Bell monitors internal quality through a network of 800 numbers created to answer employee's questions, field their complaints, remedy situations, and alert top-level management to potential trouble spots. It also conducts periodic employee roundtable meetings, interviews, as well as a comprehensive companywide survey every two or three years in order to measure satisfaction. As a result of all this work, Taco Bell's focus on employee satisfaction involves a new selection process, improved skill building, increased latitude for decision making on the job, and further automation of unpleasant "back room" labor.

Relating all the links in the service-profit chain may seem to be a tall order. But profitability depends not only on placing hard values on soft measures but also on linking those individual measures together into a comprehensive service picture. Service organizations need to quantify their investments in people—both customers and employees. The service-profit chain provides the framework for this critical task.

Service-Profit Chain Audit

A service-profit chain audit helps companies determine what drives their profit and suggests actions that can lead to long-term profitability. As they review the audit, managers should ask themselves what efforts are under way to obtain answers to the following questions and what those answers reveal about their companies.

PROFIT AND GROWTH

1. How do we define loyal customers?

Customers often become more profitable over time. And loyal customers account for an unusually high proportion of the sales and profit growth of successful service providers. In some organizations, loyalty is measured in terms of whether or not a customer is on the company rolls. But several companies have found that their most loyal customers—the top 20% of total customers—not only provide all the profits but also cover losses incurred in dealing with less loyal customers.

Because of the link between loyal customers and profit, Banc One measures *depth of relationship*—the number of available related financial services, such as checking, lending, and safe deposit, actually used by customers. Recognizing the same relationship, Taco Bell measures "share of stomach" to assess the company's sales against all other food purchases a customer can potentially make. As a result, the fast-food chain is trying to reach consumers through kiosks, carts, trucks, and the shelves of supermarkets.

2. Do measurements of customer profitability include profits from referrals?

Companies that measure the stream of revenue and profits from loyal customers (retention) and repeat sales often overlook what can be the most important of the three Rs of loyalty: referrals. For example, Intuit provides high-quality, free lifetime service for a personal finance software package that sells for as little as $30. The strategy makes sense when the value of a loyal customer is considered—a revenue stream of several thousands of dollars from software updates, supplies, and new customer referrals. With this strategy in place, Intuit increased its sales to more than $30 million with just two U.S. field sales representatives.

3. What proportion of business development expenditures and incentives are directed to the retention of existing customers?

Too many companies concentrate nearly all their efforts on attracting new customers. But in businesses like life insurance, a new policyholder doesn't become profitable for at least three years. In the credit-card finance business, the break-even point for a new customer is often six or more years because of high-marketing and bad-debt costs in the first year of a relationship with cardholders. These costs must be defrayed by profits from loyal customers, suggesting the need for a careful division of organizational effort between customer retention and development.

4. Why do our customers defect?

It's important to find out not only where defectors go but also why they defect. Was it because of poor service, price, or value? Answers to these questions provide information about whether or not existing strategies are working. In addition, exit interviews of customers can have real sales impact. For example, at one credit-card service organization, a phone call to question cardholders who had stopped using their cards led to the immediate reinstatement of one-third of the defectors.

CUSTOMER SATISFACTION

5. Are customer satisfaction data gathered in an objective, consistent, and periodic fashion?

Currently, the weakest measurements being used by the companies we have studied concern customer satisfaction. At some companies, high levels of reported customer satisfaction are contradicted by continuing declines in sales and profits. Upon closer observation, we discovered that the service providers were "gaming" the data, using manipulative methods for collecting customer satisfaction data. In one extreme case, an automobile dealer sent a questionnaire to recent buyers with the highest marks already filled in, requiring owners to alter the marks only if they disagreed. Companies can, however, obtain more objective results using "third party" interviews; "mystery shopping" by unidentified, paid observers; or technologies like touch-screen television.

Consistency is at least as important as the actual questions asked of customers. Some of Banc One's operating units formerly conducted their own customer satisfaction surveys. Today the surveys have been centralized, made mandatory, and are administered by mail on a quarterly basis to around 125,000 customers. When combined with periodic measurement, the surveys provide highly relevant trend information that informs the managerial decision-making process. Similarly, Xerox's measures of satisfaction obtained from 10,000 customers per month—a product of an unchanging set of survey questions and very large samples—make possible period-to-period comparisons that are important in measuring and rewarding performance.

6. Where are the listening posts for obtaining customer feedback in your organization?

Listening posts are tools for collecting data from customers and systematically translating those data into information in order to improve service and products. Common examples are letters of complaint. Still more important listening posts are reports from field sales and service personnel or the logs of telephone service representatives. Intuit's content analysis of customer service inquiries fielded by service representatives produced over 50 software improvements and 100 software documentation improvements in a single year. USAA has gone one step further by automating the feedback process to enter data online, enabling its analysis and plans departments to develop corrective actions.

7. How is information concerning customer satisfaction used to solve customer problems?

In order to handle customer problems, service providers must have the latitude to resolve any situation promptly. In addition, information regarding a customer concern must be transmitted to the service provider quickly. Customers and employees must be encouraged to report rather than suppress concerns. For example, one Boston-area Lexus dealer notified its customers, "If you are experiencing a problem with your car or our service department and you can't answer '100% satisfied' when you receive your survey directly from Lexus, please give us the opportunity to correct the problem before you fill out the survey. Lexus takes its customer surveys very seriously."

EXTERNAL SERVICE VALUE

8. How do you measure service value?

Value is a function not only of costs to the customer but also of the results achieved for the customer. Value is always relative because it is based both on perceptions of the way a service is delivered and on initial customer expectations. Typically, a company measures value using the reasons expressed by customers for high or low satisfaction. Because value varies with individual expectations, efforts to improve value inevitably require service organizations to move all levels of management closer to the customer and give frontline service employees the latitude to customize a standard service to individual needs.

9. How is information concerning customers' perceptions of value shared with those responsible for designing a product or service?

Relaying information concerning customer expectations to those responsible for design often requires the formation of teams of people responsible for sales, operations, and service or product design, as well as the frequent assignment of service designers to tasks requiring field contact with customers. Intuit has created this kind of capability in product development teams. And all Intuit employees, including the CEO, must periodically work on the customer service phones. Similarly, at Southwest, those responsible for flight scheduling periodically work shifts in the company's terminals to get a feel for the impact of schedules on customer and employee satisfaction.

10. To what extent are measures taken of differences between customers' perceptions of quality delivered and their expectations before delivery?

Ultimately, service quality is a function of the gap between perceptions of the actual service experienced and what a customer expected before receiving that service. Actual service includes both final results and the process through which those results were obtained. Differences between experiences and expectations can be measured in generic dimensions such as the reliability and timeliness of service, the empathy and authority with which the service was delivered, and the extent to which the customer is left with tangible evidence (like a calling card) that the service has been performed.

11. Do our organization's efforts to improve external service quality emphasize effective recovery from service errors in addition to providing a service right the first time?

A popular concept of quality in manufacturing is the importance of "doing things right the first time." But customers of service organizations often allow one mistake. Some organizations are very good at delivering service as long as nothing goes wrong. Others organize for and thrive on service emergencies. Outstanding service organizations do both by giving frontline employees the latitude to effect recovery. Southwest Airlines maintains a policy of allowing frontline employees to do whatever they feel comfortable doing in order to satisfy customers. Xerox authorizes frontline service employees to replace up to $250,000 worth of equipment if customers are not getting results.

EMPLOYEE PRODUCTIVITY

12. How do you measure employee productivity?

13. To what extent do measures of productivity identify changes in the quality as well as the quantity of service produced per unit of input?

In many services, the ultimate measure of quality may be customer satisfaction. That measure should be combined with measures of quantity to determine the total output of the service organization. At ServiceMaster, for example, measures of output in the schools and hospitals cleaned under the company's supervision include both numbers of work orders performed per employee hour and the quality of the work done, as determined by periodic inspections performed by ServiceMaster and client personnel. Similarly, Southwest Airlines delivers relatively high levels of productivity in terms of both quality and quantity. In fact, outstanding service competitors are replacing the typical "either/or" trade-off between quality and quantity with an "and/also" imperative.

EMPLOYEE LOYALTY

14. How do you create employee loyalty?

Employee loyalty goes hand in hand with productivity, contradicting the assumption that successful service providers should be promoted to larger supervisory responsibilities or moved to a similar job in a larger business unit. ServiceMaster and Taco Bell have expanded jobs without promoting good service workers. At ServiceMaster, effective single-unit managers are given supervisory responsibilities for custodial, maintenance, or other workers at more than one hospital or school. Taco Bell gives restaurant general managers a "hunting license" to help identify and operate new satellite feeding locations in the neighborhoods served by their restaurants and rewards them for doing it.

15. Have we made an effort to determine the right level of employee retention?

Rarely is the right level of retention 100%. Dynamic service organizations require a certain level of turnover. However, in calibrating desired turnover levels, it is important to take into account the full cost of the loss of key service providers, including those of lost sales and productivity and added recruiting, selection, and training.

EMPLOYEE SATISFACTION

16. Is employee satisfaction measured in ways that can be linked to similar measures of customer satisfaction with sufficient frequency and consistency to establish trends for management use?

Taco Bell studies employee satisfaction through surveys, frequent interviews, and roundtable meetings. Customer satisfaction is measured by interviews with customers conducted biannually and includes questions about satisfaction with employee friendliness and hustle.

Both the employee and customer satisfaction rankings are comprehensive and conducted on a regular basis. With these data, the company can better understand overall trends and the links between employee and customer satisfaction.

17. Are employee selection criteria and methods geared to what customers, as well as managers, believe are important?

At Southwest Airlines, for example, frequent fliers are regularly invited to participate in the auditioning and selection of cabin attendants. And many take time off from work to join Southwest's employee selection team as it carries out its work. As one customer commented, "Why not do it? It's my airline."

18. To what extent are measures of customer satisfaction, customer loyalty, or the quality and quantity of service output used in recognizing and rewarding employees?

Employee recognition may often involve little more than informing individual employees or employees as a group about service improvements and individual successes. Banc One goes one step further, including customer satisfaction measures for each banking unit in its periodic report of other performance measures, mostly financial, to all units.

INTERNAL SERVICE QUALITY

19. Do employees know who their customers are?

It is particularly difficult for employees to identify their customers when those customers are internal to the company. These employees often do not know what impact their work has on other departments. Identifying internal customers requires mapping and communicating characteristics of work flow, organizing periodic cross-departmental meetings between "customers" and "servers," and recognizing good internal service performance.

In 1990, USAA organized a PRIDE (Professionalism Results in Dedication to Excellence) team of 100 employees and managers to examine and improve on a function-by-function basis all processes associated with

property-and-casualty insurance administration, which included analyzing customer needs and expectations. The PRIDE effort was so
successful that it led to a cross-functional review of USAA's service
processing. Service processing time has been reduced, as have handoffs
of customers from one server to another.

*20. Are employees satisfied with the technological and personal support they
receive on the job?*

The cornerstone of success at Taco Bell is the provision of the latest
in information technology, food service equipment, simple work-sched-
uling techniques, and effective team training. This practice led to the
establishment of self-managing teams of service providers. Also, the
quality of work life involves selecting the right workers. Winners
like to be associated with winners. Better employees tend to refer
people they like and people like themselves. Internal service quality
can also be thought of as the quality of work life. It is a visible ex-
pression of an organization's culture, one influenced in important
ways by leadership.

LEADERSHIP

21. To what extent is the company's leadership:
   a. energetic, creative vs. stately, conservative?
   b. participatory, caring vs. removed, elitist?
   c. listening, coaching, and teaching vs. supervising and managing?
   d. motivating by mission vs. motivating by fear?
   *e. leading by means of personally demonstrated values vs. institutionalized
   policies?*

*22. How much time is spent by the organization's leadership personally devel-
oping and maintaining a corporate culture centered around service to customers
and fellow employees?*

Leaders naturally have individual traits and styles. But the CEOs or
companies that are successfully using the service-profit chain possess
all or most of a set of traits that separate them from their merely good
competitors. Of course, different styles of leadership are appropriate
for various stages in an organization's development. But the messages

sent by the successful leaders we have observed stress the importance of careful attention to the needs of customers and employees. These leaders create a culture capable of adapting to the needs of both.

RELATING THE MEASURES

23. What are the most important relationships in your company's service-profit chain?

24. To what extent does each measure correlate with profit and growth at the frontline level?

25. Is the importance of these relationships reflected in rewards and incentives offered to employees?

Measures drive action when they are related in ways that provide managers with direction. To enjoy the kind of success that service organizations like Southwest Airlines, ServiceMaster, and Taco Bell have enjoyed, looking at individual measures is not enough. Only if the individual measures are tied together into a comprehensive picture will the service-profit chain provide a foundation for unprecedented profit and growth.

Note

1. Frederick F. Reichheld and W. Earl Sasser, Jr., "Zero Defections: Quality Comes to Services," *Harvard Business Review*, September–October 1990.

About the Contributors

William H. Davidow is a general partner in a California high-technology venture capital firm, Mohr, Davidow Ventures. He is the co-author with Michael S. Malone of *The Virtual Corporation: Structuring and Revitalizing the Corporation for the 21st Century.*

Thomas L. Doorley is a founder and managing partner of Braxton Associates, an international strategy consulting firm.

Peter F. Drucker has been writing on management since he published *The Future of Industrial Man*—his second book—in 1943. "The New Productivity Challenge" was Mr. Drucker's twenty-ninth article to appear in the *Harvard Business Review.* Since 1971 he has been a professor of social science and management at The Claremont Graduate School in Claremont, California. His latest book is *Post-Capitalist Society,* published in 1993.

Founder and CEO of Satisfaction Guaranteed Eateries, Inc. in Seattle, **Timothy W. Firnstahl** is a restaurant zealot and the fourth generation of his family in the food industry. He is the author of two other *Harvard Business Review* articles, "The Center-Cut Solution" and "Letting Go."

Ronald Grzywinski is chairman of the board of the Shorebank Corporation, a Chicago bank holding company.

James L. Heskett is the UPS Foundation Professor of Business Logistics at the Harvard Business School. A member of the faculty since 1965, he has taught courses in marketing, business logistics, the management of service operations, and business policy; he currently teaches service management. His article is an outgrowth of his book, *Managing in the Service Economy* (Harvard Business School Press).

Peter T. Johnson is now an investor and a sculptor. From 1981 to 1986 he was the administrator of Bonneville Power Administration in Portland, Oregon. Before that, he spent ten years at Trus Joist Corporation in Boise, Idaho, where he was president and then CEO.

Thomas O. Jones is a senior lecturer in service management at Harvard Business School. In 1970 he co-founded Epsilon, a company that provides data base marketing services to scores of *Fortune* 500 companies, where until 1993 he served as president and CEO.

Gary W. Loveman is an assistant professor of business administration at the Harvard Business School, where he teaches service management in MBA and executive programs. For the past three years, he has been involved in a field study of enterprise reform and small business development in Poland. He is the author of a forthcoming book on the subject to be published by the Harvard Business School Press.

John E. Martin is the president and CEO of Taco Bell Corporation. He has worked in the food service industry since 1967, including holding executive positions at Burger King, Burger Chef, and Hardee's.

Nancy Nichols is a senior editor at the *Harvard Business Review*. A former reporter for the *MacNeil/Lehrer Newshour*, she has written articles for *HBR, Working Woman, The Christian Science Monitor, The Chicago Tribune,* and *Inc.* She is editor of *Reach for the Top* (Harvard Business School Press), a recently published collection of *Harvard Business Review* articles examining the challenges and opportunities faced by professional women.

Penny C. Paquette is a research associate and director of the International University of Japan Program Office at the Amos Tuck School, Dartmouth College.

James Brian Quinn is an emeritus professor at the Amos Tuck School, Dartmouth College. His most recent book, *Intelligent Enterprise: How Knowledge and Service-Based Strategies Are Revolutionizing the Economy, Strategy, and All Organizations,* won an award in the business and management category from the Association of American Publishers.

Frederick F. Reichheld is a director of Bain & Company, where he leads its Loyalty/Retention practice. His pioneering work in the area of customer and employee retention has quantified the linkage between loyalty and profits. It forms the basis of his forthcoming book on the subject of loyalty-based management, to be published by the Harvard Business School Press in 1996. His article "Zero Defections: Quality Comes to Services," co-authored with W. Earl Sasser, Jr., appeared in the recently published collection of *HBR* essays, *Keeping Customers*.

W. Earl Sasser, Jr. is the UPS Foundation Professor of Service Management at the Harvard Business School, where he serves as faculty chair of the Advanced Management Program. He has co-authored several publications in the field of service management; his most recent book is *Service Breakthroughs: Changing the Rules of the Game*.

Leonard Schlesinger is a professor of business administration at the Harvard Business School, where since 1993 he has chaired the MBA program curriculum design effort. He is the author of numerous articles and two forthcoming books, *The Real Heroes of Business*, with Bill Fromm, and *Out in Front* (Harvard Business School Press), with James L. Heskett.

Thomas Teal is a senior editor of the *Harvard Business Review*. Before coming to the magazine in 1987, he was a professional literary translator, an editorial staff member of *The New Yorker* magazine, and editorial manager of Jimmy Carter's White House speechwriting office. During the mid-1980s, he built low- and moderate-income housing for profit in Aspen, Colorado.

Michael Treacy is president of Treacy & Company, a management consulting firm based in Cambridge, Massachusetts.

Bro Uttal is a management consultant at McKinsey. His article had its origins in a portion of the book he co-authored with William Davidow, *Total Customer Service: The Ultimate Weapon*.

Alan M. Webber is a founding editor of *Fast Company*, a magazine on business and the new economy. Formerly, he was editorial director of the *Harvard Business Review*.

Fred Wiersema is vice president of CSC Index, Inc., an international management consulting firm based in Cambridge, Massachusetts.

INDEX